"In *God of All Comfort*, my friend, Scott H
cious claim: God works all things togethe
of horror can be turned into grounds o
ology of the healing and redeeming process opens up the windows of faith, hope, and love, through which the Spirit of Jesus can transform our lives in the midst of the horror of the present age."

Roland Werner, Professor of Theology,
Evangelische Hochschule Tabor (Marburg, Germany)

"An impressive interdisciplinary, theological, and pastoral approach to horror and trauma. Scott Harrower invites us into the narratives of Scripture and the Gospel of Matthew to experience a triune God who meets those on the road towards recovering safety, a story, and community."

Andrew Abernethy, Associate Professor of
Old Testament, Wheaton College

"Scott Harrower skillfully brings the pressing issue of trauma and horror into the realms of historic, Trinitarian, and creedal life of the church today. By leading us through 'horror-attuned readings' of the Gospels, he helps us to avoid the pitfalls of neglecting trauma as the present lens through which many of us read Scripture, but also reducing trauma to the only lens. I initially thought this book would be an interesting read. But Harrower made me quickly realize how necessary this discussion is to understanding Scripture, theology, and our culture soaked in misappropriations of horror. Scripture as well as the church past and present have a horror-redeeming function, and Harrower aptly helps us navigate it."

Dru Johnson, Associate Professor of Biblical and
Theological Studies, The King's College

"Horrors cause a whole range of traumas, to which only a rich and varied response will be adequate—which is precisely what we find the array of tools Harrower utilizes (including sustained interaction with horror and trauma studies). The key, he argues, is a pastoral and churchly set of practices, rooted in a coherent biblical and trinitarian reshaping of personal narratives of trauma."

Adam Johnson, Associate Professor of Theology,
Torrey Honors Institute, Biola University

GOD *of All* COMFORT

A Trinitarian Response to the Horrors of This World

STUDIES IN HISTORICAL & SYSTEMATIC THEOLOGY

GOD *of All* **COMFORT**

A Trinitarian Response to the Horrors of This World

SCOTT HARROWER

STUDIES IN HISTORICAL AND SYSTEMATIC THEOLOGY

LEXHAM PRESS

God of All Comfort: A Trinitarian Response to the Horrors of This World
Studies in Historical and Systematic Theology

Lexham Press, 1313 Commercial St., Bellingham, WA 98225
LexhamPress.com

Print ISBN 978-1-68-359230-3
Digital ISBN 978-1-68-359231-0

Lexham Editorial Team: Todd Hains, Claire Brubaker, Danielle Thevenaz
Cover Design: Bryan Hintz
Typesetting: ProjectLuz.com

This book is dedicated to those who have mediated
God's presence, care, and insight to me over many years:

Kate Harrower, Roland and Elke Werner, and Lindsay Wilson.

Thank you.

The novelist with Christian concerns will find in modern life distortions which are repugnant to him, and his problem will be to make these appear as distortions to an audience which is used to seeing them as natural; and he may well be forced to take ever more violent means to get his vision across to this hostile audience. When you can assume that your audience holds the same beliefs you do, you can relax a little and use more normal ways of talking to it; when you have to assume that it does not, then you have to make your vision apparent by shock—to the hard of hearing you shout, and for the almost blind you draw large and startling figures.

—Flannery O'Connor, *"The Fiction Writer and His Country"*

CONTENTS

FOREWORD

The brokenness of the world is patent. Indeed, stories of the brokenness are difficult, if not impossible, to avoid. A night spent watching the TV evening news or CNN or FOX or reading the New York Times or catching up with Facebook reveal the horrors. Last afternoon there was shooting in a hospital here in Chicago. A doctor was executed by an ex-fiancé. Two others were gunned down and the gunman himself was killed by the police. Domestic abuse and sexual abuse add to the dark picture. And then there are diseases that ravage our bodies. In fact, as I write I have two faculty wrestling with deadly disease. Looking out further from where I live and work there are various armed conflicts in progress around the globe. Famine, poverty, corruption in government, natural disasters are the common lot of humankind. California has just experienced horrific wildfires. Scores are dead. And then there is global warming and the threat it poses. The experience of such horrors has surely contributed to the rise of the "nones", that is, those who claim no religion at all. As philosopher Charles Taylor points out we live in a secular age. For increasing numbers the existence of God let alone a good God has become implausible. (Taylor's observations are especially pertinent to those in the West and those in the majority world with a secular Western education.)

Theologian Scott Harrower is acutely aware of the brokenness as this book shows. He is also very much aware of increasing religious skepticism in the West. Within a Trinitarian frame of reference he addresses issues of horror and trauma. He argues that horrors and trauma foster a sense of human meaningless and hopelessness. However, there is good news. God has not abandoned his creation but through Christ is realizing his project of reclaiming creation and establishing it in *shalom*. For those in his image who are caught up in the project there is nothing less than the prospect of restoration to full personhood. Matthew's Gospel in particular provides a lens with which to view the issues of trauma and of horrors that are Harrower's focus. Participation in God's kingdom work becomes the way forward for a meaningful life.

This is an altogether very useful book that is written with great empathy for those who have suffered trauma caused by the horrors. It is biblically informed, sensitive to the human condition, theologically astute, philosophically able, and a fine example of culturally engaged theology.

Graham A. Cole
Dean and Vice President of Education and
Professor of Biblical and Systematic Theology
Trinity Evangelical Divinity School

ACKNOWLEDGMENTS

This work would not have been possible without the ongoing influence of past and present teachers and colleagues. I am happy to acknowledge my PhD supervisors and other professors at Trinity International University in Illinois: Graham Cole (whose Christian personalism, understanding of providence, and use of the concept of shalom have been a longtime influence) and Thomas McCall (who together with Keith Yandell introduced me to analytical philosophy and the analytical-theological interpretation of Scripture). Kevin Vanhoozer's Prolegomena class at Trinity International University was also seminal for understanding the way by which the theological interpretation of Scripture may relate to continental philosophy. Further afield, interacting with Eleonore Stump's works and personal correspondence with her has also been very influential on my approach to knowing people and to knowing personal beings via narratives.

In Australia, a number of Australian colleagues and institutions deserve my acknowledgment and thanks. At Ridley College, Melbourne, Lindsay Wilson and Mike Bird have been constant and thoughtful companions in the process of ruminating about the problem of evil and the limitations we all experience during the course of our days in this world. Their Christian faith, prayers, insight, and perseverance have been examples of hope throughout the process of writing this book.

Douglas McComiskey from the Melbourne School of Theology has shaped my exegetical thinking in dealing with narrative and religious claims, and I appreciate his contribution. My present work departs from his in significant ways through phenomenology and epistemology, and he bears no responsibility for any shortcomings of this present work.

Ridley College provided me with a sabbatical semester during which this work was completed. In addition, together with the Australian College of Theology, it sponsored my presentation of three papers related to this project at the 2016 Evangelical Philosophical Society (EPS), Evangelical Theological Society (ETS), and Institute for Biblical Research (IBR) meetings in San Antonio. I appreciated Brian Rosner's attendance at one of these talks.

I was honored to present part of chapter 1 to the inaugural meeting of the IBR research group "Suffering, Evil, and Divine Punishment in the Bible." My thanks go to our moderator, Kenneth Litwak, and to my fellow presenters and respondents: Richard Schultz (Wheaton College, Illinois), Heath Thomas (Oklahoma Baptist University), Nathan Chambers (University of Durham), Helene Dallaire (Denver Seminary), David Starling (Morling College), Robbie Castleman (John Brown University), and Kevin Anderson (Asbury University). Special thanks go to Kevin Anderson, who thoughtfully and patiently responded to my initial paper and to a later and modified version of it. The Australian College of Theology also partly sponsored my travel to that conference, and Graeme Chatfield attended and engaged with two of my presentations. At that conference I received feedback from Jonathan King and Ingrid Faro that was particularly helpful and has influenced my thinking. My conversation with Ingrid Faro, in which she suggested that a "strong" version of healing and recovery was possible in the aftermath of horrors, kept coming to mind during the writing of this book. Following the development of this work into book form, Anne Ellison's feedback and suggestions were both insightful and sensitive to the subject matter at hand.

This work would not have been possible without the help of Gina Denholm, who helped me structure the work and express myself in a clear manner. Her sense of humor and encouragement pushed me over the finishing line. Patrick Senn also reviewed a number of earlier sections of the work—thank you, Patrick, for your keen interest in the project, eye for detail, and gentle manner.

1

INTRODUCTION

My heart sank when I noticed that *USA Today*'s lead article was "Your Definitive Guide to 2017: A Year of Hope and Horror."[1] Horrors never go away; they are always with us—destroying life and maiming human beings. I also wonder what kind of hope we can meaningfully talk about in this horrible context. The book you are reading is about horrors—what they are, what kinds of horrors there may be, and why is it that they are so deadly. Once we know what horrors are, we can do something about them, or at least ask God for help to do something about our lives when horrors invade. We care about this problem because horrors affect us all in irreversible ways, sometimes setting our lives on courses we never hoped for and even dreaded.

Horrors raise theological, existential, and pastoral questions. How is God involved in a world pockmarked by horrors? Is it possible to live meaningfully in such a random and death-directed world? Is there any hope for recovery from horrors and the traumas they generate in us? Simplistic answers to the questions raised by horrors do more harm than good, yet engaging with these questions and the nature of horrors is something that maturing Christians must face, lest our questions become roadblocks to faith. The central aim of the book is to explore how God the Trinity engages with horrors and trauma, and what people can hope for in light of this.

We all bring our own experiences and questions to bear on the reality of horrors. For this reason, reading this book will be quite an intellectually, spiritually, and emotionally involving project. You may have to take it up and then put it down for a week or two. The difficulty and personal

1. "Your Definitive Guide to 2017: A Year of Hope and Horror," *USA Today*, Dec. 28, 2017, https://www.usatoday.com/story/news/2017/12/28/definitive-guide-reflecting-horrific-and-hopeful-2017/987241001/.

nature of the subject matter need not put you off. Indeed, we need books such as this, as imperfect as it is.

WHY IS THIS PARTICULAR BOOK NEEDED AT THIS TIME?

A number of Christian and secular authors have explored horrors and trauma. However, a common denominator among these works is a lack of direct and deep engagement with the particular nature of God: God as Trinity. Though there are invaluable insights and great strengths to these works, it is hard to overlook and overcome their generalized and minimalist approach to God's nature as a Trinitarian God and the significance this has both for understanding horrors and for possible recovery from the trauma responses that horrors generate. Moreover, our Western cultural context exaggerates the shortcomings of the recent scholarship in horror and trauma studies. Our skeptical context and hyperawareness of what is perverted about the world only serve to cement the skepticisms we may have about God, the possibility of a meaningful human life, and hope for a better future for people. This context accents the need to engage with horror and trauma from a strong doctrine of God and of humanity, made in his image.

I hope to rectify this problem by taking a specifically *Trinitarian* approach to horrors and more specifically by examining how God discloses himself to people in the Gospel of Matthew. I will be attentive to how God makes himself known to people for the sake of their own recovery from horrors and for the sake of motivating them to help others in the wake of horrors and trauma.

This is a multidimensional and cross-disciplinary project. It contributes to a variety of fields that must be touched on if we are going to provide a rich exploration and description of what the life of God the Trinity means for how horrors affect human lives.

First, this project makes a *metaphysical* contribution by explaining and harnessing horror as a theological concept. In defining horrors theologically, I aim to clarify the problems—theological, existential, and anthropological—that horrors create for human persons. By providing the metaphysical premises for a model of what horrors are, I get to the root problem that recent conversations in trauma studies have left unspoken.

My hope is that a clearer theological definition of horrors will give the discussion on trauma a sharper focus.

Second, it offers a second constructive *Trinitarian* proposal for how the uniqueness of God's triadic life allows for his help in both direct and indirect manners in times of horrors and their aftermath.

Third, it explores the *pastoral* dimension of God the Trinity as caring, present, and active in the context of horrors and trauma, even if this is not immediately perceived.

Of far less importance but of interest to those who are more academically inclined is that this work engages a number of newer *philosophical* issues and methods, including new questions concerning consciousness and perspectives from both an analytical- and continental-philosophical position.[2] Finally, it makes a *literary* contribution because it points out the ways in which a horror-attuned or "paranoid" interpretation of Matthew's Gospel may resonate with contemporary trauma survivors. This yields interesting and unique results and is itself a contribution to literary studies.

HOW I HAVE STRUCTURED THE BOOK

In part 1 we look at the Edenic backdrop against which horrors should be understood. I provide a definition of horrors and the trauma responses that these may generate. Horrors are transgressive events and perceptions, large and small. These traumatize and degenerate the relational, creative, and moral aspects of human persons who are God's images. The lived experience of horrors cultivates theological, existential, and moral problems that shape how people perceive reality and other personal beings, each of which must be addressed if we are to grapple fully with horrors and trauma.

---

2. Charlene P. E. Burns, *Christian Understandings of Evil: The Historical Trajectory* (Minneapolis: Fortress, 2016), 7. I will employ phenomenological work influenced by scholars such as James J. Gibson and Maurice Merleu-Ponty at the same time as analytical work by Thomas McCall and others such as Oliver Crisp. See Stephan Käufer and Anthony Chemero, *Phenomenology: An Introduction* (Cambridge, UK: Polity, 2016); Thomas McCall, *An Invitation to Analytic Christian Theology* (Downers Grove, IL: IVP Academic, 2015); Oliver Crisp, "Analytic Theology as Systematic Theology," *Open Theology* 3 (2017): 155–56. I am also influenced by the direction set out by Michael Dauphinais, "The Difference Divine Mercy Makes in Aquinas' Exegesis," *The Thomist* 80, no. 3 (2016): 341–53. The socio-cognitive directions of this work have affinities with Risto Uro, *Ritual and Christian Beginnings: A Socio-Cognitive Analysis* (Oxford: Oxford University Press, 2016).

In part 2 I argue that the best way to deal with the questions generated by horrors is by working through stories of God's involvement in the world as it is. The story I have chosen is Matthew's Gospel. However, I note that our cultural context means that survivors of horrors and trauma will tend to read religious texts through a paranoid lens that anticipates the loss and grief they have already experienced. I therefore undertake a "horror" reading of Matthew in order to empathetically demonstrate how the violence, death, suffering, and loss in this Gospel may resonate with trauma survivors. I then ask what God the Trinity may do about this situation. I draw some keys from Matthew's Gospel and then offer an alternative, "reparative" interpretation of this Gospel. This approach to Matthew's Gospel explores the ways by which God the Trinity relates reparatively with people who have been traumatized by horrors in order to heal the relational, moral, and creative aspects of his own images.

In part 3 I follow the structure for recovery provided by Judith Lewis Herman and investigate how God enables and supports the three stages for recovery from horrors and trauma. These are *recovering safety*, *recovering the self's story*, and *recovering community*. Within this structure, I explore how the Triune God provides safety, a coherent story in which to speak about trauma, and possibilities for reconnection to the community. We examine God's indirect and direct actions of care; his visible and invisible actions; his past, present, and future presence among us; and his care for the people he loves. We will see that recovery from trauma may be possible given the cumulative manner of God's works. This Trinitarian perspective on trauma recovery is shown to be essential for realistically responding to horror-driven skepticisms about God, meaningful living, and a hopeful future.

Part 1

—

HORRORS *and* SKEPTICISMS

2

THE BACKSTORY OF HORRORS

Shalom and Blessedness

In human existence, horrors abound. Amanda Wortham writes about the contemporary pervasiveness of overwhelming evil, which she sums up as *horror*:

> Moving through this summer has felt like wandering in a mirrored maze of bad news, with each new turn giving us barely enough time to get our bearings before we have to confront another senseless horror. It's hard to know how to navigate such a brutal onslaught of tragedy; every time we attempt to move forward, our surroundings tell us that we haven't made any real progress at all. Instead, what we see insists that grief, terror, violence, and rage are destined to become a part of our cultural fabric.[1]

We all face and struggle with evil in its various forms. For this reason, we need language and concepts in order to describe the gravest problems we face.

In light of the multiple terror attacks in Paris in November 2015, French President François Hollande used *horror* as a summative category for the many evils that people perpetrated on one another and their societies.[2] His use of "horror" was echoed by many others.[3] More recently, my own

---

1. Amanda Wortham, "Reading Sideways: How Fiction Helps Us Navigate the Maze of Tragedy," Christ and Pop Culture, July 28, 2016, http://christandpopculture.com/reading-sideways-how-fiction-helps-us-navigate-the-maze-of-tragedy/.

2. Hollande : 'c'est une horreur,' " Europe 1, November 16, 2015, http://www.europe1.fr/faits-divers/hollande-cest-une-horreur-2620167.

3. "EN DIRECT – Attentats de Paris: des proches d'un terroriste arrêtés," *Le Figaro*, November 26, 2015, http://www.lefigaro.fr/actualites/2015/11/13/01001-20151113LIVWWW00406-fusillade-paris-explosions-stade-de-france.php.

hometown has experienced evils summed up as "horrors," the "Horror on Bourke Street" in 2017 providing one such example.[4]

The language of horrors is increasingly employed in the media around large-scale public tragedies, but what does this language mean? The term is often used quite fluidly. Is the language of horrors helpful? To which truths does this language refer? When is the language of horrors most appropriate and effective? Is it a metaphor, or are there reasons to believe that there are such things as horrors?

The current use of this language can serve Christians well because it stimulates us to clarify what horrors refer to. Such insight may help us come to grips with horrors, the questions they raise, and how to live with God and one another in light of them.

We can understand best what horrors are by contrasting them with the ideal state for human persons: the Edenic ideal. The Christian concepts of shalom, the God of shalom, and human beings as made in God's image establish a number of standards for life that are eviscerated by horrors.[5] When we examine these, the warrant for the truths about horrors emerges. This also aligns methodologically with trauma studies, which will become central to this book because trauma studies engages with the larger narrative of Scripture in order to deal with trauma and its theological dimensions.[6]

SHALOM: GOD'S UNIVERSE DESIGNED FOR PERSONAL FLOURISHING

The concept of shalom (שָׁלוֹם) is the background against which horrors become clear.[7] The word "shalom" (meaning "wholeness" and "peace") has

---

4. Michael Harry, "Bourke Street Tragedy: Witness Recalls Walking into a Scene of Confusion and Horror," *Sydney Morning Herald*, January 21, 2017, http://www.smh.com.au/comment/bourke-street-tragedy-witness-recalls-walking-into-a-scene-of-confusion-and-horror-20170120-gtvyom.html.

5. This section is dependent on Graham A. Cole, "Personalism," in *New Dictionary of Theology*, ed. Martin Davie, Tim Grass, Stephen R. Holmes, John McDowell, and T. A. Noble (Downers Grove, IL: IVP Academic, 2016); Juan Manuel Burgos, *Introducción al personalismo* (Madrid: Ediciones Palabra, 2012).

6. Shelly Rambo, *Spirit and Trauma: A Theology of Remaining* (Louisville, KY: Westminster John Knox, 2010), 6.

7. "Trauma returns theologians to our primary claims about death and life." However, in Rambo's work they are "narrated in the events of the cross and resurrection" (Rambo, *Spirit and Trauma*, 6).

been used by theologians to capture the ideas in Genesis 1–2 concerning the ideal environment and ways of relating between God and human persons.[8] When God blessed creation in its Edenic and wholesome state, he was conferring his approval of that state and his intention to perpetuate it: "God blessed the seventh day and declared it holy, for on it he rested from all his work of creation" (Gen 2:3 CSB).[9] God was satisfied with the sufficiency of creation; it is enough and itself has all it needs for life, which is a state of shalom—to satisfactorily have everything one needs.[10] Not only was the garden of Eden "teeming with life,"[11] but God's blessing reflects his intention for its ongoing flourishing for all involved.[12] The term "shalom" includes a perspectival sense related to the word "good"—so shalom includes the recognition that when this state of affairs is the case, then this is good.[13] Consequently, we can say that a blessed life from God, described as shalom, is the great "Good" to which God's creation is directed. Cornelius Plantinga writes:

> The webbing together of God, humans and all creation in justice, fulfilment and delight is what the Hebrew prophets call shalom. We call it peace, but it means far more than mere peace of mind or a cease-fire between enemies. In the Bible, shalom means *universal flourishing, wholeness, and delight*—a rich state of affairs in which natural needs are satisfied and natural gifts fruitfully employed. ... Shalom, in other words, is the way things ought to be.[14]

---

8. Graham A. Cole, *God the Peacemaker: How Atonement Brings Shalom* (Downers Grove, IL: InterVarsity, 2009). Yeago's methodology is helpful for carrying out this exegetical-conceptual task: D. S. Yeago, "The New Testament and the Nicene Dogma: A Contribution to the Recovery of Theological Exegesis," in *The Theological Interpretation of Scripture: Classic and Contemporary Readings*, ed. S. E. Fowl (Oxford: Blackwell, 1997), 87–102.

9. J. McKeown, "Blessings and Curses," in *Dictionary of the Old Testament: Pentateuch*, ed. T. D. Alexander and D. W. Baker (Downers Grove, IL: InterVarsity, 2003), 83–87.

10. G. Gerleman, "שָׁלֵם *šlm* to Have Enough," in *Theological Lexicon of the Old Testament*, ed. Ernst Jenni and Claus Westermann (Peabody, MA: Hendrickson, 1997), 1343.

11. McKeown, "Blessings and Curses," 86.

12. McKeown, "Blessings and Curses," 85–86.

13. Gerleman, "שָׁלֵם *šlm* to Have Enough," 1348.

14. Cornelius Plantinga, *Not the Way It's Supposed to Be: A Breviary of Sin* (Grand Rapids: Eerdmans, 1995), 10.

These are the conditions, or the ideal environment, that enable *personal* flourishing and breadth of life in common with each other. Shalom includes the best possible patterns of reciprocal relating between agents.[15] Every motivation and behavior in this dynamic and wholesome world builds up the soundness of each individual as well as the groups in the ecosystem.[16]

The ways that "shalom" is used in the Old Testament flesh out the various senses of the term and its theological use as a foundational Christian concept. The first has to do with holistic personal well-being. For example, in Genesis 29:6, when Jacob inquires as to the welfare or well-being of Laban, he asks after Laban's shalom. When Joseph's brothers come to see him in Egypt, he asks whether they are well—do they have/experience shalom (Gen 43:27). Joseph is also sent by Jacob to inquire about the shalom of his brothers in Genesis 37:14, probably in the sense of "things going well with them." In these cases, shalom "designates well-being, prosperity, or bodily health." Importantly, there is a theological driving force behind the idea of shalom; it is understood to be the outcome of a wise life that is carried out according to God's designs for it: "In the Wisdom literature the expectation exists that someone who lives in accordance with the prescriptions of wisdom will experience a long life and peace (Prov 3:2, 17). The wicked, on the contrary, will experience no peace (Isa 48:22; 57:21; 59:8). ... [Shalom] in such contexts designates a state of existence in accordance with Yahweh's created order." For this reason, shalom is associated with peace, which is "typified as a state of calmness and tranquility."[17] The apex of the emotions associated with shalom is joy (Gen 33:18).[18]

The second sense in which "shalom" is used refers to interpersonal well-being. This is a communal and interpersonal concept that is concerned with righteous relationships rather than individual well-being.[19] For this

---

15. Gerleman, "שָׁלֵם *šlm* to Have Enough," 1343–45.

16. "'The way things ought to be' in its Christian understanding includes the constitution and internal relations of a very large number of entities—the Holy Trinity, the physical world in all its fullness, the human race, particular communities within this race ... families, married couples, groups of friends, individual human beings. In a shalomic state each entity would have its own integrity or structured wholeness, and each would also possess many other edifying relations to other entities." Plantinga, *Not the Way It's Supposed to Be*, 10.

17. Philip J. Nel, "שָׁלֵם (8966)," in *New International Dictionary of Old Testament Theology and Exegesis*, ed. Willem VanGemeren, 5 vols. (Grand Rapids: Zondervan, 1997), 4:131.

18. Gerleman, "שָׁלֵם *šlm* to Have Enough," 1343–45.

19. Gerleman, "שָׁלֵם *šlm* to Have Enough," 1343–45.

reason, "shalom," Nel writes, "is also used to express the social or communal relations between friends, parties, and nations. In these contexts it gives expression to the absence of strife and war, representing, in other words, a friendly alliance."[20] For example, Hamor and Shechem use the term "shalom" when they say "these men are peaceful with us" in Hebrew (Gen 34:21). Shalom is the basis for the phrase "there will be peaceful counsel between the two of them" in Zechariah 6:13, to do with the relationship between the expected model king and an ideal priest.[21]

Thus we can say that covenantal relationships provide the security and orientation for shalom-like flourishing as well as peaceful, personal, and interpersonal "webbing together," as Plantinga puts it.[22] These promise-based relationships are successful when personal intentions and responsibilities are willingly pursued in faithful and life-enhancing ways.[23] Serene Jones writes, "When we live faithfully, we seek to mirror God's own creative intentions for the world. This is *faithful creativity*, creativity in its truest form. ... By living in conformity with God's intentions, we act in ways that please God, delight our Creator, and hence delight and enrich the whole of creation, including ourselves."[24]

Being able to act in these ways presumes that persons have the nature and qualities that will perpetuate idyllic life and life-giving conditions.[25] Not only that, it presumes they have the will and power to bring about shalom for others.[26] This relates to the third sense in which "shalom" is used: a state of affairs that may be restored in future times.[27] In the absence of shalom, it is a quality of relationships and a state of affairs that is sought

---

20. Nel, "שָׁלֵם (8966)," 4:131.

21. These examples are identified by Nel together with 1 Kgs 4:24 [5:4], 12 [26]; in "שָׁלֵם (8966)," 4:131.

22. Plantinga, *Not the Way It's Supposed to Be*, 10.

23. Sesshu Roth, "Intention, Expectation, and Promissory Obligation," *Ethics* 127, no. 1 (2016): 88–115.

24. Italics are original to Serene Jones, *Trauma and Grace: Theology in a Ruptured World* (Louisville, KY: Westminster John Knox, 2009), 104.

25. McKeown, "Blessings and Curses," 87.

26. Rochus-Antoin Gruijters, "Solidarity, the Common Good and Social Justice in the Catholic Social Teaching within the Framework of Globalization," *Philosophia Reformata* 81, no. 1 (2016): 23.

27. That is, "the state or condition that prevails when strife or war is ended." This is ש ל ם (e.g., 1 Kgs 2:5; Ps 120:6–7; Isa 59:8). Nel, "שָׁלֵם (8966)," 4:131.

after and pursued by righteous persons, especially the Prince of Peace/shalom (Isa 9:5; 53:5; contra those described in Isa 59:8).[28]

But what is it to be a person fit for shalom? Because of the intrinsically personal and interpersonal nature of God himself, we need to work out our philosophy and theology of both shalom and horrors with persons, both divine and human, as the primary reference point.[29] In order to proceed, we need to unpack how shalom, the opposite of horrors, is tied to what it is to be made as persons in the image of an intrinsically personal and interpersonal Trinitarian God.

THE TRINITARIAN GOD OF BLESSING AND SHALOM

God is the most personal being there is because he is necessarily personal "on the inside" as well as in his interactions with all other things. Graham Cole describes the warrant for believing that God is three persons: "In the canonical presentation Father, Son and Holy Spirit are speech agents (the Father in Matt 3:17, the Son in John 17:1 and the Holy Spirit in Acts 13:2). Persons are 'Thous,' not 'Its.' ... The one God is personal in three self-consciously distinct but inseparable ways as the eternal Trinity: one God in three Persons."[30] The unity of God the Father, Son, and Spirit is a dynamic relational togetherness: in God there is threefold self-consciousness and communication. This means that the life of God is shared and reciprocal.[31] He is Absolute Person, who relates internally as the Trinity and also relates personally with others.[32] The tripersonal nature of God and his qualities is the basis of the person-centric shalom he created.[33]

Because God is an incorporeal and immaterial spirit (John 4:24), his immaterial life includes an infinite degree of emotional and intellectual sharing, as well as joint attention between the divine persons. Emotional

---

28. Gerleman, "שלם *šlm* to Have Enough," 1345.

29. Burgos, *Introducción al personalismo*, 77. There are angelic persons, but they will only be treated here as they relate to divine and human ones.

30. Cole, "Personalism," 667.

31. Frame's language of God the "Absolute Personality," due to his triune personality, is helpful. John M. Frame, *The Doctrine of God* (Phillipsburg, NJ: P&R, 2002), 27.

32. Frame, *Doctrine of God*, 27.

33. Cole, "Personalism," 667.

sharing is coempathy between persons, when two persons actively and reflectively participate knowingly in the same experience as overlapping, yet discrete, subjects.[34] The three persons within God have overlapping experiences and insight into the experience of the other persons, yet they do not blend together.[35] Togetherness is the vital criterion for shared experiences. God is able to experience this because of the unity of being, which is grounded in the persons indwelling one another and being necessary for the life of the other.[36]

Love is the quality of God's Trinitarian nature. Trinitarian persons relate to each other in a loving second-person perspective: in a "you" sense, rather than in the "he, she, or it" senses.[37] This intimate sharing is demonstrated in Jesus' prayer to his Father in John 17. In this prayer Jesus speaks to the Father about a prior and preexistent relationship of shared knowledge and recognition (glory) before the creation of the world (John 17:5). He prays: "Now, Father, glorify me in your presence with the glory I shared with you before the world was created" (John 17:5 CEB). Jesus recalled the Father and Son's shared memory of a common experience in which the divine persons acknowledged each other's personhood and significance, which is what glorification is.[38]

---

34. Zeynep Okur Güney, "Collective Affinity as a Flux of You, Me and We," *Journal of Consciousness Studies* 22, nos. 1–2 (2015): 102–6.

35. I draw this from Zahavi's position on sharing emotional experience in D. Zahavi, "You, Me, and We: The Sharing of Emotional Expereince," *Journal of Consciousness Studies* 22, nos. 1–2 (2015): 84–101. Laura Galbusera summarizes it as follows: "Emotional sharing is not a fusion but must entail a plurality of subjects. … Emotional experience must be constitutively interdependent and co-regulated in order to be shared, and the subjects must be reciprocally aware of each other." Galbusera, "The (Temporal) Constitution of the 'We' between Connectedness and Differentiation," *Journal of Consciousness Studies* 22, nos. 1–2 (2015): 107–11.

36. This is secured by perichoresis in tandem with simplicity. Contemporary versions of this must wrestle with A. J. Cotnoir's proposal that "there is a viable philosophical theory of parthood, complete with a coherent and consistent formalization, that allows for *mutual parts*—distinct entities that are parts of each other. Such a view can make sense of a perichoretic relation according to which it is absolutely coherent to affirm that the three persons of the Trinity are 'in' the others." Cotnoir, "Mutual Indwelling," *Faith and Philosophy* 34, no. 2 (2017): 127. Whereas past scholars have drawn on the psychological analogy to speak of God, I am drawing on newer theories of mind, namely, consciousness studies.

37. Zahavi, "You, Me, and We," 93.

38. "In the OT the basic sense of glory is 'weight, heaviness,' with the extended figurative sense of importance, impressiveness or gravitas." John A. Dennis, "Glory," in *Dictionary of Jesus and the Gospels*, ed. J. B. Green, Jeannine K. Brown, and Nicholas Perrin (Downers Grove, IL: IVP Academic, 2013), 313. This use continues in the New Testament; for example, John's Gospel "carries over the basic uses of 'glory' in the OT and the Synoptics, such as glory as

When God focuses outward, his attention is also shared. Joint attention involves focused attention on an idea, person, or event in which one or more persons are aware that they are jointly attending to it. This is more than parallel attention, as it is an experience in which there is coordination and differentiation at the same time. Like emotional sharing, shared attention maintains personal differentiation; however, there is an unmistakable unity of a "me-and-you" within it.[39] God's shared attention is grounded in his life as the Trinity and is facilitated by the fact that the persons of the Trinity indwell one another. In addition, because God is an immaterial being, shared attention is his default manner of self-talk or internal communication; it is not foreign to him at all.[40]

Togetherness and harmony are the hallmarks of God's internal and personal life. It is unsurprising that he created a harmonious and flourishing garden of Eden. It is also unsurprising that the pinnacle of his creation was human persons, images of himself who were made to enable and enhance life. The descriptions below refer to how this was the case for the original humans before the fall, in their state of innocence.

IMAGES OF GOD AS UNIQUE AND BLESSED PERSONS

In the creation story, God says that he wants to make human beings in his likeness and image (Gen 1:26). Therefore, images of God have a nature that is fit to image God, both to each other and to the creaturely world. This nature includes relational, moral, and creative aspects that contribute to shalom, which we will now discuss.

---

social praise, honor, approval and reputation (Jn 5:44; 7:18; 8:50; 12:43), and glory as the radiant presence of God (Jn 11:4, 40; 17:5)." Dennis, "Glory," 315. Drawing on the Hebrew notion that glory refers to "a perceptible attribute, an individual's display of splendor, wealth, and pomp," theologian Millard Erickson writes that "when [glory is] used with respect to God, it does not point to one particular attribute, but to the greatness of his entire nature." Erickson, *Christian Theology* (Grand Rapids: Baker Academic, 2013), 924. In other words, recognition and greatness are the key ideas.

39. Zahavi, "You, Me, and We," 92.

40. Even after the incarnation of the Son, God's internal self-talk as the Trinity is his primary mode of inner communication.

Relational

In order to flourish, images of God need to relate communicatively and interactively with God, other persons, and their own self.[41] Emmanuel Mounier describes the fundamental importance of relatedness for human persons:

> In its inner experience the person is a presence directed towards the world and other persons, mingled among them in universal space. The person only exists thus towards others, it only knows itself in knowing others, only finds its being in being known by them. The *thou*, which implies the *we*, is prior to the *I*—or at least accompanies it.[42]

We can go further and say, with Jesús Rodríguez Lizano, that "the fundamental characteristic of [human] persons is their ability to relate to God and other persons."[43] Instead, we need to notice that the irreducibly relational nature of images of God means that they are persons dependent on other persons in order to flourish.[44]

Relationships with God are possible because humans were made to "answer and reflect him," writes Oliver O'Donovan.[45] This ability to respond to God with loyalty and trust is grounded in the fact that human persons are spiritual beings as well as physical beings—and therefore are oriented toward spirit-to-Spirit communication with God.[46] This relationship provides the person with the best possible orientation for life. In this relational context with God, says O'Donovan, "We are led to know ourselves for what we are, to come to ourselves in coming to our Father, to enact our existence truly. It is the freedom to live, the total expression of active, conscious, authentically engaged existence."[47]

---

41. Jesús Rodríguez Lizano, "El personalismo. Sus luces y sus sombras," in *El Primado de la persona en la moral contemporánea*, ed. Augusto Sarmiento et al. (Navarra, Spain: Servicio de Publicaciones de la Universidad de Navarra, 1997), 302.

42. Italics are Mounier's. Emmanuel Mounier, *Personalism* (Notre Dame, IN: University of Notre Dame Press, 1970), 20.

43. Rodríguez Lizano, "El personalismo," 301.

44. Mounier, *Personalism*, xviii–xxii.

45. Oliver O'Donovan, *Self, World and Time* (Grand Rapids: Eerdmans, 2013), 5.

46. I owe this insight to conversations with Graham Cole over many years.

47. O'Donovan, *Self, World and Time*, 5–6.

In addition to this relationship with God, other human beings are critical for the development of healthy personhood. God says that Adam needs other humans in order to flourish (Gen 2:18). People present themselves to one another face to face, which immediately establishes relationships of presence, vulnerability, and communication.[48] Ideally, the personalizing process requires interpersonal relationships by which the person becomes a loving self.[49] The corporate dimensions of personal relationality should aim toward political shalom. This is a state of affairs in which righteousness shapes order, safety, relationships, and the distribution of goods.[50]

An important aspect of relationality is the degree of intimacy and oneness that is available between some human persons. Adam and Eve are able to participate in physical sharing to the extent that they know each other and become one (Gen 2:24–25; 4:1; Mark 10:8). In order for these relationships to be life giving, they must be morally pure. Moral purity is the quality of holiness: intending the best for others and excellence in the expression of one's intended nature. Without moral purity, relationships will be marred by selfishness, transgressive behaviors, failures of responsibilities, and unequal consumption of goods.

The relationality that is possible between God and his images is deepened along Trinitarian lines in the New Testament. The incarnation reveals that human nature is able to be assumed and activated by God himself (John 1:1–18).[51] This affirms the uniqueness of human nature by demonstrating its ontological, personal, moral, and functional fittingness for a single person of the Trinity. Human beings are also fit to receive the indwelling of

48. Emmanuel Levinas, *Totality and Infinity: An Essay on Exteriority*, Duquesne Studies Philosophical Series 24 (Pittsburgh: Duquesne University Press, 1969), 66.

49. M. Nedoncelle, *La réciprocité des consciences: Essai sur la nature de la personne* (Paris: Aubier, 1942), 16, cited in Rodríguez Lizano, "El personalismo," 301.

50. Govert Buijs and Simon Polinder, "Concluding Reflections: Christian-Philosophical Reflection and Shalom Searching Wisdom," *Philosophia Reformata* 81, no. 1 (2016): 89. Here they draw on Nicholas Wolterstorff, *Until Justice and Peace Embrace: The Kuyper Lectures for 1981 Delivered at the Free University of Amsterdam* (Grand Rapids: Eerdmans, 1983).

51. Describing Leftow's view, Oliver Crisp writes: "If a human-body composite usually comprises an individual human person, in the case of the Incarnation the body and soul of Christ are conjoined with the soul of the Word to form a 'larger' person." Crisp, *Divinity and Humanity: The Incarnation Reconsidered* (Cambridge: Cambridge University Press, 2007), 64. Paul Griffiths writes: "Among enfleshed animate creatures, the human holds a special and central place, as image and likeness of the LORD, and as the kind whose flesh the LORD took." Griffiths, *Decreation: The Last Things of All Creatures* (Waco, TX: Baylor University Press, 2014), 4.

three persons of the Trinity. This further suggests the fittingness between God and his images (John 14:23–24).

Moral

The moral aspect of being an image of God refers to the manner in which the activation of a person's nature is expressed and how it affects others. If images of God are to be consistent with their design, then they should reflect, or image, God's moral qualities. These include God's holy love, which is expressed toward others as his goodness, benevolence, and faithfulness. The centrality of the holiness of God's love means that human beings may reflect God's life-giving concern. People will pursue his mission to bring about the best kind of life possible: God promotes this because he is the life giver and the light of all people (1 John 1:5–9; Ps 119:105, 130).

The ethical purity required by this moral dimension has very practical outcomes. This includes being willingly faithful to God in the context of the promise-based relationship, which extends to upholding the integrity of other persons and promoting their personal wholeness and safety, that is, shalom.[52]

Creative/Functional

God's images have creative (or functional) aspects to their nature that reflect God's purposeful and creative will and agency. For Adam and Eve, the use of this creativity revolved around bringing order to creation and contributing to its expansion. These included tasks such as tilling the ground and naming the animals (Gen 2:19–20), and making aesthetic use of the gold, bdellium, and onyx (Gen 2:11–12). Humans possess a distinct form of ingenuity by which they can advance their cultures and social good. This ingenuity motivates the development of specialized language, conceptual thought, art, music, and crafts.[53]

By carrying out these responsibilities, persons in Eden could reflect God's creative power to other creatures through their actions. In addition, Adam and Eve reflected the best of the creaturely world back to God.

---

52. Michael Scott Horton, *The Christian Faith* (Grand Rapids: Zondervan, 2011), 268.

53. This is human *ingenium*. Lodi Nauta, "The Order of Knowing: Juan Luis Vives on Language, Thought and the Topics," *Journal of the History of Ideas* 76, no. 3 (2015): 328.

Humans as images of God therefore have a mediatorial role between God and creation.[54] They were created to mediate God's perspectives to one another through their use of language and through what they do physically.[55] When people communicate God's point of view and priorities to one another, they reaffirm that humans are God's own images; this reinforces that they are "very good" and fit to experience and perceive the world in a blessed state of shalom.[56]

Perspective

Ideally, a certain kind of perspective on the world follows from being a person made in the image of God. In contrast to developing a sense of self in light of our own imaginings—as in Descartes's "I think, therefore I am"—humans can affirm "I am loved, therefore I am" in light of God and his goodness toward people.

This understanding of the human self provided a perspective on the world for Adam and Eve. Because the human individual is made in love, he or she is whole. The individual's integrity as a body and thinking soul means they are able to genuinely perceive whatever appeared to them as it truly was.[57] Humans before the fall were realists.[58] In their perfect state, they did not misunderstand the world, nor were they fundamentally skeptical about perceiving it in a successful manner.[59] The truth and fullness of perception available to people in the garden of Eden was reinforced by interactions with other personal beings, including God and at least one other person.

Perception and "being in the world" are best when they are engaged in "we" relationships with other persons, because the one thing we cannot

54. For an excellent treatment of this topic, see Erickson, *Christian Theology*, 469–74.

55. Nauta, "Order of Knowing," 332–33.

56. Maurice Merleau-Ponty, *Phenomenology of Perception*, trans. Donald A. Landes (New York: Routledge, 2012).

57. I am a body-soul dualist, not a monist/physicalist.

58. Michael C. Rea, "Authority and Truth," in *The Enduring Authority of the Christian Scriptures*, ed. D. A. Carson (Grand Rapids: Eerdmans, 2016); Peter Railton and Gideon Rosen, "Realism," in *A Companion to Metaphysics*, ed. Jaegwon Kim, Earnest Sosa, and Gary S. Rosenkrantz (Oxford: Wiley-Blackwell, 2009), 533–37.

59. Rasmus Thybo Jensen, "Merleau-Ponty and McDowell on the Transparency of the Mind," *International Journal of Philosophical Studies* 21, no. 3 (2013): 470–92.

perceive fully is ourselves.[60] We need other people to complete our perception of ourselves.[61] Hence, perception in this context includes a unity of the subjective and objective, intrinsic and extrinsic, individual and corporate.[62] Just as God's life includes shared perspective and joint attention, so does human sense-making, by which a person develops values, concerns, and cares in order to survive and mature.[63] In the state of shalom, human persons are healthily "interlocked" as this communication takes place with one another.[64] This interlocked communication is so strong that it even completes and shapes the internal communication within a person.[65]

WHAT WENT WRONG? THE IMAGES OF GOD AND SHADOWS OF GOD

The positive side of being images of God is that humans have relational, functional, and moral powers that can profoundly alter the state of affairs in the world and the perception of others. However, the shadow side is that when humans abuse their personhood, they damage each other and the world—even causing death, which is the opposite of life.

Nonrecognition and Hedonistic Transgression

The metaphysical basis of horrors lies in human transgressive motivations and behaviors toward God and, secondarily, toward other people. These stem from not recognizing the nature of different kinds of persons and from falling into illusions.[66] These replace faithfulness in attitude and action.

---

60. Merleau-Ponty, *Phenomenology of Perception*, 341.

61. Kevin J. Vanhoozer, *Remythologizing Theology: Divine Action, Passion, and Authorship*, Cambridge Studies in Christian Doctrine 18 (Cambridge: Cambridge University Press, 2010), 333; Jennifer Pfenniger, "Bakhtin Reads the Song of Songs," *Journal for the Study of the Old Testament* 34, no. 3 (2010); Susan Felch, "Dialogism," *Dictionary for Theological Interpretation of the Bible*, ed. Kevin Vanhoozer (Grand Rapids: Baker Academic, 2005), 174.

62. Merleau-Ponty, *Phenomenology of Perception*, 341.

63. "Sense making is the relational process of signification between an anonymous, self-organizing subject and the world, on which she has a certain perspective based in her self-organization, which entails certain needs and concerns." Hanne De Jaegher, "How We Affect Each Other," *Journal of Consciousness Studies* 22, nos. 1–2 (2015): 123.

64. Zahavi, "You, Me, and We," 96.

65. Contra Thomas Nagel, *The View from Nowhere* (New York: Oxford University Press, 1986).

66. Jensen, "Merleau-Ponty and McDowell on the Transparency of the Mind," 473–77.

What is nonrecognition? If glorification is the recognition of someone's weightiness or significance, nonrecognition is the opposite: it is the failure to honor another person (human or divine) with the significance that is properly due them. It does not appreciate and act out the asymmetrical relationship that is fitting for a relationship with God, nor does it enjoy and nurture life-giving reciprocal relationships with human persons. Because of the powers that are inherent to images of God, nonrecognition is always accompanied by the use of power. The use of power will attempt to subordinate other persons in master-slave relationships for the sake of the hedonistic development and the pleasure of the powerful.[67]

When God gave creative and relational powers to Adam and Eve, he gave his images the potential to affect other people and shalom. They could be vandalizers of relationships and the wholeness of other persons, thereby sabotaging shalom. For this reason, immoral perception (nonrecognition) and the immoral use of power led to humans being horror makers.[68] Ironically, their capacity to "vandalize shalom" demonstrates just how powerful the first images of God were. Such is the scope of their actions that as a result, *all* human persons and their environments are "not the way it is meant to be."[69]

Nonrecognition and hedonism come together in the great primordial sin. This was the nonrecognition of God by humans, paired with the desire to exceed the boundaries of being images of God. This meant ontological transgression—transgressing into being like God. Satan's temptation was "your eyes will be opened and you will be like God" (Gen 3:5). By acting in order that they may be gods rather than images of God, Adam and Eve tried to seize for themselves that which is most intimate to God—his divine nature. Adam and Eve attempted to transgress an ontological boundary between themselves and God. This is the gravest kind of transgression possible because of the nature of the boundary being ignored. They did not respect the integrity of God's distinct nature.

God's nature is made clear by the boundary of kind, or species, between God and humans, which plays a significant role in Genesis (Gen 1:26; 3:22; 11:7).

---

67. Raymond Belliotti, *Power: Oppression, Subservience, and Resistance* (Albany: State University of New York Press, 2016), 157–61.

68. Cole, *God the Peacemaker*.

69. Plantinga, *Not the Way It's Supposed to Be*, 7.

These passages underscore that God and humans belong to different orders of life and therefore have distinct identities and spheres of influence. The foundational creation account includes Genesis 1:26, in which God states that he will make humans "in our image, according to our likeness. They will rule." God's speech includes the contrast between God and humans, "we" and "they," which reveals an ontological fact: these referents are for two dissimilar kinds of beings. One has created the other.[70]

The ontological difference has psychological outcomes: only an asymmetrical relationship between these two kinds of beings can reflect the reality of who made whom and for what purpose.[71] Whereas God has the perfections and capacities that he displays vis-à-vis creating the cosmos—the kind of living freedom that is marked by decision, command, and generation—his images are to reflect a complementary side that comports with God's capacities: answering and enjoying.[72] This psychological boundary, and the covenantal relationship it entails, was broken when Adam and Eve doubted God's motivations, words, faithfulness, and judgments. This attempts to reduce God to faceless anonymity. He is "defaced," dethroned from having the status of the one who faces all creatures and whom all creatures should face in awe.[73]

The psychological boundary that was protected in relationship to God was breached when Eve and Adam ate of the tree of good and evil. Breaching this boundary opened up existence to psychological insecurity and incompleteness. Relational and creative chaos ensued, as power was no longer qualified by personal relationships. Persons became dislocated, both literally and figuratively, being displaced substantively, relationally, morally, and functionally.

The transgression partially succeeded, and human beings became more godlike than they were before. There was a change in the degree of their

---

70. Lyle M. Eslinger, "The Enigmatic Plurals Like 'One of Us' (Genesis i 26, iii 22, xi 7) in Hyperchronic Perspective," *Vetus Testamentum* 56, no. 2 (2006): 174.

71. Ben C. Ollenburger, "Creation and Peace: Creator and Creature in Genesis 1–11," in *The Old Testament in the Life of God's People: Essays in Honour of Elmer A. Martens*, ed. Jon Isaak (Winona Lake, IN: Eisenbrauns, 2009), 148.

72. Eslinger, "Enigmatic Plurals Like 'One of Us,'" 174.

73. Bernhard Waldenfels, "Levinas and the Face of the Other," in *The Cambridge Companion to Levinas*, ed. Simon Critchley and Robert Bernasconi (Cambridge: Cambridge University Press, 2002), 67.

knowledge and of their power to bring about good and evil: "The eyes of both of them were opened ['to know good and evil'/'obtain wisdom']" (Gen 3:5–7). However, this new state, with their bearing the sin and guilt of their actions, includes profound absences in their lives where there once was teeming life. The primary one relates to the absence of shalom with God, which then subsequently flows on to negative realities that occupy life's natural location and orientation.[74]

God Defends Himself and Defends Life as It Should Be

Despite this partial advancement, God defended the ontological, relational, functional, and psychological boundary between himself and his images. Though it was willfully and partially breached, God protected it against further human incursion. After humans ate of the tree of the knowledge of good and evil, God defended the breached boundary between himself and his images, stating that since Adam had "become like one of us, knowing good and evil, he must not reach out, take from the tree of life, eat, and live forever" (Gen 3:22). The contrast between the "the man" and "us" is ratified and defended with heightened intensity.[75] God acted to reestablish and protect the properly basic distinction between himself and his images by banishing them from the garden.[76] By doing so, God's images no longer had immediate access to his presence and words. That humans could not resist their banishment from the garden of Eden suggests that they had not fully become like God.

Life in the Devastation

As a result of being banished from the garden of Eden, people have since lived in a hostile world to which they are maladapted. They become horror makers, interested in their survival above the interests of others.

---

74. This is a revision of Aquinas's account of evil as a privation of the good. My whole treatment of horrors converses with Aquinas's work on evil; however, it departs from his in a number of ways, as will become clear. I am working in conversation with Aquinas, *Summa Theologiae*, vol. 8, 1a qq. 44–49 (London: Eyre & Spottiswoode, 1967), qq. 48–49; Aquinas, *Summa Theologiae*, vol. 18, 1a2ae. 18–21 (London: Eyre & Spottiswoode, 1966), qq. 18–21.

75. Eslinger, "Enigmatic Plurals Like 'One of Us,'" 175, 177.

76. Eslinger, "Enigmatic Plurals Like 'One of Us,'" 175, 177. I am using "properly basic" in the sense of necessarily basic, as opposed to a contingent distinction between God and humans.

Since the time that human beings vandalized shalom, life has been lived out in the realm that Paul Griffiths rightly calls "the devastation." This world of the devastation is "the damaged cosmos, the cosmos as it has become since the double fall, of humans and angels." Griffiths writes that for animate creatures such as humans, the "principal signs of the world's devastation" are "death" and "pain and suffering."[77] For inanimate things they are "annihilation by destruction" and "chaotic decay towards destruction." Hence, there is a profound absence of life. A negative presence has taken over the realm in which each particular life had its orientation, potential, and actualization. The life forms that remain are directed toward their opposite end, with the undeniable result that human persons live a "death-bounded and death-directed life."[78] This is not a metaphor but a biological reality.[79] Griffiths describes the gory reality of life within death directedness: "Traces of the cosmos' surpassing beauty remain, some evident to human creatures and some not. But for the most part, the world appears to human creatures as it is: a charnel house, saturated in blood violently shed; an ensemble of inanimate creatures decaying toward extinction; a theatre of vice and cruelty."[80]

The strange, warped, unnatural environment is one of the drivers behind the "vice and cruelty" in the warped natural environment. Once shalom is undone and chaos reigns, humans and angelic persons adapt to the harsh and hostile suboptimal environment. This adaptation does not overcome these conditions but rather survives within while bringing about horrors in interpersonal relationships.[81] In fact, the human adaptation to the suboptimal environment motivates further dreadful qualities

77. Griffiths, *Decreation*, 4. This aligns with Rambo's contention that "death in life is central to trauma." Rambo, *Spirit and Trauma*, 6.

78. Griffiths, *Decreation*, 4, 46.

79. The importance of death being understood as a cessation of life and not merely a metaphor will be important for our interaction with people working in trauma studies, for whom metaphors and the metaphorical use of "death" are important. In order to do justice to our biological reality, as well as the ways in which we experience it, we need to use a "strong" sense of death (the biological cessation of life) as well as a "weak" use of it, which refers to smaller losses and death-like experiences. Rambo, *Spirit and Trauma*, 4, 10, 23, 25.

80. Griffiths, *Decreation*, 4.

81. Marilyn McCord Adams, *Christ and Horrors: The Coherence of Christology* (Cambridge: Cambridge University Press, 2006), 39. Though Adams's point is a valid standalone insight that context drives human behavior, she does not strongly relate this to theological dimensions associated with both shalom and sin.

in relationships between human and angelic personal beings. The qualities are marked by absences, or deprivations, of what should be there—in other words, various lacks of the kind of fullness that is proper to a thing's nature. In their place we may see the presence of a negative aberration, like phantom pain in place of a limb.[82] These absences in the relational, moral, and creative aspects of personhood will be noted throughout this work.[83]

SETTING THE SCENE FOR HORRORS

Having outlined the origins of horrors, we now have a theological context for understanding what is being referred to when someone speaks of a "horror." This chapter has highlighted the importance of life, persons, and flourishing. It also highlighted how much is lost when humans take life into their own hands. This is where horrors originate from: the deathward and antipersonal nature of evil and sin. The task ahead is to clarify what horrors are. There are different kinds of horrors and different aspects to them. The next chapter provides clarity on what horrors are in order to preserve the term from being used loosely and losing any particular meaning or from being avoided altogether. The value of this is that it helps us address the many aspects of horrors as well as the many questions these raise about God, ourselves, and the point of life.

---

82. I follow Adam Swenson, who explores a positive theory of pain as it relates to privation. This draws on Aquinas's *Summa Theologia* as well as from Augustine's *Confessions* and *The Enchiridion on Faith, Hope, and Love*, both of which are placed in conversation with John Hick's *Evil and the God of Love*. Swenson, "Privation Theories of Pain," *International Journal for Philosophy of Religion* 66, no. 3 (2009): 139–54.

83. Here I am following Aquinas's privation accounts of evil, though I differ with him on a number of the details. Aquinas, *Summa Theologiae*, vol. 8, qq. 48–49; vol. 18, q. 18, art. 1–11.

3

HORRORS AND TRAUMA

What are horrors? The need to define horrors stems from the fact that they are not merely scary fantasies but are a very real part of human life and are profoundly evidenced and felt by individuals, in relationships, and in society at large in our era. How can we identify horrors, and why are they so traumatic?

Formally, horror is defined in a number of ways. From a persons's perspective, a horror may be an emotional state, for example a "painful and intense fear, dread, or dismay." It may also be a reaction such as "intense aversion or repugnance." A horror may also be a quality of a thing or person: "the quality of inspiring horror: repulsive, horrible, or dismal quality or character." Horrors, in the plural sense, are taken to refer to "a state of extreme depression or apprehension."[1]

However, the commonplace use of "horrors" seems to outrun these definitions. In truth, horrors are complex and hard to define. Theologians have recognized the insufficiency of language to speak of topics relating to horrendous trauma.[2] I therefore undertake the task of defining horrors in conversation with trauma studies. I do so for a number of reasons. First, there is an organic connection between the two because trauma is a likely (though not necessary) response to horrors. Second, trauma is often the evidence for horrors; therefore, a model of what horrors are is partly dependent on the experiences of trauma survivors and research from the

1. *Merriam-Webster's Collegiate Dictionary*, 11th ed. (Springfield, MA: Merriam-Webster, 2003).

2. For example, in the field of trauma studies, Shelly Rambo writes, "The challenge in writing about trauma is that trauma is the experience that is the most difficult to put into language and to conceptualize; it is the unimaginable territory." Rambo, *Spirit and Trauma: A Theology of Remaining* (Louisville, KY: Westminster John Knox, 2010), 10. See also Douglas E. Christie, "The Night Office: Loss, Darkness, and the Practice of Solidarity," *Anglican Theological Review* 99, no. 2 (2017): 213, 232.

field of trauma studies. Third, it is important to discuss them in close succession because the differences between them can then be made clear.

In what follows, I produce a taxonomy of horrors, which outlines a number of criteria for determining what they are. The order of the discussion is important. Though this chapter could begin by introducing trauma and how it shapes our understanding of horrors, I have chosen to outline horrors first, as they are the primary problems. This preserves the logical connection between horrors and trauma, but it also requires patience from you, the reader, as the connections between horrors and trauma, especially how they inform each other, cannot all be stated and proven at once.

This taxonomy looks backward, not forward, to form its criteria. As established in the previous chapter, shalom, in which the ideal images of God flourish as persons in the presence of one another and God, is the context against which we can understand horrors. Therefore, it is also the conceptual background for the criteria that follow. This is a creation-based (protological) rather than renewal-based (eschatological) taxonomy.

This first taxonomy is beneficial, even though it only refers to the present, penultimate state of the world. Taking the time to do this work stops us from rushing over the very painful aspects of life and hurtling unthinkingly toward a desired ending. In addition, exploring the depths of horrors also highlights the extent and intensity of action that is required of any person(s) for the sake of resolving horrors.

THE TAXONOMY

Psychiatric work has alerted us to the fact that, though they are related, there is a difference between actual horrific events and their horrific aftermath. There is a parallel here between horrors and trauma. For example, the American Psychiatric Association's DSM-5 states that trauma may be either or both an event or a perception. It is any "exposure to actual or threatened death, serious injury, or sexual violence."[3]

The spiritual dimensions of personhood and horrors are not addressed by the medical definitions of trauma. We need to recognize this boundary,

3. American Psychiatric Association, *Diagnostic and Statistical Manual of Mental Disorders: DSM-5* (Washington, DC: American Psychiatric Association, 2013), 830, cited in Nathaniel A. Carlson, "Lament: The Biblical Language of Trauma," *Cultural Encounters* 11, no. 1 (2015): 50.

because my purpose is to offer a theological account of horrors for the sake of Christian ministry—which is something the medical literature does not do. This means I will go beyond the medical definition and draw on literature from a different field (in a manner consistent with the medical definition) in order to address and include the theological dynamics at work in horrors and trauma.

Theologians working in the field of trauma studies make similar distinctions between events and perceptions in their own work.[4] For this reason, I find that, as long as the complexity and interrelatedness of various aspects of horror are acknowledged, we can begin to explain what horrors are by making a number of distinctions within the theological framework outlined above. Pointing out these particularities begins with describing two general types of horrors: the objective and subjective.[5] These can be further qualified as either gross or commonplace. It is important to note that these two types and their qualifiers can be associated with each other in a number of ways. For example, we could have an objective horror that is either gross or commonplace; we could also have a subjective horror that is either gross or commonplace.

A Horror

Something is a horror if, and only if, it includes one or more of (1)–(4) and (5):

1. it includes a degeneration of life toward death by means of replacing the makeup of a being with absences or distortions

4. Rambo, *Spirit and Trauma*, 2–4; Shelly Rambo, "Spirit and Trauma," *Theology Today* 69, no. 1 (2015): 7.

5. This reflects the strange relationship of horrors to time. A horror is an event as well as repercussive experiences related to this event at future times: trauma includes an initial event as well as its replication in the future, such as flashbacks. This second experience of the initial trauma differentiates trauma from suffering: "Trauma is not solely located in the actual event, but instead encompasses the return of that event. ... This return distinguishes trauma and suffering. Suffering is what, in time, can be integrated into one's understanding of the world. Trauma is what is not integrated in time; it is the difference between a closed and an open wound." Rambo, *Spirit and Trauma*, 19. What differentiates horrors from suffering is that horrors have repercussions that suffering may not have, such as traumatic consequences. Trauma studies usually refer to a trauma response as death's intrusion into life or a death-like experience. Rambo, *Spirit and Trauma*, 7.

of them and replacing the qualities of things with lacks or distortions of those qualities,

and/or

2. it is sourced in an objective, relationally immoral action,

and/or

3. it objectively prevents an individual from being and allowing others to be images of God in their natural and fullest sense,

and/or

4. it entails a traumatic response that diminishes the potential and actualization of personhood,

and

5. it is not possible to fully recover psychologically and relationally from these before death.[6]

Objective Horrors

Objective horrors are real events in time and space, occurring outside the mind. Regardless of their extent or the perception of their extent, something is an objective horror if it meets at least one of criteria (1), (2), (3), as well as (5).

6. This taxonomy is a revision of Aquinas's work on evil. Here I present a distortion-and-replacement view of evil. Evil replaces what should be there by taking away the full goodness of a thing and generating either a lesser version of it or something else in its place. For example, healthy skin is replaced with sores, which are imperfect forms of skin that respond to breaches of the skin. Consider a shadow: it is not merely the absence of light; it has a form and affects what is seen (such as detail and colors) on surfaces previously covered by light. Also consider an amputation: in place of a limb, there is a stump and phantom pain. The same replacement view of evil may be applied to relationships, personal character, and behaviors. I depart from Aquinas, who differentiates evil in things versus in behaviors. Thomas Aquinas, *Summa Theologiae*, vol. 8, 1a qq. 44–49 (London: Eyre & Spottiswoode, 1967), qq. 48–49; Aquinas, *Summa Theologiae*, vol. 18, 1a2ae. 18–21 (London: Eyre & Spottiswoode, 1966), qq. 18, art. 1–11. I am also drawing from Gregory M. Reichberg, "Beyond Privation: Moral Evil in Aquinas's 'De Malo,'" *Review of Metaphysics* 55, no. 4 (2002): 751–84.

As an example, let's consider a person who has been physically brutalized in a violent attack (we could think of the traumatized person in the parable of the good Samaritan—Luke 10:25–37). This person has lost teeth, lost blood, and received compound cranial fractures. This scenario entails a number of physical losses; however, the greater loss has to do with flourishing for the sake of God's glory. This relates to the first criterion, which is a criterion for being—a metaphysical criterion. This criterion is (1): "degeneration of life toward death." This degeneration is "by means of replacing substances with absences or distortions of them and replacing qualities of things with lacks or distortions of those qualities."[7]

In the scenario, the brutalized person has temporarily lost their participation and momentum in a God-given orientation, potential, and actualization toward life—which is taken to be flourishing in shalom with God and others. In its place there is a movement in the direction of physical death (the cessation of biological functioning and relationships with God and other persons) as well as in the direction of a less-than-ideal expression of the person's nature as a being.[8]

These are temporary events. The horror is revealed when we recognize that there are now absences in the constitutive features (or substance) and qualities of a person. Their essential makeup now includes deprivations and also lacks some of those qualities that are conducive to life and flourishing. For example, instead of having a full row of front teeth, there is a gap, and three teeth are missing: there is an absence of the substance of teeth. That person's face and smile are not the same; hence its qualities are affected: it is no longer a beautiful face that befits an image of God. A partly toothless face now occupies the space formerly taken up by a fully toothed

7. Brian Davies provides a helpful summary on Aquinas's position on evil and good. The first two points are important for my work here. I agree with the first but reject the second one. The one I agree with is: "(1) Evil or badness in the world exists insofar as naturally occurring substances (*entia per se*) lack goodness that is proper to them. It can also, though in a secondary sense be thought to exist insofar as *entia per accidens* lack some attribute we might want or expect them to have." The aspect I reject is underlined: "(2) Evil or badness is not an illusion. We can truly speak of it as existing or as having occurred. Unlike naturally occurring substances, thought, and even unlike accidents, evil or badness (*malum*) lacks esse." Davies then goes on to consider divine agency and to contrast evil with goodness. Davies, *Thomas Aquinas on God and Evil* (Oxford: Oxford Uninversity Press, 2011), 115, italics original.

8. As per Griffiths's realist descriptions in Paul J. Griffiths, *Decreation: The Last Things of All Creatures* (Waco, TX: Baylor University Press, 2014).

face. The fractured skull, with its accompanying neurological damage, in addition to tissue swelling and bruising, compounds the distortion. The previous face is no longer available to the individual and to the community: it is gone. The person as well as their relationships are disrupted. A horror has taken place because an absence of substance and lack of qualities have replaced what was there.

From the perspective of God's original creation, this is a horror because God created life and set up the conditions for its perpetuity and perfect actualization, not its end nor distortion. This is why the violent act meets the first criterion.

The harmful and transgressive event in itself is a horror. A violent physical assault resulting in permanent maiming meets moral criterion (2): "It is sourced in an objective, relationally immoral action."

Meeting either of these qualifies such an event as a horror. Yet this transgressive violence also introduces absences into a person's life: biological (losing teeth and two liters of blood), relational (not being prospered in personal relationships and losing trust in other persons), and psychological (losing a sense of safety and regularity of experience). Because of these absences, the violent act meets criterion (3): "It objectively prevents an individual from being and allowing others to be images of God in their natural and fullest sense." This criterion relates to a second party oppressively preventing the personal particularity of another. It occurs when one person actively impedes the differentiated ways in which people may fully be of service to the common good and God. Therefore, it is a nature-relative criterion: it considers what things should be by their nature. Naturally, when this does not occur it has ongoing individual and social consequences.

Objective horrors all meet criterion (5): "It is not possible to fully recover psychologically and relationally from these before death." This is because horrors, like trauma, entail an invasive loss of an aspect of a person's life (a form of "death") with the result that such a life is set on a radically different path: survival.[9] It is not merely unlikely that a person

9. "Trauma is described as an encounter with death. This encounter is not ... a literal death but a way of describing a radical event or events that shatter all that one knows about the world and all familiar ways of operating within it. ... The term 'survival' captures something of the suspension of life in the aftermath of a traumatic event. ... Life takes on a fundamentally different definition, and the tentative and vulnerable quality of life in the aftermath means

can return to life as it once was before horrors, but it is impossible that this be the case due to the significance of what has happened as well as the fact that memories always remain with us, even if unconsciously. Ignoring or denying the *impossibility* of returning to life as it was before a horror(s) event not only is a form of antirealism, but it is dangerous and negligent.[10]

All objective horrors (such as violent assault) qualify as objective horrors even though they do not meet criterion (4): "the traumatic perception of a real or imagined event that diminishes the personhood of an image of God." This is because objective horrors are not dependent on how they are perceived by the victim in order to be a horror.

Subjective Horrors of Perception: Fear and Despair

Subjective horrors are horrors of perception. These are located in the mind, not horrors that occur in the plane of history outside the mind. They are mind dependent and are either loosely attached to external reality or detached from it entirely. However, they are real events in the mind of a person who experiences them. They proceed from fears, including our instinctive recoiling at the unfittingness of objective horrors and other evils in the world. They are generated by the profound mismatch between our instinctive knowledge of the appropriate potential and aspirations of our bodies and psyche on the one hand, and the realities of life on the other. They are real *apprehensions* of the horrific conditions that attend much of individual and corporate human life.[11]

Subjective horrors therefore revolve around criterion (4): "The traumatic perception of a real or imagined event that diminishes the personhood of an image of God." That this is a trauma response within the victim differentiates it from criterion (3), which refers to the fact that the event in itself is an impediment to flourishing. Criterion (4) refers to the fact

that life is always mixed with death." Rambo, *Spirit and Trauma*, 4. "Although a person does not experience a literal death, the radical dimensions of the traumatic event are experienced as an end—a death." Rambo, *Spirit and Trauma*, 25.

10. "The push to move beyond the event, to a new and pure place, is not just a misconception about traumatic suffering; it is a dangerous move that threatens to elide the realities of traumatic suffering. This move also makes possible suffering's repetition." Rambo, *Spirit and Trauma*, 4.

11. Paul Hinkley, *Beloved Community: Critical Dogmatics after Christendom* (Grand Rapids: Eerdmans, 2015), 602. See also Sarah Hinkley Wilson, "Jesus Christ, Horror Defeater," *Lutheran Forum* 47, no. 1 (2013): 2–10.

that the impediment to flourishing is located in the response to horrors, which is a trauma response.

The focus of both criteria (3) and (4) is practical; it is on the fact that horrors impede actively living out the abilities God has given people for mutual benefit and flourishing. These are not merely nuisances because life is impeded and something good is replaced by something less so. For example, a nonpoisonous spider bite is not a horror, whereas a poisonous one that results in the loss of a limb and also the ability to work is a horror. Perceptions may also be merely nuisances, or they may be horrors that prevent a constructive life. Trauma responses are perceptive responses that get in the way of expressing the potential within each human nature and society.

One way to determine whether a fear or response is a horror or not is by means of another criterion to do with permanence. Fears are only horrors when they evolve to include criterion (5). When a fear introduces the kind of perception that death has irretrievably invaded and ended life's possibilities for flourishing, and that it not only threatens but necessarily undermines flourishing, then it is a horror.[12] Subjective horrors and fear have a codependent relationship. Subjective horrors are often related to fear and despair because fear is ultimately based on horror, and fear stems from "the sense of being lost in a nightmare of pointless and pervasive cruelty," as David Goldman puts it.[13] This naturally leads to questioning the goodness and purpose of the world in which we live, and by extension questioning the nature of God and human life.[14]

There is great variation in the subjective aspect of horrors, due in large part to the intrinsic variety of individual persons, their constitutions, and their worldviews. This parallels the way that trauma is a response to events that vary from person to person. Some people experience trauma in the aftermath of events, while others do not: some people experience subjective horrors as a result of engaging the world, while others do not. Marilyn McCord Adams rightly notes that that "the individuals' own estimates of

12. Here I am drawing on Rambo's idea that "death in life is central to trauma." Rambo, *Spirit and Trauma*.

13. David P. Goldman, "Be Afraid—Be Very Afraid," *First Things* (October 2009): 42.

14. Beatrice de Graff, "An End to Evil: An Eschatological Approach to Security," *Philosophia Reformata* 81, no. 1 (2016): 70–88.

how bad things are constitute weighty evidence about what is horrendous for them." She continues: "People have different strengths: some bear easily what crushes others."[15]

The importance of perception will drive much of our work in later chapters, where we deal with the questions of perception that arise from gross and commonplace horrors. These are issues relating to how God is perceived (i.e., directly present/indirectly present/absent; caring/uncaring) and how human life is perceived (meaningful/meaningless; hopeful/hopeless) in the midst and aftermath of horrors. Responding helpfully and reparatively to these questions of perception is imperative for dealing with a number of theological, existential, and anthropological questions raised by objective horrors.[16]

Gross Horrors

Gross horrors are those horrors in which the absences and lacks of what is proper to a person are most clearly visible. My use of the category of "gross horrors" includes what Marilyn McCord Adams calls "horrendous evils." These include "the rape of a woman and the axing off of her arms, psycho-physical torture whose ultimate goal is the disintegration of personality, betrayal of one's deepest loyalties, cannibalizing one's own offspring, child abuse of the sort described by Ivan Karamazov, parental incest, slow death by starvation ... being the accidental and/or unwitting agent in the disfigurement or death of those one loves best."[17] These horrors clearly meet criteria (1) and (5) in our taxonomy. They also meet criteria (2) and (3), and would almost certainly generate a trauma response (criterion [4]).

Another way to think about gross horrors is to consider the category of the worst kinds of malevolent damage that a human being can endure or do to another. Rebekah Eckert writes: "By 'horror,' I am usually speaking of violence perpetrated by humans upon humans. This would include genocide, senseless murder, rape, and torture. These are acts designed to harrow the souls of witnesses and victims, cruelty for the sake of cruelty. ...

15. Marilyn McCord Adams, "Horrors in Theological Context," *Scottish Journal of Theology* 55, no. 4 (2002): 469.

16. My work on horrors depends on and dialogues with Marilyn McCord Adams's terminology and concepts.

17. Adams, "Horrors in Theological Context," 468–69.

They are a particular kind of evil, an intention of creating as much pain as possible."[18]

Similarly, the process of death and dying is also a gross horror. It is perhaps the definitive gross horror. It ends the functional and most relational aspects of being made in the image of God; it is wholly incompatible and opposed to the purposes of life for which God created us. Death confirms the greatness of what is lost when a person dies, because their "grievability" demonstrates their ontological uniqueness.[19] In addition, at death the body is separated from the soul, rending apart the image of God and threatening God's purposes for the universe.[20]

However, horrors do not have to be gross acts of immoral violence or events that are immediately connected to the process of death. Horrors may also be commonplace horrors.

Commonplace Horrors

Commonplace horrors are frequently experienced, everyday horrors. They are less immediately and particularly devastating than gross horrors. No one is permanently maimed by each one of these. They include the horrors of exposure to the suffering of others, minor sports or workplace injuries, other nonlethal physical violence such as being punched in the face with no apparent long-term physical damage, or nonphysical violence such as being lied to or lied about. Commonplace horrors can also include relational transgressions: controlling behaviors such as stalking someone, disallowing someone from having certain kinds of friends, or preventing contact with family members. These can also include manipulative actions such as implicit threats of legal action, blackmail, or reputation spoiling.

---

18. Rebekah Eckert, "Preaching to Horror-Struck People," *Consensus* 31, no. 1 (2006): 91.

19. That people are missed and that grief follows their death and loss is a sign of their value. Sturla J. Stålsett writes that because people are "grievable," they have intrinsic worth. Stålsett, "Non/Human: Overcoming the Fatal Separation, without Diffusing the Crucial Distinction," *Studia Theologica* 69, no. 1 (2015): 25–26. Resorting to this criterion suggests the eclipse of the idea that images of God establish innate value and dignity. The "grievability" of pets also challenges the particularity of human beings as uniquely valuable persons. Stålsett, "Non/Human," 26–27.

20. This is one implication of the soul-body dualism I flagged earlier; see Joshua Ryan Farris, *The Soul of Theological Anthropology: A Cartesian Exploration* (New York: Routledge, 2017); Farris and R. Keith Loftin, eds., *Christian Physicalism? Philosophical Theological Criticisms* (Langham, MD: Lexington Books, 2017).

Commonplace horrors may also be the "smaller" events or lesser processes to do with death, such as an illness.

At first glance, one may be tempted to believe that these commonplace events and their perception are merely tragic. They are tragic departures from God's ideal, that's all. It may be tempting to employ Eckert's language of "sorrowful acts" rather than horrors.[21] However, a number of ideas internal to the taxonomy reveal the difference between merely tragic commonplace events and what we would describe as "commonplace horrors."[22]

First, such horrors are the result of transgressions, not unfortunate happenstances. They are horrors because they are indirectly related to (2): "an objective immoral violent action," because illness, death, and environmental disaster also ultimately result from a malevolent will: both malevolent demonic willing and malevolent human willing.[23]

Second, they must meet criteria (1) in our taxonomy: a degeneration of life toward death by means of replacing what was there with an absence or a distorted version of it. This is pointed out by considering the deliberate language I used above: commonplace horrors are less *immediately* and *particularly* devastating. "Immediate and particular" refers to the fact that what could be classified as lamentable tragedies if considered in isolation are in fact horrors given their frequency, pervasiveness, and compounding nature. Every person is afflicted by so many "everyday" lamentable events that these cannot be treated in isolation. Their compounding nature means that they do not remain solely lamentable; taken together, they comprise far more than the sum of their number.

A helpful metaphor for thinking about this is a thicket full of thorns. In this metaphor, each commonplace horror is like a small thorn in a thicket of

---

21. Eckert, "Preaching to Horror-Struck People," 91.

22. A fuller work would take into account the fact that horrors do not include acts of violence alone. For example, other elements that are intrinsic to human life in "the devastation" include illness.

23. Together with the horrors that describe the human violence that issues from malevolent human willing, we must include those horrors sourced in angelic will. The root cause of horrors is related to human sinfulness and angelic rebelling against God. I will assume this is the case and that it is evidenced by a series of bloody battles: the battles between spiritual forces and people, between people and other persons, and finally between a number of forces within the natural world that humans inhabit. This differs starkly from Marilyn McCord Adams, *Christ and Horrors: The Coherence of Christology* (Cambridge: Cambridge University Press, 2006), 37. However, I engage with her work because it is the standard book on horrors from a Christian perspective.

horrors. We try to walk and crawl our way through the thicket, but our very self is slowly ripped apart. Experientially, we are wearied and worn out by smaller horrors. Hope, faith, and love for God, oneself, and others fade away. In this way, the thicket of commonplace horrors flays away human psychological and relational life. Each little horror is an intrusion of death into life; hence, the sum of these is a person's movement away from life to death.[24] What makes these commonplace acts horrors in a fuller sense is their cumulative effect.

Commonplace horrors should also meet criterion (3): they restrict people from being images of God in their natural and fullest sense. This is a specific outcome of human sin, rather than another way of speaking about sin. In this sense, commonplace horrors parallel gross horrors because they unquestionably contribute to both the decreation of human beings and a failure to flourish.

Finally, commonplace horrors also meet criterion (5): "It is not possible to fully recover psychologically and relationally from these before death." Where the cumulative objective realities and subjective effects of commonplace acts intrusively damage human persons such that there is little prospect of recovery before the person experiences death, then these are considered horrors.[25]

An example of a commonplace horror from my own experience relates to the large number of nonpermanently maiming fights generated by road rage and gambling-related tensions that occur in my hometown of Melbourne, Australia. Imagine one such fight in a carpark. Is each fight merely lamentable, or is it a horror? In the light of the shalomic intention for images of God, it is a commonplace horror because it meets our criteria. It is (1) "a partial degeneration of life toward death," because it is yet another experience of the death-directedness of life—it entails relational absences and lacks. Both parties act violently (even if this is merely defensive blocking) toward another person. Such actions in the context of a perceived threat to safety are forms of antilife that recall long-past horror

---

24. Rambo successfully works with the idea of death invading life. Hence, for trauma survivors, life is lived in a midpoint between life and death. Rambo, *Spirit and Trauma*, 3, 138–41.

25. For the sake of clarity, damage is always transgressive; it always breaks down integrity barriers and boundaries in both the perpetrator and the one who is brutalized.

stories such as the violent murder of Abel by Cain. They also recall more recent horror stories in our towns and family histories.

This cluster is a degradation or decomposition of life into something less than shalom. It is clear that this kind of attack (2) "results indirectly from an objective immoral violent action." It also (3) "objectively prevents an individual from being and allowing others to be images of God in their natural and fullest sense," because it pressures people to conduct themselves in very restricted and deformed manners. And finally, (5): "it is not possible to fully recover psychologically and relationally from these before death." This experience has a compounding effect in a context such as Melbourne, which is plagued by violence, especially family violence. Though this event may not be ever-present to the mind of the person who is unwillingly involved in these fights, in this context, it will unconsciously affect behavior toward others, at least in future parallel situations. This will unconsciously be passed on to other generations, cementing its permanence in history and culture.[26]

We can't apply this set of criteria to all cases of violence and harassment. There will be some lamentable acts and transgressions that are not horrors, from which people may recover. A shouting match in the context of a sports game (especially an inherently physical contact sport, such as ice hockey) may be one such example. The context of the actions allows shouting that would usually be considered bullying to have little effect on the players because the context buffers the effect of what is said. Such an event does not fit into the horrors taxonomy.

The issue of perception is very important for dealing with commonplace horrors. This refers to criterion (4) of the taxonomy for horrors, which is "the traumatic perception of an event that diminishes the personhood of an image of God." There is a difference between gross horrors as objective events and commonplace horrors. There is likely to be a consensus that actions such as needlessly amputating the arms of a prisoner of war are gross horrors, aside from perceiving them as such. On the other end of the spectrum (we need to be aware of horrors along a spectrum running from gross to commonplace), commonplace horrors are horrors because of their withering and cumulative effect—which is as much a

26. Rambo, *Spirit and Trauma*, 21.

mental reality as a physical one. So, let's return to the example I brought in earlier: a fight fueled by road rage. I said this was a daily, commonplace event where I live. This is one fight of many; however, this single fight reminds us of past ones and anticipates one we know will involve us and/or our relatives and neighbors sooner or later. It brings to mind the fact that we live under the shadow of violence. The compounding effect of this, in addition to other local concerns such as drug use and child neglect, leads us to perceive the world as a house of horrors in which no one is safe, and life is inherently unpredictable and unstable.

CONNECTING HORRORS AND TRAUMA

Now that we have connected a medical definition of trauma with a framework for understanding what horrors are, we can enrich this by exploring a number of insights that have been pointed out by trauma studies. Trauma studies can help us to more comprehensively understand what horrors are and why they so problematically impede the actualization of life.[27] Through the presentation of scientific, intuitive, and folk beliefs, the trauma theory that emerges from this field of study confirms the existence of horrors and their traumatic aftereffects.[28]

A note on the differentiation between horrors and trauma may be helpful before I proceed. There is a genetic relationship: horrors precede the trauma response; horrors are the "traumatizing event." But whereas trauma usually refers to a temporary (which includes long-term) impeded actualization of life, horrors speak to permanent privations of life. In addition, I

---

27. "This interdisciplinary conversation around the effects of trauma and disaster draws from diverse fields of study. These include cognitive psychology, counselling, sociology, anthropology, and literary criticism. The shared hope of these investigations is to gain further understanding of the life-destroying effects of violence upon people and ultimately find processes that help people to endure, survive, and perhaps eventually thrive." Kathleen M. O'Connor, *Jeremiah: Pain and Promise* (Minneapolis: Fortress, 2011). "Trauma and disaster studies arose from the bloody smear that was the twentieth century" (O'Connor, *Jeremiah*, 2). Trauma studies have also received a strong contribution from the generation and institutionalization of feminism within the church and the university. See Gisela Matthiae, Renate Jost, Claudia Jeanssen, Annette Mehlhorn, and Antje Röckemann, eds., *Feministische Theologie: Initiativen, Kirchen, Universitäten – eine Erfolgsgeschichte* (Gütersloh: Gütersloher Verlagshaus, 2008), 291–94.

28. Daniel Nolan, "Method in Analytic Metaphysics," in *The Oxford Handbook of Philosophical Methodology*, ed. Herman Cappelen, Tamar Gendler, and John Hawthorne (Oxford: Oxford University Press, 2016), 163–69. See Nolan's work on Moorean beliefs in particular.

believe that not only is there a lack or absence of life when a horror takes place, but that in that location (the mind, or body, or a relationship) a real negative reality is introduced in the place of life's positive being.[29]

Overlap between Trauma and Horrors

There is a strong linguistic challenge present when we try to speak about evil, suffering, and its myriad consequences. Trauma theory provides us with helpful language and concepts. Some of its helpfulness is that it allows the necessary flexibility of expression that this study requires: We can speak of "traumatic events" in order to capture the strong connection between the reality of a horror and the trauma response. We can speak of a traumatized person in order to capture that people live in a state that is driven by a trauma response to horrors. Speaking in this way provides the conceptual space to recognize that horrors actively afflict persons such that they really are "traumatized." When I refer to people who are working through a trauma response, I like to speak of trauma survivors, as this picks up the fact that survival is a new reality in which these people experience the world. It also acknowledges the fact that they have much to contribute to other people who have traumatic experiences.[30] In addition to validating both the objective and the subjective aspect of horrors, trauma theory provides us with concepts that help us think about horrors as more than events: they are "open wounds"[31] and complex, long-lasting "storms."[32]

Trauma studies are also helpful to the study of horrors because they point to why we should care about the problem of horrors. Horrors are largely so problematic because they provoke trauma responses in human beings, and studies in trauma reveal the specific contours of these responses: the ways in which horrors depersonalize persons who are images of God, which in turn compounds and exacerbates the initial horror

---

29. This is an important idea that flourished in Spanish scholasticism, represented by Sebastián Izquierdo (d. 1681). See Brian Embry, "An Early Modern Scholastic Theory of Negative Entities: Thomas Compton Charleton on Lacks, Negations and Privations," *British Journal for the History of Philosophy* 23, no. 1 (2015): 22–45. The details of this need not detain us here; however, they inform the distinction between horrors and trauma as heuristic devices.

30. Rambo, "Spirit and Trauma," 25.

31. O'Connor, *Jeremiah*, 2; Kathleen M. O'Connor, "Stammering toward the Unsayable: Old Testament Theology, Trauma Theory, and Genesis," *Interpretation* 70, no. 3 (2016): 303.

32. Rambo, "Spirit and Trauma," 8.

event and experiences for the individual and for society. The twin problems of depersonalization and exacerbated trauma responses are discussed below, providing the basis from which I will discuss key theological and existential perceptions and difficulties spawned by horrors. The difficulties include doubts about the goodness of God's character, doubts about the possibility of meaningful living, and doubts about whether there is hope for a better form of human life.

Propagating Deterioration and Downgrading the Images of God

Horrors perpetuate the cascade of problems that were initiated by the primeval couple's failure to personally image God. Horrors degrade and downgrade the ways that images of God may flourish as relational, moral, and creative persons. Acts of horror, witnessing these, and being victims of them all contribute to stripping away an image's capacities for being a human kind of person by damaging the relational, functional, and moral capacities that come with being an image bearer.

This has another consequence. A diminishment in the personal capacities of a human person means that the personhood they possess, which allows them to recognize and relate to God in a life-receiving and life-giving manner, is gradually absent. A diminishment in their personal capacities will undermine their personal engagement with their divine Lover, Maker, covenant Lord, and Friend. As this engagement and security erodes, its deterioration ultimately undermines people's confidence in the goodness of God, as well as other commitments that follow on from this, including the possibility of human meaning-making and of ultimate hope.

Personal matters only get worse. The nonrecognition or misrecognition of God results in unnatural replacements for this relationship. For example, human persons and angelic persons relate to each other in distorted and compensatory manners. This is evident from the time of the seductive serpent in the garden of Eden (Gen 3), to the relationships that birthed the Nephilim (Gen 6:1–4), to the present reality of demonization and the worship of angels. These relationships devalue people as images of God, and they ultimately revolve around conflict and fear. In the midst of this, humans are brutalized by evil angelic beings and require divine rescue, both personally and cosmically.

Horrors May Generate Trauma Responses in People

Horrific events and experiences are traumatic events in that they introduce absences into places where life should bloom and are very likely to promote a trauma response. A definition of trauma that incorporates the objective and subjective sides is that it is "any serious event that threatens or affects the life or physical [I include psychological within this] integrity of a person, or a loved one. Experiencing, witnessing, or becoming aware of such an event creates intense fear, helplessness, or horror in the affected person," according to Frauke Schaefer and Charles Schaefer.[33] Though not all people will respond to horrors in the way described as trauma, the vast majority will, and for this reason it is a major public health concern.[34] From this point onward, I will focus on those people who do have this response. I will pick up the language of "being traumatized" in order to account for the unpredictability and loss of control that a traumatic response to horrors entails.

"To 'be traumatized' is, by necessity, expressed in the passive voice," writes Kathleen O'Connor, "because trauma reduces victims to a passive state. Victims are acted upon rather than actors who chose what happens to them." This passivity is reflected in the inaction that invades their mental states and beliefs: trauma "creates a kind of mental vacuum. It so overwhelms the capacities of victims to take it in, that the violence cannot be absorbed as it is happening. Traumatic violence comes as a shocking blow, a terrifying disruption of normal mental processes, distorting reality, even as it becomes the only reality."[35]

The quality of reality is disrupted, along with its foundations. O'Connor continues, "Disasters brought about by traumatic violence disturb what people think, feel, and believe. They distort perceptions and shut down ordinary life. Memories of the violence imprint themselves in the brain like a powerful ghost that returns again and again, repeatedly disordering

---

33. Frauke C. Schaefer and Charles A. Schaefer, eds, *Trauma and Resilience* (Condeo, 2012), vi.

34. The statistics on this are readily available online. I have not included them here, as they are constantly evolving.

35. O'Connor, *Jeremiah*, 2, 3. This is not a new phenomenon; see, for example, the late medieval metaphors for perception and its obstacles in the midst of suffering: the uses of "night," "wall," and "ladder."

daily life."[36] Among these consequences, trauma takes on an overwhelming quality. The nature of horrors is so appalling that the human mind cannot take it in at the time it occurs, and therefore the related traumatic effects are perpetually present and recurring.[37]

Consequently, trauma is not a temporary experience. Rather, it makes a distorting and permanent mark on people's lives.[38] Shelly Rambo describes its enduring nature by drawing on the image of life after the 2005 storm of Hurricane Katrina that hit Mississippi and subsequently led to flooding in New Orleans:

> *"After the storm" is always here.* ... It is an event that continues, that persists in the present. Trauma is what does not go away. It persists in symptoms that live on in the body, in the intrusive fragments of memories that return. It persists in symptoms that live on in communities, in ... present ways of relating. ... Life after the storm ... is not life as they once knew it.

The author then asks: "How do you account for an experience that was not fully integrated and, thus, returns? How can you heal from trauma?"[39] This may seem an impossible task because trauma's fundamental degenerative power is that it replaces potential and actual life with loss. Negative presences, such as an absent stare into the distance or eyes that never make eye contact, replace what was once geared for person-to-person relating. As a consequence, less of someone's personhood, nature, and vitality is offered toward the development of life in other people. The fullness of their being, their unique "face" or self, is less available for life and the gaze of love.[40] Various kinds of pain stemming from the loss of being inhibit

---

36. O'Connor, *Jeremiah*, 3.

37. This happens even though they are unevenly stamped in a person's consciousness, albeit in fragmentary though powerful forms. O'Connor writes: "Memories of traumatic events become fragmented, even as they take up residence in the mind where they have a life of their own. Contradictory though it may seem, these memories can be neither forgotten nor escaped, even though they exist as shattered moments of experience." O'Connor, *Jeremiah*, 3.

38. Rambo, "Spirit and Trauma," 7.

39. Rambo, "Spirit and Trauma," 7.

40. Kevin Hart writes that, for Jean-Luc Marion, "Loving turns ... not on seeing the beloved but in a crossing of their gazes that is apparent only for those intimately involved in the act of love. Two lovers *live* the invisible crossing of their gazes. ... Marion insists on the individuality of the other's face, one that cannot be substituted for another." Hart, ed., *Marion, Jean-Luc:*

a person from offering their self forward as an expression and vehicle of love.[41] Absences and pains distort perception, and as their consequence, we fall into various impersonal or contrapersonal misinterpretations of what being and life are, such as thinking "I think therefore I am" rather than "I am loved therefore I am."[42] In other words, traumatic "reductions" of a person means that there is less intentional phenomena for life, less disclosure of God's goodness through his images, and in its place there are distortions and voids. These impede processes by which a person's being develops from their nature.[43]

What was once life then becomes a "spectral existence."[44] I interpret "spectral" to have three meanings. One aspect of a spectral life refers to it being thinned out: not solid, partial and ethereal, distanced from the fullest kind of embodied life available to people. Second, spectral refers to a life that is haunted by events. Third, in place of the potential for life, a negative reality or lack is present, an absence or distortion of that which was there.[45] Given these three factors, trauma has overriding consequences for a person's worldview because it is about the nature of life itself. Rambo writes: "In the aftermath of trauma, death and life no longer stand in opposition. Instead, death haunts life. The challenge for those who experience trauma is to move in a world in which the boundaries between life and death no longer seem to hold."[46] In the light of this, we can say that in the same way that horrors lead to trauma, trauma leads to a spectral worldview.[47]

The Essential Writings (New York: Fordham University Press, 2013), 360, italics original. Adam Swenson, "Privation Theories of Pain," *International Journal for Philosophy of Religion* 66, no. 3 (2009).

41. Swenson, "Privation Theories of Pain," 145.

42. For Marion, "We encounter being in love, not in the ego. The proper formulation should not be 'I think therefore I am' but 'I am loved therefore I am.'" Hart, *Marion, Jean-Luc*, 360.

43. I draw this from Aquinas's work on Genesis, outlined in Joseph Owens, "Aristotle and Aquinas," in *The Cambridge Companion to Aquinas*, ed. Norman Kreutzmann and Eleonore Stump (Cambridge: Cambridge University Press, 2005), 38–59.

44. Rambo draws on the work of Susan J. Brisen, *Aftermath: Violence and the Remaking of a Self* (Princeton, NJ: Princeton University Press, 2003), 9, cited in Rambo, "Spirit and Trauma," 9.

45. Sebastián Izquierdo, *Pharus scientiarum*, in Embry, "Early Modern Scholastic Theory of Negative Entities," 23.

46. Rambo, "Spirit and Trauma," 9.

47. This experience of death invading life, and the impact it has on a person's prospects for living, has some parallels with the notion of *physical* "death before death," in which the process of death is slow and prolonged. Michael Banner, "Scripts for Modern Dying: The

Therefore, horrors traumatize people and consolidate a sense of horror within a person or persons.[48] This may take on a prison-like form: traumatized people experience prolonged and perpetuated internal cycles of fear and helplessness.[49]

Acknowledging the traumatic nature of horrors is important, not only because trauma theory provides great explanatory power and scope for the claim that horrors degrade the images of God, but also because it highlights the deep impact that violence has on persons.[50] This in turn sets up the constructive work of this project, which is to explore just how God might be present and active in the recovery of those who have been traumatized.

QUESTIONS UTTERED AMID DISORIENTATION

Trauma and its aftermath pose a number of questions. Will the experience of death or the experience of life have the upper hand in my mental, spiritual, work, and social life? Will the horrors of trauma be the dominant paradigm for my worldview?

The compounding disintegration caused by horrors and trauma provokes a number of Christian questions for believers who live in a horrible and traumatizing world. Where is God's care during horrors? How do Christians live after trauma? How can we integrate trauma into our lives as Christians?

These questions have not been answered well from within a Christian worldview. One of the best-known Christian researchers and authors dealing with trauma is Shelly Rambo. Rambo has worked extensively to aid the recovery of war veterans who have trauma responses to what they

---

Death before Death We Have Invented, the Death before Death We Fear and Some Take Too Literally, and the Death before Death Christians Belive In," *Studies in Christian Ethics* 29, no. 3 (2016): 254. This process is life sapping and involves deterioration and loss of capacity.

48. Traumas should never be considered at the level of an individual alone. When they occur at a larger corporate level, in this instance they are referred to as disasters; O'Connor, *Jeremiah*, 3.

49. Rambo, "Spirit and Trauma," 10.

50. The long-lasting and variegated ways in which this horror and trauma has affected people have been described using a number of tools for over one hundred years. One important outcome of this has been that a cross-disciplinary approach is required in order to study and resource these problems. For example, solely psychological or sociocultural descriptions of the dynamics of trauma and the range of its impact have been found to be an insufficient engagement. Shelly Rambo, "'Theologians Engaging Trauma' Transcript," *Theology Today* 68, no. 3 (2011): 229.

witnessed/were involved with/underwent during war. This research and clinical work has highlighted a dangerous disconnect between their experiences and the Christian worldview. Their own story does not "gel" with the larger Christian narrative and expectations and rhythms for life.[51]

What resources does the church have to offer in response to horrors and trauma? Rambo writes: "The challenge for those who take seriously the problem of trauma is to witness trauma in all of its complexities—to account for the ongoing experience of death in life. The challenge, for both, is to forge a path of healing amid all of the complexities."[52] In the chapter that follows, I outline the complexities with respect to some central theological, anthropological, and existential questions that are raised by horrors and compounded by trauma.

51. Rambo, "Spirit and Trauma," 8.
52. Rambo, "Spirit and Trauma," 9.

4

ISSUES ARISING FROM HORRORS

> "We've lost faith in faith, all hope is gone, and
> chastity is completely ... well, you know."
>
> —Tim Olds,
> "The History of the Future in Five Words"

Responses to horrors often feel inadequate: "What do you say in the face of horror?"[1] Answers must be offered, because these are aspects of our existence. If we ignore these problems, we will be antirealists. If we don't or can't address them, then our worldview is not livable and thus fails the pragmatic criterion. Sadly, experiences of horror and the realities of traumatized lives have not been substantially addressed by churches.[2] This should not be the case because the life of the church is a shared life by virtue of the communion established by the indwelling Spirit within each believer. Therefore, the body of Christ must communicate to all members that trauma is "not just your problem. It's our problem—my problem, the church's problem, God's problem. You don't need to be alone, and I hope we can work on it together. That's what faith communities do."[3] The place to start is to listen carefully to the "big three" problems raised by horrors: the theological, the existential, and the anthropological ones.

---

1. Rebekah Eckert, "Preaching to Horror-struck People," *Consensus* 31, no. 1 (2006): 91.

2. Aimee Kang, "Review of Serene Jones, *Trauma and Grace: Theology in a Ruptured World*," *Practical Matters* (March 1, 2011), http://practicalmattersjournal.org/2011/03/01/trauma-and-grace/.

3. Serene Jones, *Trauma and Grace: Theology in a Ruptured World* (Louisville, KY: Westminster John Knox, 2009), 7.

THE THEOLOGICAL PROBLEM: HORRORS AND GOD'S CHARACTER

Both Christians and non-Christians have highlighted the problem of horrors for the doctrine of a benevolent and life-giving God.[4] One of the dilemmas relates to the kind of God that God is. For some, the reality and presence of horrors throughout human history generates the argument that the God of classical theism is "*logically incompatible* with the existence of horrors."[5]

The relationship between a willing and active personal God and human suffering raises difficult questions for readers of biblical stories, such as the story of Job. Eleonore Stump writes:

> In a number of biblical narratives, not only is God a character in the narrative but he is also the character who manifestly allows or even brings about the suffering highlighted in the story. ... So it seems clearly appropriate to incorporate biblical narratives in any attempt to meld literature and philosophy in reflection on the problem of evil. ... There is therefore a certain commonsensical obviousness about bringing biblical narratives into the discussion of certain philosophical problems ... such as the problem of evil.[6]

This quote raises the stakes of the problem for those who would seek answers in a sacred text. How do we proceed if reading sacred texts may yield unwanted answers? For Stump, an answer to the problem of God's character requires biblical engagement and resolving problems within the particular story world of the texts. Stump's expectation is that a thoughtful interaction with the text will yield insights into God's character and his

---

4. Marilyn McCord Adam's *Christ and Horrors* has tremendous potential for carrying out important work on overcoming theological, apologetic, and ethical problems that arise from the presence of horrors in the world. See her threefold way of understanding the means and process through which God overcomes horrors, namely, the solidarity of the incarnate Word with other human horror participants. However, the Christus Victor theme is notably absent from her proposal, as is a strong theology of the Trinitarian nature of God. Adams, *Christ and Horrors: The Coherence of Christology* (Cambridge: Cambridge University Press, 2006), 51, 65–71.

5. Marilyn McCord Adams, "Horrors in Theological Context," *Scottish Journal of Theology* 55, no. 4 (2002): 470.

6. Eleonore Stump, "The Problem of Evil: Analytic Philosophy and Narrative," in *Analytic Theology: New Essays in the Philosophy of Theology*, ed. Oliver Crisp and Michael C. Rea (Oxford: Oxford University Press, 2009), 263.

various kinds of relationships to the world. Moreover, these insights will be theological handholds that strengthen one's worldview and personal engagement with God.[7]

The opposite view is argued by noted trauma and Old Testament scholar Kathleen O'Connor. O'Connor argues that traumatic experiences, such as Job's, are not an appropriate basis on which to make theological judgments about God. This is because Job's depiction of God arises from particular and specific traumas. For O'Connor, other books such as Genesis and Jeremiah also offer only partial reflections on what God may be like in the aftermath of traumatic experience. They are merely situation-specific reconstructions of a God, the same God whose character must be constantly renegotiated in the light of suffering. Descriptions of God are therefore human efforts to "keep God alive," a "theological survival strategy."[8] The significance of trauma in generating and coloring the text is such that these theological claims are temporary and will no doubt be revised in the future. Any proposed biblical view of God therefore has no normative status with reference to who he is, and for this reason a biblical theology of God's nature and relationships to created beings is impossible. All it does is reassure people that there is a divine being. O'Connor writes:

> The overarching purpose of Jeremiah's language is to restore Judah. It does not try to present the essence of the Deity or eternal truths about God, nor ontological insights into God's nature. ... Jeremiah's theological language is piercing, temporary, partial, a bulwark against chaos. It is culturally apt, incomplete, and provides glimpses of the Holy One to insist as emphatically as possible that God has not abandoned the people. This theology keeps God alive.[9]

Though O'Connor pitches the reconstructive theological work as a "pastoral act," one wonders whether she has gone too far. The degree of

7. Eleonore Stump, *The God of the Bible and the God of the Philosophers* (Milwaukee: Marquette University Press, 2016), 11–40.

8. Reenvisioning God is "a theological survival strategy that puts back order into a world ripped apart. ... These and other elements of the text interpret disaster, reframe it, and put it into a larger story of continuing relationship with God. They keep God alive." Kathleen M. O'Connor, "Stammering Toward the Unsayable: Old Testament Theology, Trauma Theory, and Genesis," *Interpretation* 70, no. 3 (2016): 305.

9. O'Connor, "Stammering Toward the Unsayable," 305.

changeability and arbitrariness with which she views God's identity and actions only serves to reinforce the dissonant impact of trauma and the uncertainties it creates for Bible readers.

Whereas Stump and O'Connor have focused on Bible reading and the theological problem of evil, skeptical non-Christian philosophers have laid the problem at God's feet, focusing on the apparent dissonance between the purported character of God and the presence of widespread evil and suffering in the world. For them, it is exacerbated by the claim that God is good at the same time as creating and supervising a very difficult world. J. L. Schellenberg has argued that horrors are a warrant for religious skepticism of God's existence and any claims to have knowledge with respect to things of ultimate value and good.[10] He argues that the maximally compassionate God of classical theism cannot exist given the horrors that plague human existence. His line of thinking is that it is not necessary for the God of classical theism to allow horrific suffering in the lives of humans in order to achieve their ultimate end, which is an unending and intimate relationship with him. That is, evil such as the horrific suffering of human beings is not necessary for achieving their highest good. Therefore, argues Schellenberg, the widespread phenomenon of human suffering, in tandem with divine hiddenness, demonstrates that belief in God cannot count as knowledge.

Schellenberg's exploration of the problem of divine hiddenness makes another powerful point that undermines a key Christian apologetic claim, namely, that belief in God is a reasonable and basic belief despite suffering in the world.[11] The problem of divine hiddenness refers to more than merely wondering how God, his presence, and his care relate to people in the midst of the "dark night of the soul." Rather, Schellenberg makes the fine point that even in the absence of suffering there are people who are capable, willing, and open to an intimate relationship with God, yet God does not initiate a relationship with them despite the fact that he knows

10. J. L. Schellenberg, *The Wisdom to Doubt: A Justification of Religious Skepticism* (Ithaca, NY: Cornell University Press, 2007), 243–69.

11. Daniel Howard-Snyder and Adam Green, "Hiddenness of God," *Stanford Encyclopedia of Philosophy*, April 23, 2016, https://plato.stanford.edu/entries/divine-hiddenness/. Also see W. K. Clifford's work on this in Charles Taliaferro and Paul J. Griffiths, *Philosophy of Religion: An Anthology*, Blackwell Philosophy Anthologies 20 (Malden, MA: Blackwell, 2003). A constructive analytical approach to divine presence whose method is influential on mine is James R. Gordon, *The Holy One in Our Midst* (Minneapolis: Fortress, 2016).

it is what is best for them.[12] Therefore, in Schellenberg's view, the hiddenness of God in the context of nonresistance to belief in God demonstrates that there is no such God.[13]

To my mind, the severity and rigor of this argument is only heightened in the context of natural horrors and trauma because these arise without a malevolent human will and so seem to be part of the nature of the world God made.[14] These theological questions will be addressed after exploring two further questions generated by horrors: the questions of meaninglessness and hopelessness.

THE EXISTENTIAL PROBLEM: MEANINGLESSNESS

The problems of horrors have raised existential problems as to whether life is meaningful. By "meaningful" I mean having a sense of purpose, significance, and value to others and to oneself. Joshua Seachris notes the connection between horrors and meaning: "The experience of evil links to the meaning of life, especially when one considers death and futility. ... The experience of evil is often one of those generating conditions of the question of life's meaning born out of existential angst."[15] The existential problem relates to both victims of trauma and perpetrators of trauma, yet this topic has received little attention until recently.[16]

The problems of meaninglessness are compounded by the fact that traumatized persons lose connections and confidence in other people and with themselves. As Judith Lewis Herman observes, "Traumatic events call into question basic human relationships. They breach attachments of

12. Schellenberg, *Wisdom to Doubt*, 195–242; J. L. Schellenberg, *The Hiddenness Argument: Philosophy's New Challenge to Belief in God* (Oxford: Oxford University Press, 2015).

13. Schellenberg, *Hiddenness Argument*.

14. This is highly problematic for Alvin Plantinga's claim that belief in God does not require an argument for it but that it is "properly basic." See James Kelly Clark and Michael C. Rea, "Introduction," in *Reason, Mind, Metaphysics, and Mind: New Essays on the Philosophy of Alvin Plantinga*, ed. James Kelly Clark and Michael C. Rea (Oxford: Oxford University Press, 2012), 4.

15. Joshua W. Seachris, "Meaning of Life: Contemporary Analytic Perspectives," in *Internet Encyclopedia of Philosophy: A Peer Reviewed Academic Resource*.

16. Joshua W. Seachris, "Life, Meaning Of," in *New Catholic Encyclopedia: Supplement 2012–2013: Ethics and Philosophy*, ed. Robert L. Fastiggi (Detroit: Gale/Catholic University of America Press, 2012), 1.

family, friendship, love, and community. They shatter the construction of the self that is formed and sustained in relation to others."[17]

The self's relationship to itself is also altered. Traumatic events "destroy the victim's fundamental assumptions about the safety of the world, the positive value of the self, and the meaningful order of creation." Drawing on the work of Mardi Horowitz, Herman adds that "traumatic life events ... cannot be assimilated with the victim's 'inner schemata' of self in relation to the world."[18] Such disconnection is especially acute in the face of the theological skepticisms noted above. A previously held theocentric and person-centric worldview collapses. One wonders what kind of restorative action may be pursued in the absence of the primary relationships that secure meaning.

A sense of meaninglessness has the consequence of blunting personal and purposeful action. Traumatic events undermine a person's ability to be active in the world and relate to it from a position of competence and confidence that is proper for an image of God. "Traumatic events, by definition, thwart initiative and overwhelm individual competence. No matter how brave and resourceful the victim may have been, her actions were insufficient to ward off disaster. In the aftermath of traumatic events, as survivors review and judge their own conduct, feelings of guilt and inferiority are practically universal."[19] This curtails the functional aspect of being made in God's image, which is to act creatively and purposively in order to build cultures and physical environments for the common good. Trauma curtails this by stripping a person of confidence in themselves and their actions. This truncation stunts the way in which a human being may live out their personhood. The loss of purposeful action has consequences for other people who are organically connected to horror survivors. When the sufferer is inhibited and unable to perform as they could, then various disconnections between the victim and others manifest themselves in areas such as the workplace, friendships, and social groups such as churches.

---

17. Judith Lewis Herman, *Trauma and Recovery: From Domestic Abuse to Political Terror* (London: Basic Books, 2001), 51.

18. Herman, *Trauma and Recovery*, 51, citing M. Horowitz, *Stress Response Syndromes* (Northvale, NJ: Jason Aronson, 1986).

19. "Traumatic events have primary effects not only on the psychological structures of the self but also on the systems of attachment and meaning that link individual and community." Herman, *Trauma and Recovery*, 53.

This affects communities and consolidates the personal breakdown that usually accompanies trauma.[20]

The prospects for recovery for an isolated individual who has limited capability for purposeful personal interaction and agency are very poor. The person who has been traumatized may look to extrinsic sources of hope such as friends, counselors, or special-interest groups. However, this can be a disappointing experience. Reliance on others rather than oneself may ultimately be traumatic in various ways. This is because traumatized persons may misperceive others as disproportionately harmful. There is some truth to this belief—all persons, even those who have suffered at the hands of horrors, have the potential to be active participants and perpetrators of horrors with respect to others; however, the degree of this may be overblown in the perspective of people who have been traumatized. We now briefly focus on further problems that face perpetrators of horrors.

Participation and Perpetuation of Horrors and Trauma

People who have actively committed horrors against others may be crippled by the experience as much as their victims. Adams writes, "Participation in horrors furnishes reason to doubt whether the participant's life can be worth living," because participation in actions related to a world of horrific events "engulfs the positive value of his/her life and penetrates into his/her meaning-making structures seemingly to defeat and degrade his/her value as a person." Hence, "participation in (the doing or suffering) [of horrors] … constitutes prima facie reason to doubt whether the participant's life could … be a great good to him/her on the whole."[21] This line of thinking is consistent with the clinical diagnosis of "moral injury." A moral injury occurs when people participate in "perpetrating, failing to prevent, bearing witness to, or learning about acts that transgress deeply held moral beliefs and expectations."[22] In addition to the loss of confidence in God and the self, the question of meaning also looms large.

One option may be to merely make up meaningfulness. Kain writes that "knowledge of the horror of existence kills action. … The horror

20. Herman, *Trauma and Recovery*, 51.

21. Adams, "Horrors in Theological Context," 469.

22. Shira Maguen and Brett Litz, "Moral Injury in Veterans of War," *PTSD Research Quarterly* 23, no. 1 (2012): 1–3.

and meaninglessness of existence must be veiled if we are to live and act. What we must do, Nietzsche thinks, is construct a meaning for suffering. Suffering we can handle. Meaningless suffering, suffering for no reason at all, we cannot handle. So, we give it a meaning. We invent a meaning. We create an illusion."[23]

Attempts to create the illusion that life is meaningful in the face of horror have not been entirely successful. This is borne out in a number of cultural and literary reflections on the horrors of existence. The genre of horror has played the philosophically valuable role of pointing out that life is neither stable nor secure, and that notions of meaning and hope are wholly artificial and succumb to the pressure of reality in the light of one unexpected experience. Horror-attuned fiction, or gothic horror fiction, suggests that a worldview attuned to horror is the most realistic existential perspective. The development of this genre demonstrates that the illusion has not gone unchallenged. In fact, the horror genre has become increasingly popular in the West and provides a powerful rejoinder to any fanciful and unrealistic views of God's goodness, human meaning, and hope. I will return to discuss these existential issues at length once we have covered the final major problem I will address: the sense of hopelessness generated by experiences of trauma.

THE ANTHROPOLOGICAL PROBLEM: IS THERE HOPE FOR RESTORATION TO FULL PERSONHOOD?

Is the proposition "There is hope for a better personal future" a real metaphysical possibility for horror survivors? Or does the experience of horrors and trauma disallow it?[24] What kind of perspective and skills are required to overcome this?[25] Helpful perspectives and skills often elude trauma survivors due to a profound sense of shame and helplessness, which in turn

23. Phillip J. Kain, "Nietzsche, Virtue and the Horror of Existence," *British Journal for the History of Philosophy* 17, no. 1 (2009): 155.

24. Daniel Nolan, "Method in Analytic Metaphysics," in *The Oxford Handbook of Philosophical Methodology*, ed. Herman Cappelen, Tamar Gendler, and John Hawthorne (Oxford: Oxford University Press, 2016), 163–68.

25. Stephan Käufer and Anthony Chemero, *Phenomenology: An Introduction* (Cambridge, UK: Polity, 2016), 109, 113.

means they have little expectation for a better form of life for themselves and their communities.[26]

Trauma survivors may see themselves as having failed both to defend themselves and to demand the recognition and treatment that their dignity as a person rightly deserves. This sense of inadequacy on behalf of the victim may be compounded by the subsequent inability/disinterest of others to come alongside them. A generalized sense of failure is compounded by the inability of the traumatized to seek the presence of other people. Traumatized persons can believe that they have factual evidence for "failure" if they can point to an objective event in which they were traumatized by another person. In reality, there may be no failure on their behalf because circumstances and power relationships were out of their control. Survivors may in fact have defended themselves as much as was possible at the time. There may be no truth to the fact that they did not defend themselves as a fictional ideal self "would" or "should" have. The problem is that the result was trauma, and this is what is looked to as the definitive evidence of being incapable of self-preservation. Because the interpretation of events and accompanying shame is self-generated, a person will find it hard to garner the internal resources to resist such an interpretation.

Given the purported objective basis for this claim to failure and the accompanying shame (the traumatizing horrors), then how can we possibly recover from shame and its blunting effect when it is generated by self-perception and compounded by interactions with others? Horrors and trauma point out our inability to fruitfully participate in a healthy shared world of relationships, work, and experiences. This perpetuates the "experience of disintegration when the world falls away ... as though sucked towards a drain hole. ... Shame's tonality ... begins with becoming thing-like."[27] Perceiving oneself as a thing rather than a person corresponds to numbness and purposelessness. This perception of being less than a person robs the person of a sense of their own capacity to bring about change in interpersonal relationships. Therefore, it prohibits the prospects of living

26. Aislinn O'Donnell, "Shame Is Already a Revolution: The Politics of Affect in the Thought of Deleuze," *Deleuze Studies* 11, no. 1 (2017).

27. O'Donnell, "Shame Is Already a Revolution," 3.

more fully as a person for the common good and the (seemingly remote) glory of God. This is exacerbated when others treat the survivor as a thing, an object for their use and of no value outside that. Though survivors are numb to the world in many senses, they often know when others perceive them as less than the images of God that they are.

DISCERNING A RESPONSE THROUGH STORY

In what follows I use stories in order to relate individual and group experiences of trauma with the biblical narrative. This will allow us to answer the following questions: Are grief, horror, and trauma the final state of affairs? Is there hope for a better future for the images of God?[28] Is it possible for human persons to pursue their ultimate good in the aftermath of trauma? Can a human person escape reductionism and thereby move toward becoming a flourishing person once again—a person in right relation with God, other persons, and themselves? The theological and existential aspects of this question are important too; for example: Where does the Christian God fit into this picture? Can we integrate our experiences of horrors with our orthodox and long-held beliefs about God? Can we live meaningfully in light of answers to these questions?

A leading trauma studies scholar, Serene Jones, seems to think so. Jones resists the premise that there is no hope for those who have been traumatized. She provides a powerful metaphor for how horrors and human stories are related: "Like a furnace, there is no end to the flames that violence throws out, and the stories of harm that mark our individual and collective lives are as endless in variety as they are in scope." However, Jones adds that even at the worst of times she ardently believes that "the reality of grace is vastly richer and far more powerful than the force of those flames. It is so strong that even when our capacity to narrate the good-news story of grace is destroyed (as it often is in situations of violence), the reality to which it witnesses, the unending love of God, remains constant and steady

---

28. The seriousness of losing hope is underscored by St. Hilary of Poitiers, who wrote: "If we should lose confidence in our future good, we should be guilty of unforgivable unbelief." However, he continues immediately with an offer of hope based on the good character of God: "Once our worry has come to an end, those future things which had preoccupied us will give way to the good things bestowed on us by God's goodness. On that day we will no longer be anxious." Poitiers, *Commentary on Matthew*, trans. D. H. Williams (Washington, DC: Catholic University of America Press, 2012), 83, commenting on Matt 5:13.

and ever true." In order to find hope, both survivors and perpetrators of horrors must become discerning. The goal is "to discern how this divine desire to love and heal can be spoken and lived out, concretely, in the life of faith at work in the world." Jones continues: "This is the question of how God's love might best be embodied in tangible forms that can be felt, known, and enjoyed."[29]

In part 2, I engage with and address the questions and problems I have raised in part 1. I will explore how we might perceive God's visible and invisible as well as direct and indirect works through real-world stories, and how this can be a helpful vehicle for discerning divine counterpoints to objective and subjective horrors and trauma.

29. Jones, *Trauma and Grace*, x, ix. Jones writes that expanding an understanding of both trauma and grace is required in order to understand how these are interrelated. The language of trauma is necessary because it enlarges "our appreciation for the complexities of human suffering, but also by deepening and enlivening our grasp of the amazing fullness and power of grace." Jones, *Trauma and Grace*, x.

Part 2

HORRORS *and* INTERPRETATION

5

ADDRESSING HORRORS THROUGH REAL-WORLD STORIES

The problems of horrors and the skepticisms generated by these cannot be understood nor resolved by means of abstract proposals alone.[1] Rather, narratives are the framework within which this theological, existential, and anthropological discernment must take place.[2]

Stories about the world as it is are valuable in demonstrating what real problems and real solutions look like. Working with reference to these in order to deal with challenges is superior to working with ideal or possible worlds.[3] Narratives can yield reliable knowledge in a manner that is particularly suited to those who have experienced horrors and trauma because, as Stump writes, "Narratives ... present for us direct interaction between a loving God and suffering human beings. They are, therefore, in effect, descriptions of (part of) a world in which God exists and has a morally sufficient reason for allowing human beings to suffer."[4]

---

1. Wolf Krötke, "God's Hiddenness and Belief in His Power: Essays in Honour of John Webster," in *Theological Theology*, ed. R. David Nelson, Darren Sarisky, and Justin Stratis (London: Bloomsbury, 2015); Claudia Welz, *Love's Transcendence and the Problem of Theodicy* (Tübingen: Mohr Siebeck, 2008), 4; Brian Ball, "Knowledge Is Normal Belief," *Analysis* 73, no. 1 (2013): 69–76.

2. Sönke Finnern is a model for integrating narratological, historical-critical, and theological interests in the exegetical and interpretive task. Finnern, *Narratologie und biblische Exegese* (Tübingen: Mohr Siebeck, 2010). See also Jörg Frey and Uta Poplutz, *Narrativität und Theologie im Johannesevangelium* (Neukirchen-Vluyn: Neukirchener Verlagsgesellschaft, 2012); Uta Poplutz, *Erzählte Welt: Narratologische Studien zum Matthäusevangelium* (Neukirchen-Vluyn: Neukirchener Verlag, 2008).

3. Krötke, "God's Hiddenness and Belief in His Power"; Jean-Luc Marion, *Prolegomena to Charity*, Perspectives in Continental Philosophy 24 (New York: Fordham University Press, 2002); Daniel Nolan, "Method in Analytic Metaphysics," in *The Oxford Handbook of Philosophical Methodology*, ed. Herman Cappelen, Tamar Gendler, and John Hawthorne (Oxford: Oxford University Press, 2016), 173–77.

4. Eleonore Stump, *Wandering in Darkness: Narrative and the Problem of Suffering* (Oxford: Oxford University Press, 2010), 61. For what can be discerned from the Bible and then

Stories yield both objective and subjective knowledge in the form of personal perspectives that respond to problems generated by horrors.[5] Real-world narratives about God and his images in the past may provide criteria for discerning the presence and character of God in *other stories* in which this same God relates to similar images of himself in the context of horrors.[6] This may yield a very practical ordinary or "folk" theology with which to handle everyday experiences of horrors and trauma.[7]

Another helpful aspect of appealing to narratives in order to discern how God may work to recreate faith, meaning, and hope is that narratives have an internal coherence that stops us from asking irrelevant questions. In other words, these bound and provide limits for the kinds of questions asked in the first place. The main story of a narrative offers its own validated criteria for evaluating a response to horrors. Hence, it strengthens the internal consistency and coherence of a response, making it more plausible and valuable than others. In Claudia Welz's terminology, every story that responds to horrors is an "exemplary answer."[8] This allows the story to set the rules for interpreting the phenomena that are disclosed in them. In Alister McGrath's way of thinking, this is "scientific theology," in which the phenomena at hand set the modes of knowledge and results of an investigation.[9] "Instead of fixing certain criteria for the evaluation

articulated theologically see D. S. Yeago, "The New Testament and the Nicene Dogma: A Contribution to the Recovery of Theological Exegesis," in *The Theological Interpretation of Scripture: Classic and Contemporary Readings*, ed. S. E. Fowl (Oxford: Blackwell, 1997); Millard Erickson, *Christian Theology* (Grand Rapids: Baker Academic, 2013), 53–67.

5. Stump, *Wandering in Darkness*, 61.

6. "Theodicies function as interpretation stoppers. They operate with predetermined propositions. ... What is required ... is both the tolerance of phenomena that appear in unusual ways and the passion of distinction that discerns between the ambiguity ['ambiguous appearances, in which God can reveal or conceal himself, the presence of God in history'] that can and should be dissolved in clarity, and the ambiguity that is unavoidable and remains unresolved." Welz, *Love's Transcendence and the Problem of Theodicy*, 8.

7. "Ordinary theology is what we start with, a kind of primal knowing that co-exists with the more technical and systematized knowing that is learnt through processes of education. It is the 'natural' theology for people who are on their knees 'close to mystery.'" Peter Ward and Heidi Campbell, "Ordinary Theology as Narratives," *International Journal of Practical Theology* 15, no. 2 (2011): 226.

8. Welz, *Love's Transcendence and the Problem of Theodicy*, 11.

9. Alister E. McGrath, *A Scientific Theology*, 3 vols. (Grand Rapids: Eerdmans, 2003); Elmer M. Colyer, *How to Read T. F. Torrance: Understanding His Trinitarian and Scientific Theology* (Downers Grove, IL: InterVarsity, 2001); John Webster, *Theological Theology* (Oxford: Clarendon, 1998).

of these answers beforehand," writes Welz, this story-methodology "aims at distinguishing between different points of view and at clarifying their respective normative implications."[10]

PERSONAL KNOWLEDGE OF GOD THROUGH STORIES

One of the most important assumptions at work in this book is that there is a divine personal and conscious mind responsible for the existence of human consciousness.[11] This personal mind, belonging to God the Trinity, has also generated an inspired set of scriptural texts, through which he engages personally with people's minds and perspectives (Matt 16:16–17; 2 Pet 1:20–21; 3:15–16; 2 Tim 3:16).[12] Hence I take a mind-to-mind approach to knowledge of God. This is a helpful way to prioritize a personalist focus to the question of knowing God: it works within a context of dynamic acquaintance in which there is often more to knowing than mere statements.[13] This kind of knowledge seeks to believe that which is known in an interpersonal relationship.[14] This is not a fanciful quest but is carried out within the wisdom of those who have known God in the past and gathered the Scriptures and written the creeds. It is helpful to prioritize this kind of knowledge because the Christian quest is faith seeking understanding, and faith is faith in God. In addition, this personal approach is consistent with interpreting God's great project as establishing face-to-face relationships with people.[15]

---

10. Welz, *Love's Transcendence and the Problem of Theodicy*, 11. Gotthold Lessing employed a similar criterion in his masterwork *Nathan the Wise*.

11. J. P. Moreland, "Oppy on the Argument from Consciousness," *Faith and Philosophy* 29, no. 1 (2012): 70–83.

12. Adam Green and Keith A. Quan, "More than Inspired Propositions: Shared Attention and the Religious Text," *Faith and Philosophy* 29, no. 4 (2012): 416–30 (on what this must balance see 416).

13. Michael Polanyi and Amartya Sen, *The Tacit Dimension* (Chicago: University of Chicago Press, 2009); Michael Polanyi, *Personal Knowledge: Towards a Post-critical Philosophy* (London: Routledge, 1997).

14. Green and Quan, "More than Inspired Propositions," 416; Adam Green, "Perceiving Persons," *Journal of Consciousness Studies* 19, nos. 3–4 (2012): 49–64.

15. Emmanuel Levinas, *Totality and Infinity: An Essay on Exteriority*, Duquesne Studies Philosophical Series 24 (Pittsburgh: Duquesne University Press, 1969), 66, 198. This personalist element, following Benton, Stump, and others, differentiates it from popular literary theological approaches described by Johnson: "Narrative criticism has come into favor with

These assumptions set up the priorities in my methodology, worth explaining briefly here. I will follow a "mind-to-mind" approach to knowledge, which is focused primarily on God's consciousness as he relates to and interacts with individual and corporate human minds/souls for the sake of forming beliefs and concepts that are true and helpful to them.[16]

On this model, knowledge between personal subjects involves relating to another person's consciousness and state of mind.[17] This takes account of the influence of God's mind on human ones and the response of people to his influence. Because biblical stories are inspired and communicatively employed by God's spiritual mind, then personally attuned interpretation will involve relating well to the conscious mind that inspired them.[18] This works from the principle that knowledge is gained by attending to the consciousness of other persons and in a best-case scenario involves a joint focus on events in the world.[19]

This kind of knowledge necessarily involves persons and personal knowing because it requires attentive engagement with other persons

theologians who want to work from the stories of Scripture. Literary analysis provides a particularly useful tool in that narratives have discrete structures to them and narrative logic constrains the range of meaning. Hence narratives have premises that are worked out within their own logic to necessary conclusions." Dru Johnson, *Knowledge by Ritual* (Winona Lake, IN: Eisenbrauns, 2016), 27. It also differentiates it from Greg Forbes and Scott Harrower, *Raised from Obscurity: A Narratival and Theological Study of the Characterization of Women in Luke-Acts* (Eugene, OR: Pickwick, 2015); Teun A. Van Dijk, "Narrative Macro-Structures: Logical and Cognitive Foundations," *Poetics and Theory of Literature* 1 (1976): 547–68.

16. Yeago, "New Testament and the Nicene Dogma."

17. "If propositional knowledge is a state of mind, consisting in a subject's attitude to a (true) proposition ... [then] interpersonal knowledge [is] a state of minds, involving a subject's attitude to another (existing) subject." Matthew A. Benton, "Epistemology Personalized," *Philosophical Quarterly* 67, no. 269 (2017): 813.

18. Stump argues that, in addition to propositional knowledge *that* something is the case, there also is "second-person" knowledge, "which is non-propositional and which is not reducible to knowledge *that*." Stump, *Wandering in Darkness*, 51, italics original. See also Eleonore Stump, "The Problem of Evil: Analytic Philosophy and Narrative," in *Analytic Theology: New Essays in the Philosophy of Theology*, ed. Oliver Crisp and Michael C. Rea (Oxford: Oxford University Press, 2009), 259; Gregor Damschen, "Dispositional Knowledge-How versus Propositional Knowledge-That," in *Debating Dispositions: Issues in Metaphysics, Epistemology and Philosophy of Mind*, ed. Gregor Damschen (Berlin: de Gruyter, 2009), 278–95.

19. Eleonore Stump, "Second-Person Accounts and the Problem of Evil," *Revista Portuguesa de Filosofia* 57, no. 4 (2001): 745.

and interaction with their experiences.[20] This is called shared attention.[21] For readers of the Bible who want to know God, shared attention involves the reader and God being strongly aware of one another as they cooperate in reading a text together.[22] This attention eventually leads to individual and group rituals and practices that confirm knowledge of God and in turn develop other true beliefs.[23] Therefore, biblical stories mediate the divine mind that inspired them and continue to speak today, especially through instances where God is the speaker in the story and through those historical events that surround this speech. Kevin Vanhoozer argues persuasively that the voice of God in a story, which is often that of either the Father or the Son, provides the interpretive lens for knowing God through that story.[24] Responsiveness to God's voice and his influence on our knowledge of him through stories yield an interpersonal kind of wisdom, truth, and, just as importantly, direction for action.[25]

An example of gaining access to God's perspective may be helpful. When we read about the voice of God from heaven approving of Jesus, we have access to God's perspective on a character if we share attention with God's conscious perspective for interpreting people and events.[26] Access to God's consciousness is the key to interpreting events; the apostle Peter reflects on this when he writes: "For we received honor and glory from God the Father when the voice came to him from the Majestic Glory, saying 'This is my beloved Son, with whom I am well pleased!' We ourselves heard this voice

---

20. See the conditions for this set out in Stump, *Wandering in Darkness*, 76.

21. Green and Quan, "More than Inspired Propositions," 419. This works at a personally invested level beyond the propositionalist theology of Thomas McCall, *An Invitation to Analytic Christian Theology* (Downers Grove, IL: IVP Academic, 2015), 55–56.

22. Green and Quan, "More than Inspired Propositions," 418. This is one way by which I depart from the methodology in Forbes and Harrower, *Raised from Obscurity*.

23. Johnson, *Knowledge by Ritual*.

24. Kevin J. Vanhoozer, "Theological Commentary and 'The Voice from Heaven': Exegesis, Ontology, and the Travail of Biblical Interpretation," in *On the Writing of New Testament Commentaries: Festschrift for Grant R. Osborne on the Occasion of His 70th Birthday*, ed. Eckhard Schnabel (Leiden: Brill, 2013), 269–98.

25. "Theologians must do more (but not less!) than distil clear propositions from texts in order to assess their cogency. Conceptual clarity is only the penultimate stage on the road to wisdom." Kevin J. Vanhoozer, "Love's Wisdom: The Authority of Scripture's Form and Content for Faith's Understanding and Theological Judgment," *Journal of Reformed Theology* 5 (2011): 260.

26. Vanhoozer, "Theological Commentary and 'The Voice from Heaven.'"

when it came from heaven while we were with him on the holy mountain" (2 Pet 1:17–19).[27] This powerful directing of the reader's focus secures "genuine shared attention" between God and the reader as, conscious of each other, they look at Christ. As Adam Green and Michael Quan explain, there is no sense in which God expects the reader to approach God's perspective "as if" it were so. God is taken to really be speaking and sharing his attention with the reader, whereas an "as if" perspective would not be genuine shared attention but rather a "pseudo shared attention."[28] Because God really is sharing his attention and perspective with the reader by directing them to Christ, the voice of God is an instance of God's expert opinion that counts as the testimony of an expert in this area. Because it is knowledge provided by an expert, what is known can be treated as knowledge.[29]

In a sense, this is all that Scripture does—mediate a personal encounter with God and God's knowledge of himself and all things as they relate to him.[30] Naturally, the voices of those who have known God in the past also contribute as a background chorus to God's voice. This attention-sharing approach therefore requires listening to God's voice in tandem with the perspective of the ecumenical church councils, which provides the Trinitarian and salvation-oriented framework for interpreting it.[31] Reading the Bible this way is likely to stimulate a disposition to know and relate to God personally.[32]

---

27. I take consciousness to refer to one of "so-called creature consciousness (as intransitive, involving an animal who is awake, or transitive, with consciousness as such and such) or to mental state consciousness (involving a mental state claimed to be conscious)." John G. Taylor, "The Problem of 'I,'" *Journal of Consciousness Studies* 19, nos. 11–12 (2012): 234. See also Marco Caracciolo, "Fictional Consciousness: A Reader's Manual," *Style* 46, no. 1 (2012): 42–65; Jill M. Parrott, "How Shall We Greet the Sun?: Form and Truth in Gwendolyn Brook's *Annie Allen*," *Style* 46, no. 1 (2012): 27–41; Taylor Carman, "Phenomenology," in Cappelen, Gendler, and Hawthorne, *Oxford Handbook of Philosophical Methodology*, 179–92.

28. Green and Quan, "More than Inspired Propositions," 423.

29. I.e., this is warranted and true knowledge. Matthew A. Benton, "Expert Opinion and Second-Hand Knowledge," *Philosophy & Phenomenological Research* 92 (2016): 1–4; Green and Quan, "More than Inspired Propositions," 430.

30. Green and Quan, "More than Inspired Propositions," 430.

31. Alois Grillmeier, *Christ in Christian Tradition* (Atlanta: John Knox, 1975); Grillmeier, "The Reception of Chalcedon in the Roman Catholic Church," *The Ecumenical Review* 22, no. 4 (1970): 383–404; Vanhoozer, "May We Go Beyond What Is Written After All?"

32. Damschen's work sets the directions for relating knowledge-how and knowledge-that. Damschen, "Dispositional Knowledge-How versus Propositional Knowledge-That," 279.

Such an interpersonally oriented concern for persons and relationships via Bible reading hopefully flows into a lifestyle that is pragmatically interested in others and their well-being.[33] Indeed, the test of a worldview is the degree to which that worldview is helpful for navigating reality in relationship to others. This view has a long pedigree.[34] It tests whether a worldview provides a sufficiently "helpful orientation" for trying to live context of horrors.[35] If so, it may point out the presence of God and his life-giving resources in the world.[36]

Studying a narrative in order to know God's mind, via both his historical self-disclosure and his life-giving phenomena through other people in the world, seems to be the most fitting basis for our study of how God relates to people in the context of horrors and trauma. It is a phenomenological and analytical-philosophical approach that is able to make holistic religious claims.[37]

CHOOSING MATTHEW'S GOSPEL

In order to be metaphysically consistent, a Christian exploration of the theological, anthropological, and existential dimensions of the problem of horrors needs to be rooted in its own history and traditions. This means that some premises are taken for granted and some courses of investigation are more consistent with these premises than others.[38]

---

33. Phenomenology is a movement formed around "commitment to thick, contextualized descriptions of lived experience and of the world as we encounter and understand it from a first-person point of view." Carman, "Phenomenology," 179.

34. This worldview employs the criterion of the "best lived results before God and other people" in order to demonstrate and recommend one worldview over others, it is also advocated by Gotthold Lessing in his masterwork *Nathan the Wise*. However, Lessing did not apply his theory to the different worldviews and their stories. Instead he used his theory to argue for a deliberately nondiscriminatory position on whether Judaism, Christianity, or Islam brings about the most blessed life.

35. Welz, *Love's Transcendence and the Problem of Theodicy*, 9; Johnson, *Knowledge by Ritual*.

36. Welz, *Love's Transcendence and the Problem of Theodicy*, 8.

37. I will follow Hasker, who argues that the analytic approach to philosophy of religion "offers the best means ... for clarifying the meaning of religious claims and assessing the reasons for and against those claims." William Hasker, "Analytic Philosophy of Religion," in *The Oxford Handbook of Philosophy of Religion*, ed. William Wainwright (Oxford: Oxford University Press, 2005), 443.

38. Nolan, "Method in Analytic Metaphysics."

Matthew's Gospel will be the story of choice. Limiting our use of the Bible to Matthew's Gospel is consistent with the fact that recovery from trauma takes place in small steps and slow phases. Engaging with Matthew's Gospel is one small step toward a fuller biblical engagement in which faith and theology are integrated with the problem of horrors and trauma. In other words, restricting ourselves to Matthew recognizes the limitations that accompany recovery from trauma, yet it is a positive religious coping strategy. Such a staggered approach anticipates a richer and fuller engagement with the Bible and historical reflections on it. *But why Matthew in particular*?

I am influenced by Dale Brunner's insight that at times the best way to investigate deep theological and anthropological questions is via the narrative of Scripture, and the best one by which to do this is Matthew's Gospel, "the most systematic of the Gospels."[39]

Several other factors support the selection of Matthew's Gospel. Its canonical placement accords it an interpretative role with respect to God's relationship to a dystopic human history. In addition, Matthew's historical interest and very strong interaction with Jewish texts and traditions mean that he assumes an Edenic backdrop to the story of the fall and its consequences. Finally, it seems that Matthew's Gospel is surprisingly underused in works related to theodicy.[40] My work hopes to redress this neglect by demonstrating that a biblical book other than Job or Revelation may be engaged in order to resolve key intellectual and pastoral issues related to horrors.[41]

The value of approaching the problem of horrors via a Gospel lies in that it overcomes two common critiques of Christian theodicies, as laid out by A. K. Anderson: first, that theodicy "ultimately does not contain significant connection to the thought of any particular religious community,"

39. See Dale Brunner's comments on the benefits of this in the preface to his commentary on Matthew's Gospel. Brunner, *Matthew: A Commentary*, vol. 1, *The Christbook* (Grand Rapids: Eerdmans, 2004), xviii.

40. Thomas G. Long, "Essential Books on God and Suffering (Theodicy)" *Christian Century* 130, no. 21 (2013): 33.

41. Although Adams touches on Matthew, she does not work through Matthew systematically and according to its own logic. Instead she works with clusters of texts across the canonical and apocryphal materials which are bound together hermeneutically by the theology of the book of Revelation (as well as that of Hebrews and Colossians). Adams, *Christ and Horrors*, 66–72, 74, 185, 240–43, 269.

and second that "it does not ... take sufficient account of the full depth and complexity of the suffering that the world contains."[42] Anderson continues: "To make use of a passage from Wittgenstein, one could say that in either case the end result is in some ways a smooth, ideal picture, but one equivalent to 'slippery ice' that is far removed from the actual conditions of the 'rough ground' of the everyday world in which we conduct our lives."[43]

Matthew's Gospel seems to counter these two critiques: namely, it was written as a story for a concrete religious community, and it also deals with the very complex aspects of human life. Matthew's Gospel, therefore, seems to be a candidate for Christian reflection on the nature and activity of God as well as human purposiveness and hope in the presence of evidential horrors and the trauma responses they may provoke. In what follows, I will offer two different readings of Matthew, one through the lens of horror and paranoia, and one through a renewed perspective offered by God the Trinity. The purpose of these approaches to Matthew is to demonstrate that the second approach is more theologically coherent and has more explanatory power to do with the nature of God and of people, notwithstanding the realities of horrors and trauma.

42. A. K. Anderson, "Review: Marilyn McCord Adams, Christ and Horrors: The Coherence of Christology," *International Journal for Philosophy of Religion* 64, nos. 161–65 (2008): 161.

43. Anderson, "Review: Marilyn McCord Adams, Christ and Horrors," 161.

6

THE HORROR-ATTUNED READER AND PERCEPTION

Having chosen Matthew's Gospel, we must now interpret it with respect to the theological, existential, and anthropological questions around horrors. However, we meet a very strong roadblock at this point.

There are a number of contemporary pressures on trauma survivors that could guide them to interpret Matthew in a way that perpetuates horror and trauma and undermines the life-giving proposals to which the Gospel points.[1] These pressures not only distort our perspective on reality but also exaggerate complex deficiencies and issues around horrors and trauma, even when following the approach to Scripture suggested by trauma-studies practitioners. This is what I call "the perpetuation objection."

Each person reads literature, including holy books, from a unique personal perspective.[2] An individual's interpretations of Scripture and their conclusions will resonate with their own cultural pressures and personal experiences. People interpret texts as they read them, and this is done from a predetermined point of view.[3] As Ian Boxall writes, readers have

1. Here I explore an issue that Shelly Rambo does not pause to consider for long before her own interpretation of John's Gospel, because she moves directly into her own interpretation and does not consider the question of the validity of her approach for other people from different contexts and situations of trauma. This merely reflects different primary interests and methodological strategies. Rambo, *Spirit and Trauma: A Theology of Remaining* (Louisville, KY: Westminster John Knox, 2010).

2. Dru Johnson, *Knowledge by Ritual* (Winona Lake, IN: Eisenbrauns, 2016), xvi. Johnson's work on modes of knowledge is influential on my work.

3. "We engage with text always within a particular horizon, which both limits our view—we cannot see beyond that horizon—and also affords a certain perspective and view on to the text." John Riches, "Reception History as a Challenge to Biblical Theology," *Journal of Theological Interpretation* 7, no. 2 (2013): 178.

an "active role in creating meaning through their engagement with gaps in and ambiguities of the biblical text."[4]

The subjective nature of scriptural interpretation, and of encountering God through this, is heightened for those who have suffered from horrors and trauma because of the extreme nature of horrors.[5] One of the main insights from trauma studies is that, when a traumatized person interacts with anything in the world, they do so through the lens of their own trauma. According to Shelly Rambo, trauma requires us to read the Bible through a "shattered lens."[6] We may soften this a little and say that, aside from external input, trauma survivors may often read the Gospel of Matthew in the company of traumas from their own experience and social context. The fact remains that experiences of horrors and trauma responses inhibit interpersonal openness for shared attention. This kind of coordinated attention and interest in either live people or texts written by people is too demanding. Such difficulty prevents other perspectives from playing much of a role in shaping a survivor's reading of the text.[7] Rambo deliberately wants to pursue the "shattered lens" reading of Scripture and the deconstruction this entails, because it avoids what she perceives as forms of triumphalism that arise out of the "thrust toward life."[8]

Rambo seeks to locate a trauma or shattered reading of texts at the center of theology. For her, the authorial intent behind biblical narratives does not determine the meaning of texts, but the experience of trauma does.[9] Rambo is deliberately seeking what remains in the wake of trauma, which is commendable. But is this the most life-giving way forward? Will

---

4. Ian Boxall, *Discovering Matthew: Content, Interpretation, Reception* (London: SPCK, 2014), 26.

5. Marilyn McCord Adams, "Horrors in Theological Context," *Scottish Journal of Theology* 55, no. 4 (2002): 470.

6. Rambo, *Spirit and Trauma*, 16.

7. Adam Green, "Reading the Mind of God (without Hebrew Lessons): Alston, Shared Attention, and Mystical Experience," *Religious Studies* 45, no. 4 (2009): 459–60.

8. Rambo, *Spirit and Trauma*, 7. This is not to say Rambo is uninterested in life and recovery; she is motivated by these, but does not want to arrive at these at the expense of rushing over what Scripture offers to those who live in the middle ground between death and life. My concern is that Rambo shows too much interest in remaining in this middle space and not enough interest in seeking divine assistance to move through it in a healthy and person-appropriate manner. Rambo, *Spirit and Trauma*, 17–37.

9. Rambo, *Spirit and Trauma*, 16–17.

it lead to knowledge of the one personal being we can trust and to the shalom that God may bring about?

Rambo is not alone in claiming that a trauma survivor will read a given text differently from someone who has lived a mostly comfortable, secure, and flourishing life.[10] However, my concern is that, given the overwhelming nature of trauma, if one reads the Bible through the lens of trauma this is likely to be done from an isolated perspective and without coping resources that allow for perspectives beyond those generated in response to horrors. For this reason, *I suspect such a reader may be bereft of the energy for even receiving personal knowledge of God that importantly clarifies misconceptions about him and life. I am concerned that we may read the Bible with no external perspective by which to gauge how the text and our experiences of trauma might constructively and fruitfully converse with each other.*[11] In this kind of isolated scenario, the only external input into this perspective may be by way of cultural reinforcement of the given point of view. Consequently, traumatized readers may oftentimes not have the breadth of perspective and the relational resources with which to read Matthew in a reparative and helpful manner. Indeed, there are good reasons to believe theirs will be a paranoid reading by default.

THE PARANOID INTERPRETATION

A "paranoid" interpretation of the Scriptures will very likely resonate with a trauma survivor. This is an interpretative approach to a text that inevitably finds the violence the reader and their approach skeptically anticipate.. The consequences of this are that it generates and cements the normativity of the violent and traumatic worldview it seeks to find, thereby perpetuating violence at the core of reality.[12]

Trauma scholars suggest that not only is a paranoid reading the default for a trauma survivor, but it is also an appropriate interpretative approach in order to sensitively reckon with trauma. This is what "gather at the site

10. Oral A. W. Thomas, *Biblical Resistance Hermeneutics within a Caribbean Context* (Oakville, CT: Equinox, 2010), 197.

11. Green, "Reading the Mind of God," 459–60.

12. E. Sedgwick, "Paranoid Reading, Reparative Reading," in *Touching Feeling: Affect, Pedagogy, Performativity* (Durham, NC: Duke University Press, 2003). Cited in Anne V. Murphy, "Founding Foreclosures: Violence and Rhetorical Ownership in Philosophical Discourse on the Body," *Sophia* 55, no. 1 (2016): 11–13.

of trauma" looks like as it relates to the Bible.[13] In this regard, trauma scholars are also in touch with larger cultural and social forces in the West. The warrant for a paranoid reading is strong for literary, experiential, cultural, existential, and philosophical reasons. These justifications for a paranoid reading need to be taken seriously and handled sensitively regardless of whether the reader is a trauma survivor or someone who cares for trauma survivors. I therefore unpack them at length here.

JUSTIFICATIONS FOR A HORROR-ATTUNED READING OF THE BIBLE

Literary and Biblical Reasons

Literary and cultural studies are one of the main sources for exposing and unpacking horror and trauma.[14] Literature and cultural studies reveal instances of horror and trauma in texts and also point out what particular stories and texts suggest for the recovery of individuals and communities. These enable reflection on trauma in ways that process the events and, as Christopher G. Frechette and Elizabeth Boase write, "facilitate recovery and resilience."[15]

A small number of scholars have read the Bible with their eyes open to horror and trauma. Importantly, they do so for reasons internal to the Scriptures themselves. Stories, metaphors, and ideologies within the Bible intrinsically include elements of horror and trauma. These require a "horror-attuned" or "paranoid" reading of the texts.[16] Amy Kalmanofsky writes: "Though the Bible and a movie such as her Texas Chain Saw Massacre might seem unrelated, theories of horror provide valuable insight into the ways

13. Rambo, *Spirit and Trauma*, 30–31; see also n43.

14. Christopher G. Frechette and Elizabeth Boase, "Defining 'Trauma' as a Useful Lens for Biblical Interpretation," in *Bible through the Lens of Trauma*, ed. Elizabeth Boase and Christopher G. Frechette (Atlanta: SBL Press, 2016), 4.

15. Frechette and Boase, "Defining 'Trauma,'" 10.

16. Kathleen M. O'Connor, *Jeremiah: Pain and Promise* (Minneapolis: Fortress, 2011); O'Connor, "Stammering toward the Unsayable: Old Testament Theology, Trauma Theory, and Genesis," *Interpretation* 70, no. 3 (2016); Amy Kalmanofsky, *Terror All Around: Horror, Monsters, and Theology in the Book of Jeremiah*, The Library of Hebrew Bible/Old Testament Studies 390 (New York: T&T Clark International, 2008). Andrew Ng, "Revisiting Judges 19: A Gothic Perspective," *Journal for the Study of the Old Testament* 32, no. 2 (2007): 199–215; E. T. A. Davidson, "The Comedy of Horrors," *Proceedings* 23 (2003): 39–54.

both texts engage and terrify their audience. They help to understand the nature of biblical horror and the objects that provoke horror, as well as the ways texts work to horrify their audience."[17] In other words, relating well to these texts requires reading them, or at least portions of them, with a horror-attuned reading.

Experiential Reasons

Reading the Bible with a hermeneutic that is attuned to horror is appropriate for those who have suffered horrors. However, it may not be for those who have not, as these people will not be able to engage with such dimensions of the story. E. T. A. Davidson argues that a person's life experience determines whether they are sensitive to the presence and extent of horrors in biblical texts. He begins his argument by noting that horror stories are intrinsic to narratives in the Bible, such as the book of Judges. He notes, however, that though the book of Judges contains a great deal of death and mayhem, "what is so strange is that this devastation, destruction, slaughter, and carnage have largely been ignored by interpreters. Mutilations abound, but ... readers pass by them impassively." Davidson claims that these elements are overlooked because many readers have simply not suffered horror and trauma. Drawing on Elaine Scarry's work *The Body in Pain*, he promulgates her view that "the denial of pain in literature and in life" occurs in cases where one is not a sufferer or has not suffered. In other words, unless "one is the sufferer, one cannot enter into the other person's suffering."[18] His work is helpful because it highlights that experiences of

17. The author writes: "In this study I examine the nature and structure of the rhetoric of horror in the book of Jeremiah. I seek to understand what scared Jeremiah's audience as well as how the prophetic text worked to provoke fear in its audience." Kalmanofsky, *Terror All Around*, 1. Kalmanofsky describes her procedure as follows: "Applying horror theory to the book of Jeremiah, the first part of this study identifies and analyses the emotional response of horror reflected in Jeremiah. I examine words and images that convey Israel's terror in Jeremiah and throughout the prophets and consider what it is to feel horror in the context of the Bible. The second part of the study focuses upon the objects that provoke horror—Jeremiah's monsters. Using horror theory to identify monsters, I will address the nature of monsters and the monstrous in Jeremiah. In the third part, I consider the formal textual elements of a text that provoke horror and include a close rhetorical analysis of Jer 6 as an example of a horror text. ... The final part of this study will consider the literary and theological implications of Jeremiah's monsters and his rhetoric of horror." Kalmanofsky, *Terror All Around*, 1–2.

18. Davidson, "Comedy of Horrors," 39. See also Kalmanofsky, *Terror All Around*.

horror and trauma are a significant factor for the reading strategy with which one approaches the Bible. He develops this insight as follows:

> Most scholars have interpreted Judges as a chronicle of history. Most of them, in my experience, do not factor into their interpretations the strangeness and the humor that pervade the book. ... We see only what we are prepared or taught to see. ... When we read the Bible, we focus on our own topic of interest, on what we are looking for, such as the status of women, or the theological message, or what we can learn about history. In doing so, we become blind to everything else.

Davidson then provides the following illustrations of his claim that reading the Bible is a highly personal and selective undertaking. "As with the Rorschach test, if we see the inkblot as a rabbit, we can no longer see it as a duck."[19] In other words, it takes a certain kind of experience to read horror narrative and to understand the generative power of horror within biblical stories. Indeed, only experiences of horror and trauma can unlock this aspect of biblical stories. Therefore, those who have been victimized by horrors and suffered trauma have good experiential reasons for reading the Bible through a paranoid horror hermeneutic. Indeed, they will appreciate aspects of the text that are often ignored or overlooked. What oft-ignored events, consequences, metaphors, suffering, and moods would a horror-attuned reading of Matthew notice? What helpful though overlooked aspects of the story are available for horror victims?

An Example of Local Cultural Reasons

The justification for a personal horror-attuned reading of the Bible will have many individual and local cultural expressions. In order to illustrate this, I turn to my own local Australian cultural context and examine the paranoid reading in Australian history and literature.

Australian authors have written horror-infused fiction as both a reflection on and coping mechanism within the realities of a horror-plagued history and environment. This is driven by the central place of fear and emptiness within the national consciousness. In her introduction to *The*

19. Davidson, "Comedy of Horrors," 41.

Best Australian Stories of 2015, Amanda Lohrey writes about the prevalence of fear and hollowness in the Australian consciousness. For her, the stories in this publication share a common theme: fear. She writes: "While the stories in this collection vary greatly, what they do have in common is an element of danger. At the heart of all stories is a concealed threat, a latent danger that tests our perception of the world, along with our nerve."[20]

Lohrey states that, though fear is a creative impulse in Australian literature, it has the potential to shatter us without remainder:

> If there is nothing to fear then there is no reason to read on, but while fear is generative of story it is not enough in itself to create a satisfying reading experience. A story that is wholly paranoid in character cannot render truth, because experience is complex, shot through with light as well as burdened by darkness. The paranoid narrative seeks to exploit our fears for cheap effects ... but it leaves a hollow feeling, as nourishing as a cake made of sawdust and ashes.[21]

Australian gothic literature has captured this sense of fear and hopelessness. The Australian spirit and our national fears are often expressed as gothic horror fiction of various forms.[22] In Australian gothic literature, indeed in most gothic literature, "several themes or features immediately come to mind: ghosts from the past (literal and metaphorical) rising up to oppress the stories' protagonists; a sense of discomfort, of being unwholesome, resulting from breaking social taboos; overwhelming darkness, hopelessness, claustrophobia, and disintegration."[23]

Australians have so many problems and pains yet have so few resources to help us. Australians have sadly found that we cannot turn to others, as much as we talk up "mateship." It is not that people don't want to help; it's

20. Amanda Lohrey, "Introduction," in *Best Australian Stories (2015)*, ed. Amanda Lohrey (Collingwood, Victoria: Black, 2015), viii.

21. Lohrey, "Introduction," viii.

22. Nick Cave, *And the Ass Saw the Angel* (London: Penguin, 1989).

23. Hannett continues: "Australia's colonial/convict history is an obvious source of inspiration for this type of horror—but there are so many Australian gothic stories set in the colonial period that we'll have to save discussing them for another time. Instead, I want to focus on stories that feature 'the vastness of this land'—either as a backdrop to dark short stories, or as a fundamental part of the horror itself." Lisa L. Hannett, "Wide Open Fear: Australian Horror and Gothic Fiction," This Is Horror, http://www.thisishorror.co.uk/columns/southern-dark/wide-open-fear-australian-horror-and-gothic-fiction/ (accessed Dec. 12, 2015).

just that their help is not enough. Consider the latest book from Australian author and musician Nick Cave, *The Death of Bunny Munro*.[24] At the end of a disastrous life and series of events, an anonymous and somewhat repellent ambulance driver lends a hand. She helps the bloodied protagonist stand up for a moment, but the moral of the story has been told: his life tells us he will surely fall again and busy people such as the ambulance drivers and attendants only help in the short term. Furthermore, as much as they may help out occasionally, people will continue to damage each other. Life is ultimately about loss and fear.

An Australian may realize that people cannot ultimately help them. This may be realistic and the best response to their environment, in which people have limited resources in the first place and are under threat themselves, so sharing with others and caring for them is a step too far. In other contexts, this may cause people to turn to nature and wonder whether perhaps nature can provide aid and healing. Yet in the Australian context this is not the case, because Australians relate to nature as an oppressive, strange, and threatening entity. Tehani Wessley's assessment of Australia's nature is this: "There's simply something about the vastness of this land and the many weird, wild and dangerous creatures that populate it that lends itself to terrifying tales."[25] Lisa Hannett writes that at the core of "manifestations of Australian gothic" is the idea that nature is a bizarre enemy that is set against human beings. Hannett states: "Underlining human and supernatural threats is nature itself, harsh and unforgiving; over it all hangs an endless, suffocating sky. The settings in these narratives are more than just unsettling or uncanny; there's an *unheimlich* quality to this country's wilderness, which makes it clear that most characters—human or otherwise—are unwelcome. Leave, they seem to say. You don't belong here."[26]

If people and nature are no help to Australians in the midst of lives plagued by horrors, then we may cling to some hope that perhaps God can help us. In *Prayers of a Secular World: Australian Poems for Our Times*,

24. Nick Cave, *The Death of Bunny Munro* (New York: Faber and Faber, 2009).

25. Tehani Wessely, introduction to *Australis Imaginarium* (Mawson, ACT: Fablecroft, 2010), cited in Hannett, "Wide Open Fear."

26. Hannett, "Wide Open Fear." She continues immediately: "Many of them depict rural isolation: people alone in the desert, in the bush, by the sea."

Jordie Albiston and Kevin Brophy write that Australians are slowly realizing that perhaps we discarded too much when we threw religion away. We need to reformulate our relationship with God.[27] This raises the painful question of how such a reformulation could be achieved in an Australian context, where there is so much violence and horror to lament. Surely a God reinvented within this context would be a reflection of the traumatic context: he/she/it would be a monster. What kind of God would be present, could be prayed to, could have poetry written to him in the context of fear, meaninglessness, and hopelessness? Is there a possible world in which a good God exists and provides hope and meaning for life despite the presence of gross and commonplace horrors that afflict the images of God? The Australian context therefore supplies *another* good reason for approaching any religious text through the lens of paranoid horror.

Broader Cultural Reasons

There is a widespread and broad cultural attunement to horrors in the Western world. Horror and trauma-related cultural products such as online serials, TV series, movies, magazines, and even tattoos have currency today. For this reason, it is not surprising that many readers will bring a horror-attuned reading strategy to the Bible. The recent development in interest and energy with respect to gothic studies has served to expand its cultural force, Andrew Ng writes:

> The gothic can no longer be seen as merely a "genre." Instead, it has become a mode of critical expression in its own right as well, benefiting from the perspicacity of various theoretical purviews including feminism, Marxism and (especially) psychoanalysis, all of which combine to intensify its work of excavating the deep structures of discourses. As an aesthetics, it enables the articulation of what is otherwise unutterable, providing a discursive space for epistemologically and ontologically problematic configurations to be represented, and vexing the dominant discourses which seek to

27. Jordie Albiston and Kevin Brophy, *Prayers of a Secular World: Australian Poems for Our Times* (Carlton South, Victoria: Inkerman & Blunt, 2015).

> repress it. ... Moments of crises ... disrupt the subject's coherence and confront his or her symbolic interpellation with a gaping void.[28]

Given the widespread popularity of horror and related genres, the task of theology today must engage with this new horror-sensitive context and propose constructive sources of hope and renewal.

Here I have suggested that a horror-attuned reading culture is native and hence appropriate to postcolonial Australian approaches to texts; this kind of reading of texts and reality is demanded in the Australian context. Readers in other contexts may have to look deeper at their own history and context in order to be informed about their own pervasive traumatic history in order to read the Bible in a manner that is in realistic conversation with horrors.

Existential Reasons

Given the presence of horrors in the world, there are good existential reasons for reading the Bible and other books as horror fiction. The prevalence of horrors explains why we respond to stories of horror even if we know they are not true per se. Amanda Wortham argues that a valuable response to pervasive horrors is "looking sideways at fictional stories to see how they run parallel to our own. In reading and studying fiction, we can discover our place within the stories and histories that shape our reality." Therefore, she argues, fiction "helps us navigate the maze of tragedy." Wortham points out that horror fiction, including classics such as *Frankenstein* and more recent dystopian works such as *Mockingjay*, promotes a deeper engagement with our plagued reality rather than an escape from it. She writes: "Fiction is not, at best, an escapist's *modus operandi*. Fiction does not allow us to ignore reality; rather, it is a tool for the wise, the desperate, and the bewildered. It gives us a frame of reference beyond what we see directly in front of us, and allows us to connect, to explore solutions safely and hypothetically." During seasons of overwhelming and unrelenting horrors, "when reality seems all too much to bear," writes Wortham, "fiction offers us a fresh framework, a way to think *around* our problems with distance, comparison, and critical analysis. Through reading, we inherit the wisdom

28. Ng, "Revisiting Judges 19," 200.

of the ages—a balm and treasure for our current social ills."[29] This explains why readers and viewers of horror are afraid of stories even though they know that these are not real.[30]

Horror stories are coherent with the shameful isolation and abandonment that many traumatized people experience as repercussions of horrors. These interpretations of reality stem in the first place from the inadequacy and failure inherent in traumatizing interpersonal relationships and by the lack of care by others in the aftermath. According to Aislinn O'Donnell, these include feelings of "social isolation, and a painful sense of being positioned as an object, thing-like or invisible." A horror-attuned reading also sits well with the shame we feel about the state of the world as a whole.[31]

Philosophical Reasons

So far, I have outlined good experiential, existential, and cultural reasons that suggest a reading strategy for the Bible that has much in common with the gothic horror genre. These reasons are corroborated by a number of philosophical lines of thought. The strongest reason given is that it is an epistemological "good." It opens our eyes to the truth about the instability of our existence.

Phillip Nickel explains this idea as follows:

> I will argue that there is something good about horror—I mean, aesthetically interesting and epistemologically good. ... By the threats it presents to the everyday life of the viewer, horror gives us a perspective on so-called common sense. It helps us to see that a notion of everyday life completely secure against threats cannot be possible, and that the security of common sense is a persistent illusion.[32]

---

29. Amanda Wortham, "Reading Sideways: How Fiction Helps Us Navigate the Maze of Tragedy," Christ and Pop Culture, July 28, 2016, http://christandpopculture.com/reading-sideways-how-fiction-helps-us-navigate-the-maze-of-tragedy/. See also the Australian novel *The Book Thief* by Markus Zusak. My thanks go to Anne Ellison for pointing out this Australian gem to me.

30. Noël Carroll, *The Philosophy of Horror, or, Paradoxes of the Heart* (New York: Routledge, 1990), 10.

31. Aislinn O'Donnell, "Shame Is Already a Revolution: The Politics of Affect in the Thought of Deleuze," *Deleuze Studies* 11, no. 1 (2017): 2.

32. Phillip J. Nickel, "Horror and the Idea of Everyday Life," in *The Philosophy of Horror*, ed. Thomas Richard Fahy (Lexington: University Press of Kentucky, 2010), 17.

Not only do horrors expose our faulty belief that the word is a safe place, but they expose the faultiness of our beliefs and the foolishness of choosing these clearly illusory beliefs. Nickel continues: "The idea of security in the everyday is based on an intellectually dubious but pragmatically attractive construction. ... This is not because such reliance is rationally compulsory, but because we choose it as the most easy and natural strategy. ... [It is] an epistemological choice." It is a choice to live according to beliefs that do not count as knowledge; it is a form of antirealism, "a construction."[33]

This antirealism may bring some temporary psychological relief from the truths about the world. The creation of artificial intellectual and social structures provides the illusion of safety. Their benefit is existential, even if it is ultimately illusory:

> It is necessary that we construct an idea of the everyday in which the intellectual backing for our practical trust feels secure, even when we know it is not. We must fabricate for ourselves a sphere in which we will not be attacked in our kitchens or showers, in which our own bodies will not turn suddenly against us, and in which the birds perched on the jungle gym are benign. There are a number of psychological reasons why this construction of the everyday is necessary, but one is simply that we cannot focus on all the possible paranoid scenarios at once.[34]

We find ourselves in a bind, knowing the truth but not being able to handle it, so we take refuge in fantasies of safety. Ironically, the drive to reinforce this illusion leads to the consumption of more horror literature and film. Sadly, it is not often appreciated as a wake-up call but instead reinforces the belief that bad things happen to other people and that we can watch them from a safe distance.[35]

---

33. Nickel, "Horror and the Idea of Everyday Life," 30.

34. Nickel, "Horror and the Idea of Everyday Life," 29.

35. For example, consider the stories of the Brothers Grimm—these are stories we tell to others (told to children). More recently we have the Malifaux world stories, whose motto is "Bad Things Happen" (these are told to adults). "People watch something in the theater because it resonates with something outside the theater. To see the cinematic representation of horrible things may be frightening, but the viewer knows that it is safe. And the sense of safety we derive from watching make-believe things helps us tolerate the prospect of real things." David P. Goldman, "Be Afraid—Be Very Afraid," *First Things* (October 2009): 42. I owe the insight to do with the Brothers Grimm to Anne Ellison.

THE TRAUMA HERMENEUTIC

Practitioners in the field of trauma studies have identified "trauma hermeneutics." This is a valid "hermeneutical lens for biblical interpretation," write Frechette and Boase. This is a Christian form of the paranoid reading. Trauma hermeneutics stem from the medical, psychological, and sociological "recognition of trauma as a distinct type of suffering that overwhelms a person's normal capacity to cope." What makes life after trauma unique is that the unconscious processing of a trauma or traumas shapes the way in which information about the world is interpreted. Trauma thus forms a point of view from which individual and corporate life is interpreted.[36] This is a trauma hermeneutic, or, in my own preference, a "horror reading."

There are three reasons for choosing to speak about a horror reading. First, the phrase "horror reading" more closely relates trauma to the fundamental problem of horrors. Second, the term "horror" is more evocative than the sanitized word "trauma." Third, horror has a longer artistic history in Western culture, which can function as a helpful touchstone in this conversation.

Drawing from trauma studies, we can say that this horror hermeneutic predetermines the way a text is read, as do the hermeneutics that stem from trauma. This, write Frechette and Boase, "shapes the specific thoughts and feelings that emerge into consciousness after sensory input, over time giving rise to conscious assumptions about self and world." It destroys the assumptions that "the self has agency and dignity, enjoys solidarity with trustworthy others (human and divine), and inhabits an environment that is relatively safe are fundamental to maintaining identity and a felt sense of well-being." These are replaced by an opposite, toxic assumption that "dignity, trust, and solidarity" are fantasies. The result is that the self and the world it inhabits are haunted by trauma, and there is no one who can trustworthily help the victim recover.[37]

The intractability of the trauma hermeneutic is consolidated by the kind of hermeneutics that are suggested by prominent trauma practitioners for those who have suffered. These principles can be described as "limiting the story" and "the mirror reading."

---

36. Frechette and Boase, "Defining 'Trauma,'" 3, 4.

37. Frechette and Boase, "Defining 'Trauma,'" 5.

Limiting the Story

Limiting the story selectively receives some Scriptures as helpful and not others. The operative assumption appears to be that only some Scriptures are sensitive to trauma, and thus only some are helpful for recovery from trauma. Instead of approaching the Gospels as coherent literary units, trauma theorists tend to read them very selectively.[38] The general tendency for trauma theorists is to focus their work on those parts of the Gospel stories that speak about Jesus' death and trauma, his death on the cross, his experience of being dead (Holy Saturday), and his perpetual wounding.[39] For authors such as Jones and Rambo, the operative interpretation is to underemphasize Jesus' life after his death; this means that his resurrection and his victory over death are only a minor consideration. Serene Jones comments: "Neither Shelly [Rambo] nor I do much with the resurrection. The closest that I come to the trauma of the resurrection is the end of Mark's Gospel where there is no more than a gesture to it." Jesus' resurrection is taken to be entirely weird for all those within the narrative itself, including Jesus, who is "barely recognizable."[40] Mayra Rivera-Rivera states: "I read those [postresurrection] stories as more ambiguous and uncertain."[41] These interpretive concerns are carried through to a very "tempered" theology of the Spirit.[42] For some, there is little or no reference to God the Trinity, renewal, or new creation.[43] The cumulative effect of interpreting the narrative of Jesus so selectively is that only certain aspects of the Christology in the Gospels are available to us. These operative assumptions shape the perspectives of the readers who take them on

38. For example, see how Rambo engages with John's Gospel in Rambo, *Spirit and Trauma*.

39. Shelly Rambo, "'Theologians Engaging Trauma' Transcript," *Theology Today* 68, no. 3 (2011): 228.

40. Jones is cited in Rambo, "'Theologians Engaging Trauma' Transcript," 226, 228.

41. "You recall that in those stories Jesus is barely recognizable—and he apparently walks through walls! What if we accepted the strangeness of these stories? Could those narratives help us re-encounter the strange narratives of communities that have been oppressed, who have gone through severe and catastrophic events, stories that witness to the elusive presence of ancestors?" Cited in Rambo, "'Theologians Engaging Trauma' Transcript," 228.

42. Rambo, "'Theologians Engaging Trauma' Transcript," 227.

43. O'Connor, "Stammering toward the Unsayable."

board, including what they look for from God within their recovery from horrors and trauma.[44]

These hermeneutical practices are a stark contrast to the interpretive approaches that seek to know God personally through the breadth of a scriptural narrative, such as Eleonore Stump's approach (outlined above). The contrast set up between the work of Stump and others in trauma-theory circles will play out in two rival interpretations of Matthew presented in oncoming chapters. The cumulative effect of trauma theorists' tendencies to limit the scope of Scripture goes hand in hand with the belief that people can never "get over" trauma.[45]

The Mirror Reading

Another effect of bracketing off Jesus' resurrection, ascension, sending, and work of the Spirit is that it sets up the second aspect of a trauma hermeneutic—the mirror reading.

Renowned trauma practitioner Serene Jones offers to trauma survivors the mirror reading within what she believes is a limited range of christological texts available to those who have suffered trauma. For Jones, the "mirror reading" is a reading of biblical narratives that focuses on how a traumatized person may have aspects of their traumatic experiences reflected in texts or images that refer to traumatized biblical characters.[46] These "mirror-effect" readings are similar to a distinctive aspect of the art-horror genre, also called the mirror reading.[47] The mirror reading

44. For a model of trauma theory applied to spiritual counseling with those experiencing PTSD, see Steven Ballaban, "The Use of Traumatic Biblical Narratives in Spiritual Recovery from Trauma: Theory and Case Study," *The Journal of Pastoral Care & Counseling* 68, no. 4 (2014): 1–11. Though his model is helpful in these specific instances, I am not convinced that this approach, taken as the sole approach to the usefulness and interpretation of Scripture, offers clients all that God has to say to them personally through biblical stories.

45. Serene Jones states: "Trauma is not something you really ever 'get over,' but rather one develops a capacity to bear it. An account of trauma cannot ever be reduced to a happy narrative of redemption, but it leaves you hanging. ... For many, the lived experience ... [of the ultimate truth] in resurrection is never going to be the case." Rambo, "'Theologians Engaging Trauma' Transcript," 227. M. Shawn Copeland speaks about "living-with-trauma" in Rambo, "'Theologians Engaging Trauma' Transcript," 228.

46. Serene Jones, *Trauma and Grace: Theology in a Ruptured World* (Louisville, KY: Westminster John Knox, 2009), 82.

47. Carroll, *Philosophy of Horror*, 18. These mirror readings are not duplications of the emotions of the characters in a horror story but rather parallel them.

and the limited texts employed by trauma theorists go hand in hand and stem from pastoral practice: wounded persons tend to gravitate and resonate with a limited number of biblical texts. This mirror effect limits the Scriptures that are employed in spiritual healing. However, is this constraint on the scope of the available Scriptures necessary in every case?

Jones finds historical warrant for the mirror reading in the writing of Reformation-era pastor and theologian John Calvin. Jones draws on Calvin, who employs the image of a mirror for how the language and emotion of the Psalms form a mirror in which we see our own experiences reflected. Calvin writes that the Psalms display the full scope of those emotions that flay and scar our souls.[48]

Jones then moves to use the passion of Christ as a mirror of and for the traumatized soul, because there are a number of dimensions of trauma that may be reflected in a passion play or another story of Jesus' torture and death. The passion of Christ and a contemporary experience of trauma both contain an original violent event and transgressive violation of personal boundaries. They also both involve the absence of the self—Jesus descends to Hades, and the victim often does not remember the violent events. Furthermore, in both cases the factual events and the interpretation of them take on significance and outcomes that transcend mere factual history. Finally, Jones notes that the public retelling of both the passion and a personal traumatic story share the potential for meeting the criteria for healing after trauma: owning the story publicly as not-a-secret and being believed, with the consequences that the violence is exposed and the victim may healthily integrate the trauma into their past as they begin to flourish in the present.[49]

Jones reasons that the particularity of each person's experience of trauma means that, the cross will not mirror all aspects of trauma for every person. This may appear to be a limitation on the mirror reading. However, Jones reasons that because the cross has been interpreted in diverse manners in the past, this is valid today also. Even cases of contradictory interpretations are not problematic because her aim is not to interpret the cross in a way that could be described as true knowledge. Rather,

48. Calvin, *Commentary on the Psalms*, cited in Jones, *Trauma and Grace*, 51.

49. Jones, *Trauma and Grace*, 78–79.

her aim is to position the traumatized interpreter in a relationship to the cross in which they can see it being relevant to them, whether this be as a sign of survival or victimization.[50]

Importantly, Jones deploys two theological convictions that restrain the breadth of interpreting the cross in the light of trauma: God's "No" to evil and his embodied "Yes" to being graciously loving.[51]

Apart from these restraints, however, Jones has little to offer on what God may resolve or achieve in a person's life, and also what may come about as persons collaborate with God's grace in their lives. This is acutely demonstrated in her exegesis of Mark's Gospel, where Jones finds neither theological hope nor resolution but rather a call to enter into the silence brought about by trauma and also into others' silence—the kind of silence embodied by the women at the end of the story and the silence enjoined by the story's abrupt ending.[52]

Jones's proposal offers little that is unique and true to the victim of trauma from a Christian perspective. Perhaps a better way of describing the mirror reading is to name it the limited mirror reading. Slim portions of the story of Jesus are examined in order to see our own stories reflected back to us in part. It offers very little in terms of framing survivors' lives with a sense of divine help for establishing what survivors need: safety, a coherent self-understanding, and reintegration with the community.[53]

---

50. "If the trauma-drama narrative is unstable and multivoiced, it is also clear that theological interpretations of the cross are varied and mutable as well. As a theology professor, I know well the long list of models that Christian communities have used to explain how God saves the world through an event of traumatic violence." Jones, *Trauma and Grace*, 81.

51. Jones, *Trauma and Grace*, 81. I question whether the polyphony of biblical texts, such as those narratives with which Jones interacts, necessarily means these are unstable. What is the significance of historical events themselves such as a resurrection from the dead? What is the value of authorial intent, and the affirmative value of the history of the text's editing and the reception by interpretive communities? Aren't these all historically grounded and purposeful activities with ideological ends? Unless their ends were "instability" itself, then Jones's thesis may require revision. Gospels do have stable claims even in the midst of appalling historical events. See C. Kavin Rowe, *Early Narrative Christology: The Lord in the Gospel of Luke*, Beihefte zur Zeitschrift für die neutestamentliche Wissenschaft und die Kunde der älteren Kirche 139 (Berlin: de Gruyter, 2006); Rowe, "Biblical Pressure and Trinitarian Hermeneutics," *Pro Ecclesia* 11, no. 3 (2002): 295–312.

52. Jones, *Trauma and Grace*, 81–97.

53. Herman writes, "Recovery unfolds in three stages. The central task of the first stage is the reestablishment of safety. ... The second stage is remembrance and mourning. ... The third stage is reconnection with ordinary life." Judith Lewis Herman, *Trauma and Recovery: From Domestic Abuse to Political Terror* (London: HarperCollins, 1992), 155, 214–36.

The meaning this method purports to offer trades on a very limited view of the person and work of Christ.

What, then, does the limited mirror reading offer the traumatized person for the sake of recovery from trauma and comprehension of their horrors? It suggests the primary value of the sufferings Christ is validating the experience of trauma in others. It also exposes and rejects the kinds of violence that reduce the health and dignity of a human person. In addition, some would argue that it provides a sense of Jesus' solidarity with those who suffer.[54] However, our current literary, cultural, and philosophical context problematizes these contributions by exaggerating their hesitation to draw on the life of Jesus more constructively. This compounding effect will be demonstrated in our next chapters.

Questions Arising from the Trauma Hermeneutic

While both limiting the scope of Scriptures and engaging in mirror reading have some commendable motivations and outcomes, I believe they may also have the effect of compounding trauma and yielding a lack of purposeful resolution to theological and anthropological questions that establish the context for recovery from trauma. Our investigation above points to a problematic thesis embedded in the work of some leading trauma practitioners: namely, that for those who have experienced trauma the most helpful reading of the biblical texts occurs when trauma-relevant texts are read through the lens of trauma and horror.[55] This leads to a burning question. If read in such a way, does a Gospel, such as Matthew's Gospel, reinforce and propagate a horror reading of reality? Does it thereby unwittingly undermine and inhibit possibilities of personal and worldview recovery?

Even apart from deliberately approaching the Gospel of Matthew through the lens of horror, it's interesting to note that this Gospel shares many formal and material features in common with horror literature.[56] These include the massacre of children, profound loss, spectral beings such

---

54. Jones, *Trauma and Grace*; Michael E. McGowan, "Trauma and Grace: Psychology and Theology in Conversation," *Pastoral Psychology* 58, no. 2 (2009): 167–80; Christie, "Night Office."

55. Rambo, *Spirit and Trauma*, 16–17, 111–41. See also Adele Reinhartz, "Incarnation and Covenant: The Fourth Gospel through the Lens of Trauma Theory," *Interpretation* 69, no. 1 (2015): 35–48.

56. A strong case for this is made in Scott Harrower, *Magical Realism, Horror and the Weird Gospel* (forthcoming).

as angels and demons, a beheading, oppressive power systems, distressed people, torture, and suicide.

If it is true that Matthew accommodates such a horror-attuned reading because of its literary features, then we must ask whether it welcomes such a reading from an ideological perspective as well.[57] This raises a potentially problematic issue for Christians. Does Matthew—and its ideology—perpetuate the prevalence, dominance, and damage of horror in our world? In other words, is Matthew a "text of terror"?[58] If Matthew is indeed a text that perpetuates a fearful and horrific view of reality, cynicism about people and skepticism about the existence or character of God will poison a Christian's worldview. It would serve a paranoid reading of reality and not a reparative one.[59] A horror reading of texts and the world will generate and cement the normativity of the violent and traumatic worldview it seeks to find, thereby perpetuating violence at the core of reality.[60]

Further consequences would follow if Matthew affirms such a paranoid view of reality and of the best way to be read as a Gospel. For example, at an ideological level, it would only serve to confirm J. L. Schellenberg's perspective that "skeptical realism" is the most appropriate approach to the existence of the God of classical theism.[61] At a pastoral level, it strips people of the potential to find hope and meaning—other than in arbitrary constructions of their own. The last thing traumatized people need is a Gospel that only reinforces the worst aspects and experiences of their existence.

AN APPROACH TO A HORROR READING OF MATTHEW

Before exploring how Matthew's Gospel is well placed to answer these questions, I want to outline a strategy for a horror reading of this text. The best

57. When I refer to Matthew, I mean the Gospel of Matthew.

58. The phrase "text of terror" is powerfully deployed as a descriptive term in Phyllis Trible, *Texts of Terror: Literary-Feminist Readings of Biblical Narratives* (Philadelphia: Fortress, 1984).

59. This results from reading texts and the world from a perspective that E. Sedgwick names "paranoid." Sedgwick, "Paranoid Reading, Reparative Reading," cited in Murphy, "Founding Foreclosures," 11–13.

60. Sedgwick, "Paranoid Reading, Reparative Reading."

61. J. L. Schellenberg, *The Wisdom to Doubt: A Justification of Religious Skepticism* (Ithaca, NY: Cornell University Press, 2007).

way forward is, first, to note the genre and structural elements of gothic literature; second, to be attuned to its common themes and characters; and third, to see how the worldviews and messages with which horrors deal are communicated through these stories.

To do so, I draw on the central features of gothic horror literature. This body of literature is explored because, as suggested by Wortham and others, it pushes us to confront and resolve the horrors of existence, and the questions these raise about the nature of human dignity and experience. Engaging with this literature provides a helpful reading strategy by which to explore Matthew's Gospel in search of answers to these questions.

A gothic horror reading strategy ensures that traumatic horrors and suffering aspects of Jesus' life and those of his earliest followers are taken into account in the development and defense of a theology of the nature of God, human meaning, and hope. This is very important for dealing with these theological issues in a realist (rather than antirealist) manner. A realist approach is consistent with the view that the Gospels are based on testimonial witness. It is not a form of religious antirealism.[62]

Wortham reminds us that, for those "living after the storm" of trauma, Bible reading serves as a text in which to bring together two horizons, the theological and the existential. When people find themselves overwhelmed by horrors and traumas, readers "would do well to remember that the maze we find ourselves in now has a Master, that He designed our path with careful patterns and reiterations of His truths. To engage good and truthful stories about human nature is to engage His good work, to

---

62. "Religious non-realism holds that 'God' should not be understood as referring to a metaphysical God existing independently of our conceptualizations." Erica Appelros, *God in the Act of Reference* (Aldershot, UK: Ashgate, 2002), 177. Appelros is a religious nonrealist who attempts to avoid the following alternatives, which seem to be the only avenues open to religious nonrealists in the context of the dualism as she has outlined. "There are ... seemingly only two alternatives left for the religious non-realist for how to understand the reference 'God.'" Appelros writes that the first option is the one whereby "the referring practice involving 'God' can be interpreted as not referring to anything real, in line with talk about other non-existing fictional characters such as Anna Karenina and Sherlock Holmes. Engaging in religious practice is then like being inspired by great literature, or being carried away by compelling myths." The second is "to interpret religious language as indeed referring to something, although not God, but, for instance, emotions, an internalized father figure, neural transmissions, or sociological values." Appelros ultimately describes her position as "closely related to internal realism." *God in the Act of Reference*, 180.

watch His kingdom appear parallel to our own broken world."[63] Such an answer requires an engagement that is deeply informed by an awareness of what to look for in the realm of horrors, lest we become complacent with traumas and not notice them due to their common occurrence. This is achieved by a reading strategy that seeks out the core themes and tropes within horror literature.

Across the subgenres of horror stories and horror-inclusive stories (such as Matthew's Gospel), horror literature has, according to Thomas Richard Fahy, "two central elements: (1) an appearance of the evil supernatural or of the monstrous (this includes the psychopath who kills monstrously); and (2) the intentional elicitation of dread, visceral disgust, fear, or statement in the spectator or reader."[64] Hence, horror literature ultimately serves the emotions and feelings it conjures up in the reader/hearer. John Clute says that these revolve around powerful emotions such as fear: each "horror story makes its readers *feel* horror."[65] Clute writes: "A 'pure' horror tale may occupy the same region as a supernatural fiction—this world is being encroached on by another ... but is shaped *primarily* to convey the affect of horror. Thus the pure horror story is normally structured so that its protagonist and its readers share the same reactions." Readers and protagonists share the feeling of horror for the good reason there is a real "threat to one's body and/or culture and/or world," and also that "there is something inherently monstrous and wrong in the invasive presence."[66]

The wrongness of the invasive presence often has to do with distortion of something originally good, for example, the distortion of the images of God. An example of this occurs when people are not trustworthy reflections of God's character but are devious or deceitful. Such characters

63. Wortham, "Reading Sideways."

64. Fahy continues: "On this understanding, some of the most popular and critically acclaimed works of art and entertainment contain elements of horror. It is instantiated not only in contemporary film but in the whole history of literary and representational art (Dante's *Inferno*, Shakespeare's tragedies, paintings by Caravaggio and Goya, to mention some obvious examples)." Fahy, *Philosophy of Horror*, 15. On the different kinds of subgenres of horror see Viktória Prohászková, "The Genre of Horror," *American International Journal of Contemporary Research* 2, no. 4 (2012): 132–42.

65. Gothic horror literature is a hybrid of Romantic, horror, and fantasy literature. John Clute, "Horror," in *The Encyclopedia of Fantasy*, ed. John Clute and John Grant (Exeter, UK: Orbit, 1997), 478, italics original.

66. Clute, "Horror," 478, italics original.

undermine other people rather than enabling them to flourish and develop as servants of God and the world. The outcomes of this are shambling and shallow versions of what could have been the case in a best-case scenario. The context for the horror story is also distorted—it is "toxic and non-optimal," as is the context of life outside the garden of Eden.[67] "What generates the frisson of horror is an overwhelming sense that the invaders are obscenely, transgressively impure," writes Clute. He continues: "The monsters of horror are befoulers of the boundaries that mark us off from the Other. ... They may be neither one thing or another, so that they violate the decorum of species, of role, of fittingness to place."[68]

These elements generate a profound sense of outrage, according to Michael Schrauzer:

> The outrage in horror is especially important. Gruesome monsters and sadistic murderers are certainly frightening, but behind the fright is the conviction that such things just should not be. Vampires are not only scary, they are wrong. ... Psychopaths are inhuman. Torture, murder and death itself are profoundly outrageous. These horrors violate our deepest intuitions about how the world ought to operate, about good and evil, crime and punishment, and what it means to be human.[69]

The outrage felt by readers has to do with transgression and deviance. One of horror's main themes is transgression. Ng underscores the centrality of transgression and its significance for generating the key events in horror stories: "The gothic, among other things, is about transgression ... the breaking open of texts to reveal their hidden and otherwise indescribable instances of terror. This is why moments of crises which disrupt the subject's coherence and confront his or her symbolic interpellation with

67. Marilyn McCord Adams, *Christ and Horrors: The Coherence of Christology* (Cambridge: Cambridge University Press, 2006), 37–39; Matthew Forrest Lowe, "Book Review: Marilyn McCord Adams, Christ and Horrors: The Coherence of Christology," *Religious Studies and Theology* 26, no. 2 (2007): 267–69.

68. Clute, "Horror," 478, italics original.

69. Michael Schrauzer, "Sin Is the True Horror," *The Catholic Answer* (September-October 2012): 32.

a gaping void (familiarly conceptualized as the sublime) are especially prominent."[70]

Horror literature focuses on "weird" people and stories that cannot be described according to known categories or known typologies. Transgression takes on a living form, often in the shape of fringe people and fringe experiences. Ng writes, "The gothic is also about liminal positions, a discourse that situates the subject on the threshold of humanness. The gothic monsters, for example, simultaneously human and abhuman, remind us of our precarious identity, which is always threatening to slip into otherness."[71] This genre helps us give form to the strange things that replace "life." These provide us with images and symbols that show us what the absences of life's actualization and potential look like. For example, the nothingness that occupies the space for fruitfulness that is proper and fitting for a human takes the form of a haggard woman. The strangeness of life after the fall is embodied in the way that people are "other" with respect to how they were intended by God. When this otherness is given a form and "being," it is profoundly threatening and scary, which helps explain and illustrate what life is like. The genre of gothic horror takes these kinds of deviances and aberrations to be its central horrors. These novels suggest that the abnormality and deviance we see in the creatures that populate its stories are partial reflections of the physical, social, and psychological contradictions that all readers embody and struggle to contain.[72] The profound philosophical entailment of this is that in gothic horror, according to Ng, "there are no stable foundations."[73]

In sum, the horror genre's aim to elicit fear as evil is given form via distorted versions of good things. Our horror reading strategy involves reading the text for places where it resonates with horror themes such as unknown threats to well-being, secrets, perversion, subhuman behavior,

---

70. Ng, "Revisiting Judges 19," 200.

71. Ng, "Revisiting Judges 19," 201.

72. Jerrold E. Hogle, "Introduction: The Gothic in Western Culture," in *The Cambridge Companion to Gothic Fiction*, ed. Jerrold E. Hogle (Cambridge: Cambridge University Press, 2002), 12. "The Gothic clearly exists, in part, to raise the possibility that all 'abnormalities' that we would divorce are part of ourselves deeply and pervasively (hence frighteningly), even while it provides quasi-antiquated methods to help us place such 'deviations' at definite, though haunting, distance from us." Hogle, "Introduction," 14.

73. Ng, "Revisiting Judges 19," 201.

and hidden truths. Reading horror is meant to be a profoundly emotional and unsettling experience. The reader should be affected and changed by such an experience. The intensity of the genre means that one is affected by it, even in immediately unknown ways.

In the chapter that follows, I will carry out a horror reading of Matthew in the spirit of Zöe Lehmann Imfeld, who promotes "a skillful marriage of literature and theology" in the context of postmodern caution not to rush to the assumed answers too quickly and at the expense of thorough investigation. This is a "hospitable" interaction between literary theory, biblical text, and theology—a critical yet welcoming conversation in which the theological dimensions and conclusions of texts are valued.[74] This dynamic approach is demonstrated in Kalmanofsky's procedure of studying horror and the horrible in Jeremiah with the help of horror literary studies.[75] I plan to do in select chapters of Matthew what Kalmanofsky does in her work on Jeremiah 6.[76] The goals (fear and outrage) and central concerns (transgression and deviance) of horror literature need to be borne in mind as we do this.

As we turn to a horror- and trauma-informed reading of Matthew's Gospel, we will note the fears and revulsions the text generates in us as it details transgression and deviance rather than shalom and blessing for the images of God.

---

74. Zoë Lehmann Imfeld, Peter Hampson, and Alison Milbank, "Hospitable Conversations in Theology and Literature: Re-opening a Space to be Human," in *Theology and Literature after Postmodernity*, ed. Zoë Lehmann Imfeld, Peter Hampson, and Alison Milbank (London: T&T Clark, 2015), 4.

75. "Having examined the nature of horror and the horrible in the book of Jeremiah as a whole and considered the literary strategies designed to engage readers in the horror genre, I will now present a close rhetorical reading of one horror text: Jer 6." Kalmanofsky, *Terror All Around*, 104.

76. There are good literary reasons for reading Matthew's Gospel as a supernatural horror gothic text. I believe Matthew's stories and themes lend it to be thoughtfully approached as an anticipatory form of "the supernatural gothic, in which the existence and cruel operation of unnatural forces are asserted graphically." Carroll, *Philosophy of Horror*, 4. Matthew Lewis's *The Monk* is an example of what Carroll describes above. He notes that the ending of this book revolves around the "appearance of the demon and the gruesome impalement of the priest at the end," and as such "is the real harbinger of the horror genre." Carroll, *Philosophy of Horror*, 4.

7

A HORROR READING OF MATTHEW

As we have seen, the metaphysical reality of horrors produces strong literary, cultural, experiential, philosophical, and trauma-related reasons for a horror reading of texts. I carry out such a reading of Matthew's Gospel in what follows.

For readers unaccustomed to a horror perspective, some of the material that follows may be offensive and shocking. This is deliberate and is intended to stimulate you, the reader, to ask why such a reading should not be the case. Pushing you to develop your own reasons for a different reading of the Bible, a life-giving one, is the first step in overcoming a horror reading of the Bible and of life more generally. In order to overcome horrors, a reader must eventually, with the aid of God and other persons, develop a perspective that anticipates shalom in their own life.

In addition to responding to the good literary, experiential, cultural, philosophical, and trauma-related reasons for the horror reading, I have a number of aims that will suggest ways forward beyond the horror reading itself.

The first aim of this horror- and trauma-attuned reading is to demonstrate that this kind of reading does indeed perpetuate the view that human existence is permanently and irretrievably marked by horrors and trauma. The power of this reading lies in that it reinforces a paranoid approach to life and God because it underscores the normativity of "death in life" that lies at the center of traumatic experiences.[1] It seems to reinforce that our

1. "I am seeking a picture of redemption that adequately accounts for traumatic suffering, that speaks to divine presence and power in light of what we know about trauma. This picture of redemption cannot emerge by interpreting death and life in opposition to each other. Instead, theology must account for the excess, or remainder, of death in life that is central to trauma. This reconfiguration of death and life, viewed through the lens of trauma, unearths a distinctive theology that can witness the realities of the aftermath of trauma." Shelly Rambo, "Spirit and Trauma," *Interpretation* 69, no. 1 (2015): 12.

worldview should be the imagination of disaster. A mirror reading of a text will find the violence it skeptically anticipates within the text and its imaginative world.

This point means that, given a trauma and horror reading, Matthew as a standalone text, and aside from its instrumental use by other persons, does not resist or subvert the kinds of themes that gothic horror authors such as Flannery O'Connor suggest are actually faithful descriptors of reality and human existence. Matthew on its own does not have the power to overturn the commonplace and gross horrors that present the world as a carnival of perverted persons whose master emotion is fear and who abuse their power with respect to others at the same time that they are victimized. This suggests that Matthew's Gospel needs to be used instrumentally by a person or persons in order to communicate its intended message to a traumatized person who is looking for hope. A private reading will not be reparative on its own.

The horror and trauma reading of Matthew emphasizes just how much the reader of Matthew must overcome in order to interpret Matthew as *good news*. It also points out how much help we need from God and other people in the Christian community. Matthew only bears good news if it is illuminated by divine and human presence, if and only if it is read in such a way that it surmounts most of the violent horrors, traumas, and skepticisms that present themselves as intrinsic to human life.

There is also an explorative reason for undertaking this reading of Matthew. To my mind, a horror and trauma reading will inevitably uncover previously underexplored and underappreciated aspects of the author's story.[2] Because this approach to Matthew is driven by the argument and intuition that life is essentially traumatic, this reading will pick

2. In times of horror and trauma, people may benefit from a reading strategy that functions as a medium through which to approach resources that can help us. Gothic literature can help us because it enables us to read about the difficult and bizarre experiences of others in such a way that we can at once project our difficulties onto characters in past stores while at the same time allowing their stories to shape our interpretation of own. See Jerrold E. Hogle, "Introduction: The Gothic in Western Culture," in *The Cambridge Companion to Gothic Fiction*, ed. Jerrold E. Hogle (Cambridge: Cambridge University Press, 2002), 6.

up neglected theological and emotional dimensions within the text.[3] In addition, such a reader may expose a number of assumptions that have been smuggled into other, more conventional, readings of Matthew. Indeed, a horror reading of Matthew is ironically a fresh and honest approach to this Gospel that may expose unfounded and presumed interpretations by other readers.[4] The pastoral aim of this reading is to create empathy for the traumatized reader by noting examples in the narrative that may be profoundly unhelpful to a person who has experienced horrors but may go unnoticed by a well-meaning person who is trying to help them.

Finally, I take the suggestions of scholars working in the field of trauma studies to their radical conclusions by following their proposals for a mirror reading in the context of bracketing off important elements in the text such as resurrection, the Spirit, and victory. This demonstrates the limitations of these "trauma hermeneutic" approaches. The details of this are important too: much of what is lost by way of this approach involves the personal dimensions of how God and people relate to each other within his renewing kingdom.

My procedure draws from Amy Kalmanofsky's approach to the book of Jeremiah, which is informed by insights from horror literary theory. This leads to asking questions such as the following: "How does this text horrify its readers? What images are used to express and elicit horror? With whom is the reader aligned? How does the text establish this relationship?"[5] Where these are found, I note how they work to develop ideologies related to skepticism about God's goodness, the meaningfulness of human life, and hope.

I need to be clear upfront that I do not hold the views of the horror reading that follows. Overcoming the horror reading is carried out in later chapters of this book, and you may want to turn to this as you go.

---

3. "This study ... provides a powerful glimpse into the emotional life of the Bible's audience—which may include its current readers by examining what moves and terrifies them." Amy Kalmanofsky, *Terror All Around: Horror, Monsters, and Theology in the Book of Jeremiah*, The Library of Hebrew Bible/Old Testament Studies 390 (New York: T&T Clark International, 2008), 2.

4. Ian Boxall, *Discovering Matthew: Content, Interpretation, Reception* (London: SPCK, 2014), 27.

5. Kalmanofsky, *Terror All Around*, 104.

A HORROR READING OF MATTHEW

Matthew's Gospel follows the formal plotline of gothic horror: it will (1) uncover the extent of evil, (2) confirm its presence, and (3) finally confront it.[6] This takes place as (1) the intentions and actions of all kinds of personal beings—including demons, the devil, human rulers, mobs, and the friends and family of Jesus—are exposed, and (2) the presence of these evils is confirmed in their malicious failures to relate to Jesus, God, and each other in personal, moral, and creative ways. As the story proceeds, Matthew will employ compilations of images that show these events are true; this serves as the "rhetoric of horror." These will evoke the reader/hearer's "composite emotional response."[7] Matthew will finally move to (3) in which there is a sad, gory, and scary clash between Jesus and horror makers. It ends in doubt and absence.

The Genealogy

The first of these compilations is Matthew's selective genealogy. The genealogy will tell a story of woe. It will establish the emotional mood and historical expectations that foreground the bizarre events that swirl around the conception of Jesus.

Another Messiah among Pretenders

The genealogy begins with "An account of the genealogy of Jesus Christ, the Son of David, the Son of Abraham" (Matt 1:1). It is a story of images of God who need rescue from each other's actions. Some have taken the mantle of savior on themselves and without a calling from God to do so. The genealogy's use of the term "messiah" brings to mind the rebellious and frenzied messianic claimants of the author's age. These were the kind of wonder-workers that Jesus and others warned against (Matt 24:14), for example, the "Egyptian who led four thousand terrorists into the desert" (Acts 21:38).

Jesus is introduced in the context of disorder, pretention, and deluded claims of salvation. For the reader this means that claiming that Jesus is a

---

6. Noël Carroll, *The Philosophy of Horror, or, Paradoxes of the Heart* (New York: Routledge, 1990), 109–11.

7. Kalmanofsky, *Terror All Around*, 11.

messiah is not persuasive per se; rather, it is a dubious claim that others took on with deadly results for themselves and their followers. This puts pressure on the story to define Jesus' unique status among other messiahs. Sadly, the genealogy that follows only serves to undermine any expectations that a messiah may yield hopes for human living and meaningfulness.

An Ancient and Degenerate History

One of the key features of horror literature is that it trades on "deep fears and longings."[8] Matthew's Gospel does this as it depends on deep theological and existential longings for God and his blessings, as well as for meaningful lives and hopeful futures for human beings. These longings will be matched by profound fears that are exposed in the genealogy that opens this Gospel. Matthew's story opens with a haunting record of human disaster stories. He records the story of those with whom God made a personal covenant from Abraham, through the line of David, to the exile, ending at the stepfather of Jesus (Matt 1:1–17). The personal, moral, and creative aspects of the people involved in these covenants with God were to serve God's project of a world full of life and peace. Dynamic abundance and vitality should be the hallmarks of this extended family history. In its place, the genealogy retells the history of a doomed nation and its exile. It is a historical affirmation of the senselessness of humans and their cultures, even those who call on God. It refers to historical horrors and echoes the subjective experiences of those who had to endure them and their aftermath. In this light, fear about the present and the future has a good grounding.

Even the so-called people of God suffer from perennial national confusion and insecurity in a world of horrors. These facts from history cannot be ignored or undone; these realities are our haunted inheritance, and we are doomed to repeat this history. According to the taxonomy for horrors proposed earlier in this work, the Abrahamic people have experienced horrors at a macro level. They have experienced (1) "a degeneration of life toward death," via degenerative conflicts with neighboring states such as those described in the book of Joshua, which were (2) "sourced in an objective, relationally immoral action," which is recorded in the Old Testament, such as the ambition of rulers, expressed in wars aimed at oppressive and

8. Hogle, "Introduction," 4.

self-serving regimes. The traumatic outcomes included (3) "prevention from being and allowing others to be images of God in their natural and fullest sense," as they lost the vitality of their faith and possibilities for flourishing, as attested in the book of Isaiah. By Jesus' day, the leadership of the covenant people lived in fear and under oppression, meeting criterion (4), "the traumatic perception of a real or imagined event that diminishes the extent of the personhood of an image of God." Clearly, this nation will never recover the glory it momentarily experienced under Solomon; hence it meets criterion (5): "It is not possible to fully recover psychologically and relationally from these before death."

The genealogy is a record of this macrohorror, akin to a longer-term record of genocide. Appreciating this fact evokes one of horror's core elements: cognitive dissonance between life as it is and life as it should be, which is amplified given that this all relates to God's chosen people.[9] If this is the way God cares for his own, then how about the rest of us? Who is worse off: Those who believed God was on their side or those who never knew this God in the first place?

The genealogy echoes and recalls the stories that take their point of departure from God's covenant with Abraham, which was intended to restore Edenic shalom to all the world. Shamefully, all of these people and their efforts were eventually swallowed up by failure, trauma, and death. Even those who momentarily brought security from affliction, such as David, turned on their fellow images of God in transgressive ways: he was a murderer, thief, liar, and adulterer.

What happened to the Edenic and new-Edenic hopes for human flourishing in personally moral social-political cultures? What is the legacy of the images of God, so wonderfully endowed with unique relational, moral, and creative abilities? Is this all that comes from thousands of years of their existence? Yes, it is. And this is highly recognizable, because this is the way the world is. The carnival of failure described by the genealogy is not an antirealist tale; it is metaphysically sad realism because it is a shrunken version of what should be. The sense of contrast with what

9. E. T. A. Davidson, "The Comedy of Horrors," *Proceedings* 23 (2003): 41; István Czachesz, "The Promise of the Cognitive Science of Religion for Biblical Studies," *The Council of Societies for the Study of Religion Bulletin* 37, no. 4 (2008): 102–5.

should be is apparent by what is missing. Because it is a story of horrors in the place of life, it is a story shot through by relational, moral, and creative absences, as generations of personal and moral failure have blasted pellets of emptiness into these people. It is a history of deviance. This is a fearful and outrageous flip side of shalom brought about by the shadowy lives of the images of God.

The Absence of Life

This is not a story of long-term national flourishing. Israel does not develop to the extent that it provides a model of life with God for other nations. Instead, Israel's fragility and the impermanence of life are striking. The genealogy refers to the national history of thousands, perhaps even millions, of people who die. Death is the prominent power in the genealogy. Each person dies, returning to nothingness; a number of the persons recorded were assassinated. What of the wholesome shalom in which people and all forms of life were to flourish? Are the images of God precious? If so, why are they all dead? Was there no one to care for them and protect them from physical, relational, and historical oblivion? At this point the reader is tempted to abandon any expectations of a flourishing life in the company of God and other persons.

The Absence of God and His Visible Care

All people—including those in the story and the reader—yearn for secure relationships. The prospect of this is dashed by the genealogy. Expectations for divine care or human sociocultural care should be abandoned as delusions.[10] "From the height of Israel's political and spiritual glory under King David," writes Frederick Dale Bruner, "Israel first gradually then precipitously declines until she falls into the pit of exile, losing her land, temple, kings, and thus, seemingly, almost all of God's promises."[11] It is oxymoronic to think in terms of God's chosen people: the reader searches the ruins in vain.[12] Israel's loss of God and his promises undermines the nation's

10. Kathleen M. O'Connor, "Stammering Toward the Unsayable: Old Testament Theology, Trauma Theory, and Genesis," *Interpretation* 70, no. 3 (2016): 307.

11. Frederick Dale Bruner, *Matthew: A Commentary* (Grand Rapids: Eerdmans, 2004), 121.

12. Judith Lewis Herman, *Trauma and Recovery: From Domestic Abuse to Political Terror* (London: Basic Books, 2001), 77.

confidence in their ability to live in such a righteous manner that could provoke God to act on their behalf. More importantly, it confirms that God's presence could not live among them.

The mention of characters involved in the Babylonian exile brings to mind the theological confusion and a crisis of worldview for all Israelites. Even the prophets had to understand God anew in the face of gory national cataclysms. Their hope was to maintain two propositions: "that God is alive even though every faith tradition of the past has been smashed to pieces like their environment, and, second, there is a cause and effect in the world, order in the midst of chaos," writes Kathleen O'Connor.[13]

However, that God is alive and that there is order is not clear from Matthew's genealogy. The genealogy reflects theology written in the mode of survival. O'Connor states: "Jeremiah's literary artistry is a mode of survival, an expression of hope, even when the words themselves are hopeless."[14] This authorial attempt for the sake of coping is a reflection of the creative capacity of humans. Matthew, like the prophets who came around the times of exile, was trying to survive and adapt protectively to the violent realities outside Eden. In the same manner, the readers of this text recognize that the story that is told is epistemologically sound, because they themselves live in this same kind of brutal world.[15]

This quest for survival is merely an extension of the struggle and despair that follow on from being expelled from Eden. Cycles of struggle recur endlessly. Within these cycles, God is certainly alive, but perhaps only tangentially present and interested in the misery of human life. Perhaps his active care is dissuaded after a series of apparently failed covenants. This creates a tension in the later Old Testament literature: God is able to bless but somehow is not doing so.[16] The deep question this

---

13. The exile hovers over Matthew's horizon as a national disaster and theological horror. See Kathleen M. O'Connor, *Jeremiah: Pain and Promise* (Minneapolis: Fortress, 2011), x.

14. O'Connor, *Jeremiah*, x.

15. O'Connor, *Jeremiah*, x.

16. O'Connor describes this tension: "Jeremiah promises a future beyond the death of the nation, a future that is uncertain, open-ended, and just over the horizon. The future will come because God, whom they thought had punished them, failed them, or left them, was still there, still loving, and still yearning for them. Jeremiah does not explain suffering in any satisfactory way ... (no biblical book does), but the book pledges that God will make a future and points the way toward it." O'Connor, *Jeremiah*, x.

generates is whether God is a kind of monster. He is a monster whose actions reveal that he is an uncanny mixture of opposites: care and neglect, promise and punishment, blesser and blighter. His monstrosity could be argued along a spectrum: at one end, perhaps, he is uncaring where he should be caring; at the other end, he is more actively against his own people.

Ultimately, we need to make a call about who is primarily responsible for the objective and subjective horrors described and referred to in the genealogy. Only once this is done can we move to bracket this person off from relationships with others in the hope of restoring order, a sense of safety, and reintegration into the way things should be for human persons. But if God is not the depersonalizing and traumatizing monster in this story, then who is?

The Absence of Morality and the Abuse of Power

In the context of a horror reading, historical events seem to be primarily driven by transgressive abuses of power. The unrelenting story of the struggle over self-rule and subsequent communal imprisonment is a far cry from ideal covenantal relationships and shalom.

The captivity referred to in the genealogy is particularly deviant and outrageous. Captivity is a deviant form of person-to-person relationships. The integrity and vulnerability of the other person is ignored as they are treated like an object rather than as a subjective person. These relationships are perversions of the relational and moral aspects of being made in God's image. Ironically, being made in the image of God is what allows one party to enslave another, because this perverted behavior is the evil use of the creative or functional aspect of human agency.

Captivity, says Judith Lewis Herman, "brings a special type of relationship, of coercive control." This coercive relationship has profound consequences for undermining belief and trust in God above other powerful gods, persons, or institutions. This is because one of the effects of coercion is that "the perpetrator becomes the most powerful person in the life of the victim, and the psychology of the victim is shaped by the actions and beliefs of the perpetrator."[17] Hence the boundary between being human

17. Herman, *Trauma and Recovery*, 75.

and being God is porous and scarily unstable. A powerful consequence of this in Israel's history was that when the nation played the power games of their geographical neighbors, they were ultimately enslaved by those nations' actions and their evil gods. The theological dimensions of this are important because skepticism about Yahweh and his character abound when the nation faces oppression in the name of other divine beings.[18]

The Absence of Meaning and Hope

The skepticism that the genealogy yields with respect to God and his character is closely related to skepticism about the possibilities of living a meaningful or hopeful human life. As the genealogy recounts the history of God's people, it recalls that Israel's own kings were often also oppressors. This point is made by both the inclusion of evil characters such as Joram (Matt 1:8) and Manasseh (1:10), as well as by the omission of known historical kings, whose lives were outrageous in their depravity and deaths.[19]

In addition to Israel's internal oppressors, the genealogy notes foreign oppressors such as the Babylonian overlords (1:12). Tyrants and oppressors aim at "the creation of a willing victim," says Lewis Herman. This is a common feature of all tyrannical rule, and the postexilic literature witnesses to this: "The desire for total control over another person is the common denominator of all forms of tyranny. Totalitarian governments demand confession and political conversion of their victims. Slaveholders demand gratitude of their slaves. Religious cults [Israel in Jesus' day] demand ritualized sacrifices as a sign of submission to the divine will of the leader."[20] The personal and theological debasement required by this kind of oppression has multigenerational effects on its victims. Sadly, oppression of this sort is commonly witnessed throughout the Old Testament and the New Testament, and in the period of early Christianity.[21]

18. This sets up a gloomy mood tinged with hope: "The tears of Jeremiah, God, the people, and the earth itself flow across the book, promising to awaken hearts turned to stone by brutality." O'Connor, *Jeremiah*, x.

19. D. A. Carson, *Matthew*, 92; Bruner, *Matthew*, 13.

20. Lewis Herman, *Trauma and Recovery*, 75, 76.

21. C. Kavin Rowe, *World Upside Down: Reading Acts in the Graeco-Roman Age* (Oxford: Oxford University Press, 2009).

Ironically, it is not merely a distortion and perversion of the victims, but it also creates a sick alteration in the oppressor—the oppressor becomes dependent on the victim. "Hostages, political prisoners, battered women, and slaves have all remarked upon the captor's psychological dependence upon his victim," writes Lewis Herman.[22] Because the oppressor is not being personalized in the context of healthy relationships and action with other persons, oppressors need victims to validate them on a number of levels. Hence, oppressors themselves sadly become prey to transgressive relationships of their own devising. This suggests that meaningful living and hope for the future also elude those who sit atop the structures of human power when they rule without respect to the relational, moral, and creative aspects of who persons are.

In sum, the genealogy generates objective and subjective macrohorrors. Objectively, it claims that all the historical interactions between persons leading up to the life of Jesus have added up to the loss of life, persons, relationships, moral strength, and human ingenuity. Every simple relationship between persons has added up to failed social structures.[23] Events such as betrayal, murder, abuse, unfaithfulness, the worship of false gods, and pagan sacrifices provide the basis for this fact. The victimization of Israel by other nations highlights the failure of people to relate to God and to other persons as images of God. This story serves to anticipate further loss and violence, which is horribly fulfilled in the torture and death of Jesus. For this reason, it is reasonable to conclude that there is no such thing as shalom and that people will not flourish: neither then nor now. This overwhelming truth is compounded by the ludicrousness of asking what kind of events could overturn this objective account of history as the basis for beliefs about God and persons.

Subjectively, the whole genealogy is shot through with a sense of what Robert Harris terms "unease and foreboding."[24] This is compounded by the

22. Lewis Herman, *Trauma and Recovery*, 75–76.

23. Andrew Beveridge, "Social Theory Two Ways: John Levi Martin's Structures and Actions," *Historical Methods* 45, no. 4 (2012): 179. In the constructive portion of this work I will draw on complexity and chaos theory for historical investigation in order to argue for a different perspective on chaos and social order.

24. Robert Harris, "Elements of the Gothic Novel," Virtual Salt, June 15, 2015, https://www.virtualsalt.com/gothic.htm. Harris's work has been a powerful influence on my thinking in terms of the gothic genre.

genealogy's ending on the name of a man who was famously murdered unjustly, which indicates the mood according to which the story should be read. This has a powerful subjective effect on the reader. In the genealogy there is no protagonist with whom we share the sense of danger and disruption of normality. Rather, we have a shared horror experience with the objectivity of history. This shared horror between Matthew's story and the reader anticipates further absence of God and his care, interpersonal abuses, and a lack of theological and personal meaning and hope.[25] The power of this lies in that there are no counterfacts for these beliefs and emotions. Thus, it is realistic and entirely appropriate to feel personal dread, caused by the threat of destruction.[26]

Mary: A Woman Transgressed, Terrified, and Displaced

Horror literature usually includes women who are often endangered, confined, and anxious.[27] Mary seems to play this role in Matthew and to experience a number of relational, moral, and creative failings and absences in personal relationships. These affect her and her family profoundly.

The Weird Absence of Stability

Mary's story opens with a very strange event, a virginal conception of a divine-human child. Such a rupture of the ordinary expectations to do with pregnancy, biology, and human-to-divine relationships is traumatic.[28] It is so out of the ordinary that even its purported explanation is unsettling. There is little detail for the context of the story, which means there are no good points of reference for understanding what is happening.

Transgression is one of the hallmarks of gothic horror literature. This involves one agent pushing past boundaries that should not be crossed. Often this involves victimizing another person. The genealogy records the names of five women who were part of sexual transgressions of their

---

25. O'Connor, *Jeremiah*, x; Kalmanofsky, *Terror All Around*.

26. "Shared horror is evoked in the text through … the recognition of a threat to one's body and/or culture and/or world." John Clute, "Horror," in *The Encyclopedia of Fantasy*, ed. John Clute and John Grant (Exeter, UK: Orbit, 1997), 478, italics original.

27. Hogle, "Introduction," 9–10.

28. Adele Reinhartz, "Incarnation and Covenant: The Fourth Gospel through the Lens of Trauma Theory," *Interpretation* 69, no. 1 (2015): 39–40.

own doing or also at the hands of others. They were also displaced and victimized. They are each related to sexual transgressiveness: prostitution (Rahab and Tamar), inappropriate marriage (Ruth?), and adultery (the wife of Uriah). A horror reading of Matthew's story of Mary in the infancy section of his Gospel appears to perpetuate this reality.

In Matthew, Mary is presented in line with these transgressed and displaced women. She is not sexually transgressed; however, she does have God's will imposed on her in a way that seems to cross the divine-human boundaries that he himself protected in the garden of Eden. This is a theologically inconsistent event, with a weird product: Jesus. Terrifying events around the conception of Jesus leads to perpetual displacement: Mary will become an outsider in her native community. She does not have the internal capacity to deal with this well, as she does in Luke's Gospel. There she is a vibrantly active protagonist: not only does she welcome the news of the immaculate conception, but she is the Gospel's lead interpreter of Scripture and salvation history.[29] This is not the case in Matthew.

The Absence of the Basic Boundary between Humans and God

This is an action by the holy in which the boundaries between God and humans are transgressed. When this kind of boundary transgression was attempted by people in the garden of Eden, people were punished for trying to become gods. Oddly, there is a suspension of justice here. The divine becomes human. "Immanuel," God with us, comes about in a person who is conceived by the Holy Spirit within a woman. I do not want to be crass or disrespectful in any way, but the traumatized reader will notice that Mary has experienced an intimate transgression and breach of biology and expectations. This contributes to "the atmospheric element of fear and dread."[30]

The Absence of Relationships

The consequences of this transgression are all-encompassing for Mary. An apparent victim of fate, like the author of *Frankenstein*, Mary loses her past

---

29. Greg Forbes and Scott Harrower, *Raised from Obscurity: A Narratival and Theological Study of the Characterization of Women in Luke-Acts* (Eugene, OR: Pickwick, 2015), 43–60.

30. Harris, "Elements of the Gothic Novel."

life as she is taken to that strangest of lands, Egypt. There she will live as a foreigner under the threat of death (2:13). Even upon her return to the land of her forefathers, she is relocated a number of times by troubling circumstances, revelations from the monstrous realm of angels, and fears. Finally, she arrives at a backwater, Nazareth (2:23).

The key question here is whether Mary has experienced a horror, be it objective or subjective. According to the first criterion of our taxonomy, we have to ask whether in the conception of the child by the Holy Spirit she has experienced a horror. Her pregnancy itself does not immediately meet any of the other criteria, (3)–(5), in our taxonomy. So, though it is a transgressive event, it is neither an objective nor a subjective gross horror.

However, the aftereffects of this pregnancy meet a number of criteria that establish it as a cumulative commonplace horror. Consider the following immediate consequences of the pregnancy: losing Joseph's trust and commitment, being hunted by Herod with murderous intent, and fleeing from persecution to numerous locations. Were any of these something that (1) "includes a degeneration of life toward death"? Certainly, Mary did not flourish as quickly and as fully with Joseph in their native land as they would have hoped for. Has she experienced an action that (2) "is sourced in an objective, relationally immoral action?" What motivates Herod's actions is perverted atheistic jealousy. This criterion is certainly met.

The trauma of the cumulative horrors is compounded by the fact that Mary would have consciously experienced criterion (4), "the traumatic perception of a real or imagined event that diminishes the extent of the personhood of an image of God," when she is hunted murderously by Herod, and later in the story when her son is crucified. Being hunted down by Herod and fleeing to multiple places did not provide Mary with the security to express her creativity in ways of her choice because her actions had to revolve around cultural adaptation and survival away from the support of her extended family. The loss of her son later in the narrative, first to what she perceived as mental illness or possession, then to a Roman crucifixion, diminishes the extent to which her son could relate to and contribute to her particular development as a person.

Mary's experiences in the aftermath of her persecution by Herod are so profound in terms of the years and locations during which she was made to live away from her home and family that her life meets criterion (5): "It is not possible to fully recover psychologically and relationally from these before death." Therefore, in light of this event alone, Mary has suffered from commonplace horrors as a consequence of fleeing from Herod, and this in the context of gross horrors (killing boys) by Herod.

Other criteria are also met in different ways: for example, being at least temporarily at odds with her fiancé meets criterion (3): "It objectively prevents an individual from being and allowing others to be images of God in their natural and fullest sense." Trust between Joseph and Mary is interrupted, and Joseph secretly plans to divorce her. A deep fissure appears in their relationship, which affects all persons involved. This is physically embodied in that face-to-face (literally), personalizing sexual intimacy with Joseph cannot be consummated.

Herod and the Immoral Use of Power by Images of God

Herod is presented as a paradigm example of a horror maker. He meets our criteria for horrors by generating them. He has the malevolent will in which objective relationally immoral actions are sourced (criterion [2]). His actions degenerate life toward death (criterion [1]), which clearly introduces a move away from allowing others to be images of God in the fullest sense (criterion [3]), leading others to traumatically perceive real or imagined events that diminish the extent of the personhood of an image of God (criterion [4]). His actions include murder, from which "there is no possible full recovery from these before death" (criterion [5]).

Herod "secretly" gathers together the religious leaders who could point him to the child he wants to kill (2:7). Herod has no regard for this child as an image of God, nor does he regard God's commandment "do not murder" as applicable to himself (Exod 20:13). Herod will kill children, and do so liberally. When this puppet-king is duped by the wise men, he is filled with "rage." He commands his troops to massacre boys: toddlers and babies under two years old (Matt 2:17). These boys experience the immoral use of human power and creativity; they are not treated as precious persons. Militarized people rip them from the grasping hands and arms of their mothers, fathers, and siblings. Death reigns, and life is crushed underfoot in order to satiate the powerfully oppressive. In the larger scheme, nothing changes; people die senselessly and away from God's care. Hence, the "weeping and mourning" cannot be consoled: "She refused to be consoled, because they are no more" (2:18). Mary is doomed to raise her child in this woeful context.

Joseph

Joseph fills a classic role in horror literature. He allows the ordinary reader to engage personally with the story because he is the ordinary person with whom the reader can identify. Joseph is the common man who has no control of the strange and unexpected events that will overwhelm him. He is subject to objective horrors: his fiancée falls pregnant to a spirit, he has numerous dreams in which ethereal beings address him and command him to act, he is hunted by a murderous king, and he must flee from his homeland.

These objective horrors are compounded by further injustices: he cannot consummate his sexual desires and life-giving hopes with Mary, his new wife. He has to raise another's child as his firstborn son. Joseph subsequently vanishes from the story. His character arc is never resolved; he is just another victim of the randomness of how cruelly people relate to one another. Joseph experiences both objective and subjective horrors according to the terms of the taxonomy for horrors presented earlier in this book. If we take being murderously hunted by Herod as an example, we can say that Joseph experienced horrors. His experience fulfills criterion (2) because it is sourced in an objective, relationally immoral action. It meets criterion (3) because he must abandon his ancestral family, land, and workplace in order to survive. It meets criterion (4) because he cannot engage the full range of his personal, moral, and creative aspects of who he is in the native context in which these will flourish, including marriage and his homeland. Finally, his experiences also meet criterion (5) because having to move to different locales and spend many years away from his homeland exhausts years of his life, which cannot be recovered.

In addition, there is a twist to his story. Joseph's innocence comes into question by his participation in a deviant religious act. When the magi from the East worship Jesus, Joseph stands by and does not refuse nor resist these actions. He allows the strange baby to be worshiped by the kings from the East. The worship of Jesus would not be allowed by any law-abiding Jew. By accepting gifts from the kings, Joseph appears complicit in a deviant religion—a hallmark of horror literature.

Jesus: The Unfamiliar "Abhuman"

Jesus appears to be typical of a quasi-human monster of horror fiction. He does not have full parental lineage, nor is he purely a spiritual being. He is a being on the fringes of humanity.[31] Jesus is the kind of being that invokes caution and fear. This is because Jesus embodies two things at once, paradoxically relating opposite states to one another. For example, these types of beings may be both alive/dead, human/nonhuman, attractive/repellent.[32] These figures are weird, uncanny versions of familiar creatures. In them, Jerrold Hogle writes, "the deeply and internally familiar ... reappears to us in seemingly external, repellent, and *un*familiar forms."[33] Jesus is a strange version of a human being whose nature parallels the sense evoked by the genealogy: life is essentially unpredictable and under threat.

The strangeness of Jesus' origins means that the classic question, "Who do you say I am?" takes on a spectral tone when Matthew is read through the lens of horror and trauma. Jesus is conceived within a human mother by the "Holy Spirit" (1:18–20). What kind of being is "he"? Jesus' conception is not natural; it is supernatural, because it did not involve a human father. The author tells us that "it was discovered before they [Mary and Joseph] came together that she was pregnant by the Holy Spirit" (1:18). The conception of a child by the Holy Spirit is the central mystery around which the plot will revolve. Is the Holy Spirit his father? What kind of father is he if Jesus' origins involve an uninvited transgressive action by a spiritual entity?[34] This unbidden action creates a disturbing and deep "atmosphere of mystery and suspense," according to Andrew Ng. Like a work of gothic fiction, Matthew's chapter is "pervaded by a threatening feeling, a fear enhanced by the unknown. ... Often the plot itself is built around a mystery, such as unknown parentage ... or some other inexplicable event. People

31. "The Gothic is also about liminal positions, a discourse that situates the subject on the threshold of humanness. The gothic monsters, for example, simultaneously human and abhuman, remind us of our precarious identity, which is always threatening to slip into otherness." Andrew Ng, "Revisiting Judges 19: A Gothic Perspective," *Journal for the Study of the Old Testament* 32, no. 2 (2007): 201.

32. Hogle, "Introduction," 6.

33. Hogle, "Introduction," 6.

34. Ng, "Revisiting Judges 19," 200.

disappear or show up dead inexplicably."[35] A feeling of unease and dread hovers over the unsettling questions around Jesus' identity and purpose.

As a supernatural character, Jesus will behave in, or be the recipient of, shocking behaviors, "gross violence of physical or psychological dissolution," which transgress conventional behavioral norms.[36] This is what occurs: Jesus' unusual behavior and teaching will be shocking to his hearers, and their behaviors toward him will be murderous. Due to his otherness, he will be scapegoated and crucified.[37] Jesus will die because he tries to do what protagonists in horror literature often try to do, as Hogle says: he attempts to resolve the "unresolved crimes or conflicts that can no longer be buried from view." He will not be able to overcome a culture marked by trauma, secrets, transgressions, corruption, and deviance.[38]

Jesus' Objective Horrors

Because of their weirdness, or otherness, uncanny characters such as Jesus are often scapegoated by other people, often their own kin.[39] In this story Jesus is scapegoated on the cross. From a divine perspective he is the scapegoat who is banished and spurned in order to bear Israel's consequences for her woeful internal history and failed relationship to God. On a more mundane level, petty religious groups will unjustly misinterpret Jesus, lie about him, and blame him for being a chaotic figure so that they may preserve their social prestige and power. Elites and mobs will fabricate meaning and sense for themselves to the point that, like King Herod, they will kill someone else to hold onto power. They will willingly act immorally and impersonally in order to maintain their deceitful and ultimately deathly cause.[40] Their cause will end in cannibalism and flames in the year AD 70, when besieged Jerusalem was overrun and destroyed by Roman troops.[41] With the horrible history of his own people as a guide to his fate,

35. Harris, "Elements of the Gothic Novel."

36. The first of these is known as "terror" gothic, while the second is known as "horror" gothic. Hogle, "Introduction," 3.

37. Hogle, "Introduction," 6.

38. Hogle, "Introduction," 2.

39. Hogle, "Introduction," 5, 6.

40. Lewis Herman, *Trauma and Recovery*, 101.

41. Thomas Scott Cason, "Victims and Not Violators: Scapegoat Theory and 3 Maccabees 7:10–17," *Journal for the Study of the Old Testament* 41, no. 1 (2016): 117–33.

Jesus became a victim of his people as well as to the Roman oppressors. His nonviolent life and work was a great contrast to the response he received from Israelites as well as from the Romans, yet it did not prevent him from being victimized and generating followers who expected victimization (1 Pet 2:21–23).

Jesus' Subjective Horrors

Throughout the Gospel of Matthew, Jesus is treated in a number of anti-personal ways. He has to overcome a strange crossroad experience of the devil. Self-interested people continually harass him, as do demons. He has to withdraw from the public on a number of occasions. Even his very small band of followers ultimately betrays him. His only hope seems to be his intimate relationship with his Father in heaven. However, this relationship is destroyed to the point of abandonment, cementing deep pessimism about the care of God and prospects for meaning and hope for human beings.

The struggle between the Father and Son at the garden of Gethsemane has powerful connections with horror literature, as Hogle points out. This struggle is immediately connected to Jesus' death. Horror literature employs struggles such as the ones between sons and fathers, or women and their captors, to reflect the unavoidable reality of chaos and death. This "deathly chaos" is the foundational premise for reality.[42] This is a primordial chaos form that we try to escape in order to be a person, yet which we cannot ultimately resist. Primordial, destructive violence is the backdrop for all human existence; indeed, all existence is a losing battle against this.

The result of this context and contest with death is that people perpetually fail to live up to full personhood in a zone somewhere between death and semilife. For this reason, they cannot consistently act in such a way as to perpetuate life and a full expression of their identity as God's images. People are always on the precipice of extinction, and doomed to fall off it into oblivion, because they are pitiful, threatened, and fragile creatures.[43] Though scientism may claim that the universe is merely material and indifferent to human existence, the experience of it and the anticipation of its

42. Hogle, "Introduction," 5.
43. Sadly, we are threatened the most by other people.

end are appalling to us.[44] In this context, questions about God's care and prospects for human meaningfulness and a better future are futile.

Jesus' Final Hours and Horrors

Nameless Soldiers as Horror Makers

Torture is one of the most powerful and visible ways by which persons reduce the physical, social, and psychological states of other persons. It embodies a number of antitheses to the ideal nature of personal relationships: it is the opposite of persons relating to each other in ways that shape and mold fullness of personhood and life in one another. This is what we see in the soldiers' treatment of Jesus in his passion. First, he is whipped, which is best described as a scourging. Then,

> the governor's soldiers took Jesus into the governor's residence and gathered the whole company around him. They stripped him and dressed him in a scarlet robe. They twisted together a crown of thorns, put it on his head, and placed a staff in his right hand. And they knelt down before him and mocked him: "Hail, King of the Jews!" Then they spat on him, took the staff and kept hitting him on the head. And after they had mocked him … they led him away to crucify him. (Matt 27:27–31)

Torture is also diagnostic of the nature of human beings. The actions of Jesus' torturers meet the criteria for being horrors in the same way that Herod's did. In addition, what these torturers do to others reveals a number of absences in their lives that set the conditions for their horror-making work. There is the absence of the moral capacity to pursue another course of action, and the absence of the relational "gravity" that persons in God's image should feel for one another, whereby they are drawn to meaningful and loving interaction. In their acts of brutalization, torturers not only embody the opposite of this friendly state, but they revel in it; these are an occasion for creativity. When Jesus' Roman guards turn torture into an enjoyable activity, they are making deviant and perverted use of their human creativity.

---

44. Jason Colavito, "Oh, the Horror!," *Skeptic* 15, no. 3 (2010): 21–23.

The horrors involved in the torture and murder of Jesus should generate one of the primary outcomes of horror literature: outrage. This is because, as Michael Schrauzer writes, "Torture, murder, and death itself are profoundly outrageous. ... Encounters with them leave us feeling unsettled and terrified, but underneath it all, righteously angry."[45] Adding to the outrage is that Jesus is abandoned by his friends and he believed he was abandoned by God.

The Crucifixion as a Gross Horror

The crucifixion of Jesus is a horror. Its horribleness is compounded by a number of absences.

A befouled man hangs on a cross. Old blood crusts and mingles with the new. He claimed to be the Son of God. Where is the heavenly voice that affirmed Jesus as the "beloved Son"? Where is God now? The mob witnessing the crucifixion of Jesus understands the incoherence of Jesus' lonely death and his claim to be especially related to God: "He trusts in God; let God rescue him now—if he takes pleasure in him" (27:43). If only God would care for him, or love him now. But he does not. God speaks not; he cares not. He is not here. He is absent and inactive in this place. Most likely, God has changed—as all other persons do—and he no longer cares.

On the cross, Jesus experiences the abandonment of God. The degree of the absence of God's presence and blessing stands out. Jesus experiences this absence as the greatest contrast to the presence and blessing of God demonstrated in Eden. Nature embodies the absence of God's blessing and shalom on the crucifixion of Jesus. Nature seems to say "No!" to this event: "From noon until three in the afternoon darkness came over the land" (27:45).

Nature speaks, but God does not. If God's consciousness has not ceased, and his great-making properties, such as omniscience, remain the same, then he is conscious of human suffering.[46]

---

45. Michael Schrauzer, "Sin Is the True Horror," *The Catholic Answer* (September–October 2012): 32.

46. Based on his research and clinical experiences related to near-death experiences, van Lommel locates consciousness in nonlocal space. This is compatible with locating consciousness in the soul: "One cannot avoid the conclusion that endless or non-local consciousness, with an apparently unaltered 'Self-identity,' has always existed and will always exist independently from the body, because there is no beginning nor will there even be an end to our consciousness. There is a kind of biological basis for our waking consciousness, because

Jesus' first-person perspective on reality includes the belief that he is abandoned by God: "About three in the afternoon Jesus cried out with a loud voice: 'Elí, Elí, lemá, sabachtháni?' That is, 'My God, my God, why have you abandoned me?'" His self-awareness and awareness of the external world involve no positive contact with God, and God does not positively relate to him at the moment. Jesus' cry of abandonment reflects our intuitive beliefs about the way the world is; he is not speaking about abstract concepts at this point.[47] The sense that God has abandoned him means that Jesus cannot sense God; on an immediate and psychological, God is not present with him at all. The abandonment by God is a truth, as it relates to Jesus' present experience on the cross.[48] God is not accessible personally at this time. He cannot be known as a personal being. Nor can God be known through his acts; he is entirely absent: subjectively unavailable and imperceptible because he is inactive.

Two conclusions about Jesus' perception lie before us, and both have disheartening results for beliefs about God's care for people. One conclusion may be that Jesus was simply not conscious of God's care for him, and hence he was wrong to claim he was abandoned. In this case, God's care is not sufficiently robust to make any difference at all in Jesus' suffering. Another option is that Jesus was right to claim he was abandoned, because though there may have been larger conceptual and theological reasons for believing that God was caring for him, he did not find these sufficient to explain his experience without calling it abandonment. So, either God is insignificant at points of horrible suffering and trauma, or God truly does not significantly care for people in the midst of horrors. Both of these options are epitomized in the experiences of Jesus. Whether this is taken

during life our physical body functions as an interface or place of resonance. But there is no biological basis of our whole, endless, or enhanced consciousness because it is rooted in non-local space. Our non-local consciousness resides not in our brain and is not limited to our brain. So our brain seems to have a facilitating and not a producing function to experience consciousness." Pim van Lommel, "Non-local Consciousness," *Journal of Consciousness Studies* 20, nos. 1–2 (2013): 39.

47. I am employing the distinction between intuitive cognition and conceptual cognition from William Ockham. See Susan Brower-Toland, "William Ockham on the Scope and Limits of Consciousness," *Vivarium* 52 (2014): 200–201.

48. William Ockham, cited in Brower-Toland, "William Ockham on the Scope and Limits of Consciousness," 200n7. He draws a strong distinction between abstract and contingent truths as they relate to perception.

as a generalizing truth is up to the interpreter. If Jesus is abandoned, won't those who are less faithful to God be equally abandoned by God?

Zombies on the Prowl

Around the time of Jesus' death, the dead are awoken from their slumber in death. Subsequently the undead roam the ancient city and seek out particular people: "The tombs were also opened and many bodies of the saints who had fallen asleep were raised. And they came out of the tombs after his resurrection, entered the city, and appeared to many" (Matt 27:52–53). This is terrifying and very unsettling. One can only imagine the fear of those who were sought out by these zombies. How did they respond when the undead came knocking on their doors and windows, calling out their names with newly moving vocal chords? What would have happened when eye contact was made between the zombies and the living?

It is as if the genealogy of the dead, which opened this story, has strangely and eerily come alive. Death itself is embodied in these people; it walks about and haunts others in the bodies of these people. This creates profound confusion about the order of life and its predictability. The boundaries between living and dead are now porous, and there is nothing to make sense of this weird quirk in history. This is another senseless and disturbing event that cements confusion and fear at the core of the Jesus story.

The End

Even though he is seen after death, Jesus is not the same person but a spectral version of the man who had been Jesus of Nazareth. He is barely recognizable. At the supposed high point of the narrative, when he is worshiped on the mountain before his disappearance, some of his followers doubt. At that point, Jesus offers them a new vision of who God is and points people away from the faith of national Israel as they have known it. He then promises to be with them, at which point he disappears. He never returns, leaving the majority of them to be killed by various people groups around the Mediterranean.

EVALUATION OF THE HORROR READING

The horror reading has a number of strengths to it. It affirms the horrific nature of the world of human interactions with other humans, angelic beings, and nature. Such a paranoid reading of the Bible can conceivably be viewed as the most realistic, and hence philosophically superior, adaptation to the hostile environment by victims of horrors seeking a biblical response.

However, there are overwhelmingly negative results for the reader who adopts this interpretation of Matthew. This reading confirms suspicions that people are very likely abandoned by God and thus live meaningless and hopeless lives. Hence, it does not establish the grounds for feeling safe in the world. The randomness and vulnerability of life in the story suggest that there is no point in trying to integrate the horrors we experience into a coherent story of our own: life is fragmented and weird. Neither can meaningful relationships be formed with other people: humans wear masks that cover up their true intentions, and they cannot be trusted to care for others beyond what benefits themselves.

The results of the reading are surprisingly nihilistic, serving to strengthen the theological, existential, and anthropological skepticisms that arise from horrors. This reading does this in a number of ways. Theologically, it suggests that God is not able to bring about shalom once again. God must be unconcerned, and coldheartedly so, about human affairs. He is possibly too weak to make a difference in the world; therefore, he is not a reliable character and is a disappointment (in contrast to commonplace Christian assumptions about God being benevolent and powerful). The story has nothing to offer in terms of the anthropological question; a horror interpretation of the story undermines hope for a better personal future and restoration to full personhood. With regards to the existential question, life is meaningless, and all pretensions at meaningfulness are just that: pretensions. Such a reading may therefore contribute to readers giving up on the pursuit of living full human lives.

The paranoid reading results from allowing a human being to be the central personal reference point from which to view reality. The problem with this centralization of the self is that it results in a dictatorship of one or more individuals and their actions over a given person.[49]

49. When a person's will is not vitally connected and shaped by other loving persons, the dictatorship (*Diktatur*) of relativism and the unchecked selfish perspective will rule ruthlessly. See Benedict XVI, *Licht der Welt* (Freiburg im Breisgau: Herder GmbH, 2010), 70.

Each person who follows this line of priority and thinking is ultimately oppressed by their own view of reality. It is an inescapable self-imprisonment within the larger cosmic enclosure.[50] What can be done to prevent this solipsism and further trauma and horrors? Not much, because humans are persons without alternatives. We have no choice but to perpetuate the past unless we are able to receive external aid for knowledge and metaphysical renewal.[51]

This reading shows that offers made by trauma studies—the limited use of Scripture and the mirror reading—are not sufficient to redress the pervasiveness of horrors and their traumatic and overwhelming effects, nor the skepticisms that arise. There are strong limitations to what trauma studies has to offer.

I seek to address these limitations by undertaking to answer a central pastoral-theological question, asked by Serene Jones: "*How do people, whose hearts and minds have been wounded by violence, come to feel and know the redeeming power of God's grace?*" Jones has called for those working in the area of trauma "to discern how this divine desire to love and heal can be spoken and lived out, concretely, in the life of faith at work in the world." According to Jones: "This is the question of how God's love might best be embodied in tangible forms that can be felt, known, and enjoyed."[52]

It is through understanding God as Triune that we can begin to address and resolve these questions. Following Jones's lead, I explore the personal ways that God the Trinity works through direct and indirect as well as invisible and visible means to restore people from horrors and trauma.

---

50. Albert Keller, "Der Mensch ohne Alternative," in *Structuren der Wirklichkeit: Leben im Geist*, ed. Paul Imhof and Gabriel-Alexander Reschke (Taufkirchen: Via Verbis Verlag, 2005), 65.

51. See the three theses to do with freedom, the other, and the necessity of love in this equation. Keller, "Der Mensch ohne Alternative," 74–76.

52. Serene Jones, *Trauma and Grace: Theology in a Ruptured World* (Louisville, KY: Westminster John Knox, 2009), vii, ix, italics original. Jones writes that expanding an understanding of both trauma and grace is required in order to understand how these are interrelated. The language of trauma is necessary because it enlarges "our appreciation for the complexities of human suffering, but also by deepening and enlivening our grasp of the amazing fullness and power of grace." Jones, *Trauma and Grace*, x.

8

A BLESSED READING OF MATTHEW

In the preceding chapter, we carried out a horror reading of Matthew via a trauma hermeneutic. It has some value and may be reflective of current cultural sensibilities; however, it is problematic as it does not enable the reader to move through trauma to recovery. A number of trauma approaches to biblical texts deliberately want to stick to human experience and are not keen to move beyond these by emphasizing the help of the church or the Spirit in biblical interpretation. In this chapter, I want to consider a different hermeneutic: the "blessed" perspective. This serves as a critique of the horror reading and sets up the final section of the book, which focuses on the outworkings of this blessed reading for recovering from trauma.

Jesus' perspective is that God himself, and his church, will enable his disciples to experience, know, and speak about him in ways that go beyond the limited cognitive powers of an individual cognition.[1] In stark contrast to trauma approaches to biblical texts, this perspective anticipates the possibility of a radical change in a person's perspective on reality, primarily via the invisible actions of God's Spirit. God's Spirit helps people understand what kind of God he is and what kind of direct and indirect works he does in order to restore human vitality. Jesus calls this the "blessed" perspective, the perspective enabled by God himself, which will be the key to a true interpretation and reception of Matthew's message.

1. This constructive work on cognition, perception, perspective, and Gestalt psychology is drawn from Stephan Käufer and Anthony Chemero, *Phenomenology: An Introduction* (Cambridge, UK: Polity, 2016).

The rest of this chapter will explore what such a perspective involves, how it comes about, and what meaning it has for readers who have suffered horrors and experienced trauma.

THE "BLESSED" READING

A Change in Perspective

The blessed perspective on the story of God's involvement in the world, as recorded in Matthew's Gospel, comes to light in the story of God's work to enable Peter's confession of who Jesus is (Matt 16:13–20). This is one of the most important stories in Matthew because it serves his aim of providing a powerful and life-changing answer to Jesus' question "Who do you say that I am?" (16:15). It powerfully demonstrates a change in perspective. Though we can't argue that Peter has a trauma perspective in the same way we can about people today, his perspective would have been shaped by the difficulties involved in Roman occupation, a corrupt temple system, and the struggle for a livelihood. When Jesus asks this question, Peter answers by saying: "You are the Christ, the Son of the living God" (16:16). This response indicates that Peter did not interpret Jesus as his contemporaries did, as merely a wisdom teacher or a sage or a prophet. This answer is also surprising given Peter's failures of perspective on a number of occasions throughout the Gospel.

Something has changed; Peter has been freed from his previous misperceptions and misconceptions of Jesus. A life-giving shift has occurred. But how did this change within Peter's perception occur? Why does Peter have this perspective? We may never know all the reasons why the shift occurred; however, a key part of this includes a gift from the "Father who is in heaven."[2] The invisible Father's actions lie behind Peter's new and accurate perspective. Jesus says to Peter: "Blessed are you, for flesh and blood have not revealed this to you, but my Father who is in the heavens" (16:17).

2. This section does not intend to give the impression that people who approach biblical texts via a trauma perspective only do so because God has not revealed himself to them. I want to avoid the impression that the only problem for trauma sufferers is that they haven't grasped this truth. This is not the case. What I am doing here is pointing out one large piece of the complex involved in a change of perception: divine aid to see Jesus anew and what this reveals about God, people, and meaningful hope for life.

Peter's reoriented perspective on Jesus is the proof of God the Father being interested in Peter and able to secure an attentive relationship between himself and Peter. This is because Peter's perspective is drawn into God's focused attention and hence into a temporary yet deeper mind-to-mind communication with God. This is not to say that it was permanent before the indwelling of the Spirit. The Spirit gave Peter an insight rather than coming to dwell within Peter. Indeed, Peter reverts to his confused state throughout the story and even denies Jesus, so this episode is only a temporary suggestion of what may be a convincing and enduring shift of perspective for mature Christians. It is a goal toward which we can move and grow in grace.

Mind-to-Mind Knowledge of God

Successful perception of another person is a highly relational mode of knowledge in which seeing and interpreting requires the attentiveness of both persons involved in that relationship. One of the reasons why perception shaped by horrors is unsuccessful for generating knowledge that may function as the basis for recovery is that it is a lonely interpretation of the world and as such is subject to the uncertainties of a solitary mind trying to navigate unnatural circumstances. The problem of a mostly isolated perspective points out that we need other personal minds to help us successfully interpret one another and ourselves. Hence, the depth at which we engage with and interpret one another affects the degree of success in perception.[3]

In order to know God and his perspective, people need to access his stream of consciousness or to have it opened up to them.[4] Engagement with God requires more than being able to state things about him: it involves a person-to-person relationship in which his perspective is understood and

3. Ola Sigurdson, *Heavenly Bodies: Incarnation, the Gaze, and Embodiment in Christian Theology*, trans. Carl Olsen (Grand Rapids: Eerdmans, 2016), 151–54, 181–82.

4. Developed from William James, *Principles of Psychology*, 239: "Consciousness ... does not appear itself to be chopped up in bits. ... It is nothing jointed; it flows. A 'river' or a 'stream' are the metaphors by which it is most naturally described. *In talking of it hereafter, let us call it the stream of thought, of consciousness, or of subjective life.*" Cited with italics in Rebecca S. Ravue Davis, "Stream and Destination: Husserl, Subjectivity, and Dorothy Richardson's *Pilgrimage*," *Twentieth Century Literature* 59, no. 2 (2013): 312.

appreciated.[5] Merely relating to propositions about him from a first-person or third-person perspective (such as "I believe X about him") is insufficient to claim to be knowledge of God—it may be knowledge "about" God but not "of" God as a personal being.[6]

This full and necessary kind of knowledge requires a mind-to-mind relationship with God. Matthew Benton writes: "If propositional knowledge is a state of mind, consisting in a subject's attitude to a (true) proposition ... interpersonal knowledge [is] ... a state of minds, involving a subject's attitude to another (existing) subject."[7] This kind acquaintance allows for understanding God's perspective, and therefore how he may be involved in healing traumatized lives. It requires getting to know him as a personal reflective being, a communicative "you," in a dynamic "I-to-you" relationship. For this to be successful, someone has to initiate interpersonal awareness between the knower and the known.[8] God initiates the interaction and cooperatively works with the degree of a person's response to him. How this dynamic relationship between God and people occurs exactly varies from person to person. The point at hand is that God initiates a process of knowing him that requires our attention and commitment.

The relationship between Jesus' human mind and his divine mind demonstrates that there may be a strong, attentive, and engaged relationship between God's mind and a human mind. There was an asymmetrical relationship in which the knowledge from Jesus' divine mind would occasionally break through to his human mind.[9] In these cases, Jesus' human

5. Sigurdson, *Heavenly Bodies*, 49, 77.

6. Eleonore Stump, *The God of the Bible and the God of the Philosophers* (Milwaukee: Marquette University Press, 2016).

7. Matthew A. Benton, "Epistemology Personalized," *Philosophical Quarterly* 67, no. 269 (2017): 814.

8. Eleonore Stump, "Second-Person Accounts and the Problem of Evil," *Revista Portuguesa de Filosofia* 57, no. 4 (2001): 745. She continues by saying that a "second-person experience is an experience one has when one has conscious awareness of another consciously aware person."

9. "In the case of God Incarnate, we must recognize something like two distinct ranges of consciousness. ... The divine mind of God the Son contained, but was not contained by, his earthly mind, or range of consciousness. That is to say, there was what can be called an asymmetric accessing relation between the two minds." Thomas V. Morris, *The Logic of God Incarnate* (Ithaca, NY: Cornell University Press, 1986), 102–3. See also Oliver Crisp, *God Incarnate: Explorations in Christology* (London: T&T Clark, 2009).

mind would receive expert secondhand knowledge from God.[10] Jesus also knew that God the Spirit would share God's perspective with believers. This knowledge brings a previously unavailable perception of the character and activity of the Father, Son, and Spirit. It also includes an awareness of the mediums by which he conveys this knowledge—be they direct or indirect—as well as the kinds of knowledge and extent of knowledge that he shares.[11]

Mind-to-mind knowledge, or perhaps better, Spirit-to-human-spirit knowledge, affects how a person interprets the Scriptures and what they say about God's present activity in a world of trauma and horrors. For believers, a Trinitarian interpretation of Jesus is required. It is Trinitarian in two ways. First, Jesus is understood as God the Son incarnate, as recorded in the New Testament and anticipated in the Old Testament. Second, this revelation is received in humble dependence on God to bring about a change in the believer's perspective as he invisibly and intimately accompanies a person's or church's Scripture reading.

Australian-Hungarian psychiatrist Paul Valent writes that there is an important tradition of witnessing to the trauma of others that draws on divine help. Valent refers to the whole truth that Jesus reveals about himself and ourselves, which needs to be taken into account as a historical model of drawing on God to bring relief from suffering and experience the love of God. Valent draws from Jesus' words in John 18:37 that he has "come into the world to testify to the truth. ... Everyone who is of the truth listens to my voice." Trinitarian Christians may take a theological rather than historical lead from this verse and Valent's work and argue that Valent is correct theologically. The significance of this for recovering from horrors is that whole truth revealed to us—not just those parts of Jesus' life that resonate with out past and present experiences—are important for knowing God and what this means for people in the midst and wake of horrors. The Trinitarian aspect of this change particularly relies on God's truth revealed through Jesus as well as his Spirit enabling us to hear and respond to one another's responses to horrors. Hearing each other well

10. Matthew A. Benton, "Expert Opinion and Second-Hand Knowledge," *Philosophy & Phenomenological Research* 92 (2016): 492–98.

11. Adam Green, "Reading the Mind of God (without Hebrew Lessons): Alston, Shared Attention, and Mystical Experience," *Religious Studies* 45, no. 4 (2009): 465.

involves factual and empathetic listening in which we are operating with both the right and left sides of our brains.[12]

This compassionate kind of relating between people is likely to occur as they become aware of the invisible and visible ways by which God brings about new life to people by offering them safety, a larger story, and a community of faith, hope, and love. This evolution in the Christian life is detailed in the final chapter of this book and provides concrete evidence for religious claims that overcome skepticisms about God's goodness, the possibility of a meaningful life, and hope for a better future for people.[13]

Reorienting Perception through Jesus

Peter's insight into the person of Jesus is a demonstration of the knowledge that may come about for those who are engaged in a mind-to-mind relationship with God. Peter is able to do more than see Jesus as a meek and humble man. Peter perceives that Jesus' life has qualities that exceed and overrun what can be immediately seen.[14]

Some of these qualities are revealed in the phrase "You are the Christ." At this point Peter perceives Jesus as the historical physical being (a personal phenomenon) who best reveals God's character and perspective. Jesus' approval of Peter's confession underscores God's affirmation that Jesus is anointed by the Spirit, and this brings clarity of perception.

The association between Jesus and renewing power is evident in stories in which Jesus brings about freedom from spiritual blindness as a precursor to living as an image of God should. For example, consider the case of the men who lived in the wilderness under the oppression of demons (Matt 8:28–34; Mark 5:1–17; Luke 8:26–39). They surely lived with a horror view of the world, yet this was transformed by Jesus. The story opens with Jesus being confronted with men who are horror makers: "They were so violent that no one could pass that way" (Matt 8:28). These men are isolated and live where dead bodies are laid: such a life is a relational and aesthetic

12. Paul Valent, "Bearing Witness to Trauma," in *Encyclopedia of Trauma: An Interdisciplinary Guide*, ed. Charles R. Figley (London: Sage, 2012), 38, 40.

13. William Hasker, "Analytic Philosophy of Religion," in *The Oxford Handbook of Philosophy of Religion*, ed. William Wainwright (Oxford: Oxford University Press, 2005), 443.

14. Thomas Aquinas, *Commentary on the Gospel of St. Matthew*, trans. P. M. Kimball (Bristol, UK: Dolorosa, 2012), 560.

wasteland. At least one of them self-harms: "Night and day among the tombs and on the mountains, he was crying out and cutting himself with stones" (Mark 5:5). They relate not only to people in a distorted manner, but to evil angels too: they are demonized and made to be mouthpieces of demons (Matt 8:29). However, after Jesus frees them, their perception changes: "The man who had been demon possessed [was] sitting there, dressed and in his right mind" (Mark 5:15). This man in turn is able to understand this and testifies to others that this was the case (Mark 5:20).

This story fleshes out the blessed perspective in that Jesus has the power to overcome those perspectives and influences that create relational, psychological, and physical absences in people's lives. It dramatically models a rapid transition from a trauma interpretation of life to a different one in the wake of Jesus' presence and healing.

Peter and the demonized men may not have been aware of all the dynamics going on within them; however, the point is that their perspective was changed by Jesus, with a new orientation for life in both cases.

If Jesus can do this with respect to Peter's perspective and that of the demonized, *then he may do so for other people today too despite great internal or external resistance*. It may not be as dramatic or as quick, though it may occur either way.[15]

Peter also identifies Jesus as "the Son of the living God." This is what distinguishes Peter's confession from others who have called him "son of God." This latter title was often meant in a secondary sense of "you are god-like" or "approved of by God." We see this in the kinds of titles given to or claimed by Roman emperors. Rather, Peter confesses the unconditional divinity of Jesus, as Thomas Aquinas notes. Jesus is identified as God. At a theological level, this passage suggests that just as God delighted in creating humans through the Son, he delights in remaking them through the Son. The demonstration of this is clear: God the Son brought new life

15. This work of Jesus has been as demonstrated through the ministry of Johann Blumhardt (d. 1880) and more recently in the ministry of Roland and Elke Werner, which I have myself witnessed. Friedrich Zündel, Christian T. Collins Winn, and Dieter Ising, *Pastor Johann Christoph Blumhardt: An Account of His Life* (Eugene, OR: Cascade Books, 2010); Vernard Eller, Johann Christoph Blumhardt, and Christoph Blumhardt, *Thy Kingdom Come: A Blumhardt Reader* (Grand Rapids: Eerdmans, 1980); Roland Werner, *Die Christus-Treff Story—Die Geschichte einer Gemeinschaft im Aufbruch* (Neukirchen-Vluyn: Neukirchener Aussaat, 2002).

into those experiencing objective and subjective horrors: the demonized, the ill, the outcasts, and even the oppressors themselves.[16]

As a brief way of flagging what this means for us today, this evidence means that answering the question of God's relationship to horrors must take the person, life, and works of Jesus as its starting point.[17] Jesus is the "radiance of God's glory and the exact expression of his nature" (Heb 1:3). An open and personal engagement with the stories of Jesus and himself, rather than the worst of our personal experiences, should focus our search for answers. A Trinitarian perspective undergirds this claim: because Jesus' nature, qualities, and powers are those of Yahweh, the Creator of all things, he has the power to restore humans from horrors, trauma, and the corresponding toxic skepticisms. By seeking a reorientation of our conscious relationship to reality through Jesus, we may encounter the personal Trinitarian power to restore shalom and blessedness to the entire created order, including the images of God.

The Hermeneutical Principle: "The Living God"

Peter states that Jesus is the Son of the "living God." This statement is made in the context of a lethal struggle between life and death: Jesus points out Hades as an enemy of life (Matt 16:18) and also states that he will suffer, die, and yet be raised again (16:21).

Describing God as the "living God" is the interpretive key to understanding God's life and what his attention aims toward. God is the source of life, and he attentively and interactively aims to give life to others. This echoes the pervasive idea that God is the fountain of life (Ps 35:10).[18] The life of God, which is life in its fullest expression, is also the unending, life-giving source for a new perspective on himself. God's stance for life is a stance against death, horrors, and trauma. This means that actions that lead to death, horrors, and trauma cannot be attributed to God as his ideal, even when God destroys people and places in biblical books such as Joshua. Nor can they be said to occur in a manner that denies that they are evils—these offend and sadden God even if he uses them as means himself.

---

16. Aquinas, *Commentary on the Gospel of St. Matthew*, 562–63, 561.

17. The identity between God and Jesus was affirmed by the earliest Christians: Heb 1; Eph 2.

18. Aquinas, *Commentary on the Gospel of St. Matthew*, 562.

The believer therefore needs to interpret the world with eyes that see life where it is present. Seeing is always an act of both noticing and interpretation. Perception driven by the living God will therefore be an act of deliberate interpretation and affirmation of life, even when it occurs in the feeblest forms: "Faith is the *specific way* in which religious people actually experience what is happening."[19]

Faith chases after the "living God" perspective revealed in a blessed interpretation of human experience. Faith leads to the creation of cultures and artifacts that reflect these beliefs, which in turn become means of communicating the blessed perspective to others. This culture employs, as Risto Uro puts it, "not only Christian words, but also images and embodied acts that both articulate the meaning of 'God' for Christianity and form the Christian experience."[20]

Blessed Are You

Receiving the divine insight into the identity of Jesus is a blessing: "Blessed are you," Jesus says to Peter (Matt 16:17). Jesus shares his perspective with Peter, inviting him to see that something special has come about for Peter. Jesus directs Peter to focus on what Jesus is focusing on: Peter has God's perspective on Jesus. This shared attention and perspective on Jesus includes God's insight and is not sourced in provisional and doubtful human ruminations on the world, as the horror reading is. Whereas mere reason brings neither peace nor intellectual security, blessed knowledge begins to "satisfy a natural desire" for God's perspective, which will ultimately occur in the beatific vision in which we see all things at their best and also through God's eyes. Aquinas comments on the Old Testament grounds for this: "Eye hath not seen, nor ear heard: what things God hath prepared for them that love him" (Isa 64:4). Therefore, in this life, inasmuch as a man can perceive more of this knowledge, he is more blessed; "Blessed is the man that findeth wisdom" (Prov 3:13).[21]

19. Sigurdson, *Heavenly Bodies*, 275, italics original.

20. Sigurdson, *Heavenly Bodies*, 275. See also Risto Uro, *Ritual and Christian Beginnings: A Socio-Cognitive Analysis* (Oxford: Oxford University Press, 2016).

21. Aquinas, *Commentary on the Gospel of St. Matthew*, 563.

Beyond "Flesh and Blood"

Jesus tells Peter that what he knows about Jesus via a shared perspective with God is opposite from a mere "flesh-and-blood" viewpoint. A flesh-and-blood perspective only perceives Jesus from a mundane, human point of view.

The flesh-and-blood perspective is like the horror perspective because it is merely sense perception reinforced by cultural assumptions. These perspectives infer knowledge in historically and experientially conditioned manners, rather than via the knowledge of one who is not limited by history and culture. A flesh-and-blood perspective limits itself to what we know by nature alone, which is driven and determined by the frailty of the flesh and blood.[22]

On the other hand, a blessed perception shares God's perspective beyond what mere flesh and blood can see and interpret. God shares his awareness with Peter in order to speak of Jesus in a larger way, referring to his "flesh, blood, and divinity," as Aquinas writes. When Peter's sense perception is enlarged by God's own, it breaks with a minimalist interpretation of Jesus' identity—and, by extension, God's identity.[23]

An expanded and fresh perspective of Jesus' identity as the Christ has consequences for human self-understanding. The coming of the Christ demonstrates that history is not subject to random forces but is ordered and purposeful under God's direction. This divine revelation means that Jesus' disciples have a historical warrant in the person of the Christ for a new interpretation of history in the light of God's character. God is faithful to his promises to bring about rescue and restoration via the Christ. Hence, the disciples will no longer view the plane of history and God's character through what can be known by flesh and blood (16:13–20).

A flesh-and-blood reading of Matthew's Gospel is a reading that expects nothing from God in the realm of history. It is a cynical reading that only expects to find more of the godless history that has come before it.

22. Aquinas, *Commentary on the Gospel of St. Matthew*, 563.
23. Aquinas, *Commentary on the Gospel of St. Matthew*, 563.

A TRINITARIAN BLESSING: ITS BASIS AND MODE

Human persons, on their own, cannot know who Jesus is. The Father in heaven has four unique capacities that mean he can communicate who Jesus is. First, he has the true and otherwise inaccessible knowledge of the Son.[24] Second, the intimacy of the Father-Son knowledge makes it appropriate for the Father rather than anyone else to make him known. Third, as God it is the Father's role to make known those things that are mysterious to human beings.[25] Fourth, the Father has the will to make him known.

However, the perspective-giving work of the Father cannot be understood in a sense that does not include a Trinitarian account of God. The knowledge of the Son is tied up with knowledge of the Father, who gives knowledge of the Son. The gift of knowing the Father presumes and requires the work of the Son in determining who receives the gift of revelation. Jesus said: "All things have been handed over to me by my Father; and no one knows the Son except the Father; nor does anyone know the Father except the Son, and anyone to whom the Son wills to reveal him" (Matt 11:27).

In tandem with this work of the Father and the Son, the role of the Holy Spirit is important for a rehabilitative reading of Matthew. Understanding who Jesus is, and articulating how he is related to God and history, requires the help of the "Spirit of the Father" (10:20).

Importantly, the help of the Spirit enables understanding and articulation of truths in a world of horrors and trauma. The Spirit of the Father gives disciples the words they need: "For you will be given what to say at that hour, because it isn't you speaking but the Spirit of your Father is speaking through you" (Matt 10:19–20). In this way the Spirit of the Father fulfills two roles: (1) the Spirit enables understanding and speaking for disciples and (2) the Spirit enables revelation to nondisciples with the hope that their worldview will be transformed (10:5). The truths that Jesus teaches are the facts that the Spirit uses to redescribe the world for

24. "For no one knoweth the Son, but the Father (Lk. 10:22)." Aquinas, *Commentary on the Gospel of St. Matthew*, 563.

25. "There is a God in heaven that revealeth mysteries (Dan. 2:28)." Aquinas, *Commentary on the Gospel of St. Matthew*, 563.

those whose perspective is evolving, "What I tell you in the dark, speak in the light. What you hear in a whisper, proclaim on the housetops" (10:27).

An interesting point in the text confirms the role of the Holy Spirit in giving Peter his true knowledge of Jesus. Jesus replies to Peter's statement with, "Blessed are you, Simon son of Jonah" (16:17). "Son of Jonah" means "son of the dove," a reference to the Spirit, who anointed Jesus and secured his human knowledge. Therefore, knowing that Jesus is the Son of the living God is a perspective that corresponds to and is accompanied by being blessed as a son of the dove, or the Holy Spirit.[26]

God's knowledge and power, together with his Trinitarian actions, have profound implications for what Christians can know and how they know it. This has to do with God's attributes and power to bring about change, but also with the effects of interpersonal interaction: the mind-to-mind relationship. The divine mind not only communicates the truth to his own people but also changes their minds in order that they may apprehend and understand the truth.[27] Christians depend on the mind of God for a true perspective on the world and for him to change the functioning and outcomes of Christian thinking.

In sum, Jesus suggests that Trinitarian interpretation of himself is a means by which God shares his perspective with people. This requires a neurological change and healing of the soul.

HISTORICAL ATTESTATION TO SHARING IN GOD'S BLESSED PERSPECTIVE

Given the subjectivism that plagues trauma survivors, it is reasonable to ask whether the blessed perspective argued for above is merely another reactionary and hopeful perspective imposed onto the text of Matthew's Gospel. One control for this possibility is to check whether God has shared this particular way of seeing with other Christians across time. A criterion by which to test this would be to ask whether the same early church that received Matthew and other Gospels as authoritative also received

26. "Because Peter had confessed Him to be the Son of God; now Jesus calls him son of the dove, namely, the Holy Ghost, because his confession could only be made by the Holy Ghost." Aquinas, *Commentary on the Gospel of St. Matthew*, 562.

27. A. N. Williams, *The Architecture of Theology: Structure, System, and Ratio* (Oxford: Oxford University Press, 2011), 221.

the rules for interpretation that reflect the blessed perspective. If so, then the blessed interpretation has historical pedigree and in addition will have contours that demand attention.

Indeed, this is the case: the belief that God the Father, Son, and Spirit brings about the blessing of a new perspective on Jesus and the works of God is widespread. For example, in Luke 24 alone, there are two stories in which Jesus redirects the attention of some of his followers in order that they share his perspective.

The first story in particular directly resists and overcomes a horror reading of Jesus' torture and death. It is initially dominated by Jesus' terrible and disappointing death. Despite the associates of the disciples reporting an empty tomb, the missing body, and a vision of angels claiming Jesus is alive (Luke 24:23–24), they focus on Jesus' death and crucifixion (24:20). The disciples speak about hope for themselves, Israel, and Jesus in the past tense: "We had hoped that he was the one that was going to redeem Israel" (24:21). Jesus then uses the Old Testament and his own words to explain who he is; however, they do not respond immediately (24:26–28). Their understanding is only activated by divine intervention in the context of reenacting the Last Supper (24:30).

The subsequent story also points to God invisibly opening God's mind to disciples of Jesus. In this story Jesus appears to his disciples and announces to them his shalom (Luke 24:36)—that elusive fullness of life within which images of God can develop and flourish. Thus, the Edenic possibility of blessed life with God and one another is offered to human persons once again, and in a new and definitive manner, after the resurrection.

Interestingly, the disciples cannot receive this greeting and promise of peace, and are thus "startled and frightened, thinking they saw a ghost" (Luke 24:37). Following this, Jesus assures them of his identity and of the promises that lie behind his death and resurrection (24:44). However, once again, this is not enough to overcome the recent horrible events they have witnessed and yield comprehension. Jesus has to open their minds, to create a shared perspective with them through the invisible involvement of his Spirit.

By his Spirit, Jesus directs and secures their attention toward events in the world in a way that parallels his own divine perspective. First, he "opened their minds to understand their minds so that they could understand the Scriptures" (Luke 24:45). Second, he points to the promised Holy Spirit, who will enable continued understanding beyond that immediate point in time. As the promise and the power of the Father, the Holy Spirit will enable knowledge of Jesus as the Son of the living God for many people into the future (24:49).

This Trinitarian perspective on the true knowledge that leads to life, despite a world of horrors, is reinforced in the sequel to Luke: the book of Acts. On numerous occasions, the Spirit enables an understanding of who Jesus is (Acts 1:4; 2:17–18, 33, 38; 5:32; 10:44–47; 11:15–16).

Matthew's hope for a blessed reading of his Gospel and of Jesus also overlaps with Pauline theology, which is keenly attuned to horrors. Matthew's description of blessed knowledge via Trinitarian action is consistent with Paul's prayer for a transformed life as a result of the renewal of the believer's mind by God (Rom 12:2). For Paul, this renewal is contrasted with the patterns of thinking that conform to the fallen state of affairs in the world. Paul describes the *universality* of horrors at great length in Romans 1 and 2.

Having a mind conformed to our suboptimal context of horrors is not fitting for people and is traumatic.[28] The renewal of our minds means that the Christian develops a new "theological instinct." About the theological instinct, T. F. Torrance writes: "What really counts in the end is whether a person's mind is radically transformed by Christ and so spiritually attuned to the mind of Christ, that he or she thinks instinctively from the depths of their mental being in a way worthy of God."[29] This means that both our reasoning about and our language for God will be "baptized" and not imprisoned by horrors and trauma.[30]

The New Testament point of view on the new perspective given by the living God continued into the second generation of Christians. Immediately

---

28. Marilyn McCord Adams, *Christ and Horrors: The Coherence of Christology* (Cambridge: Cambridge University Press, 2006).

29. Thomas F. Torrance, Atonement: The Person and Work of Christ, ed. Robert T. Walker (Downers Grove, IL: InterVarsity, 2009), 445.

30. He continues: "Either you think from out of a mind centred in God through union with the mind of the Lord Jesus, or you think from out of a mind centred in yourself, alienated from God and inwardly hostile to the Truth incarnate in the Lord Jesus, that is, in a way that is finally governed by the unregenerate and unbaptized reason." Torrance, "Reconciliation of the Mind," 203.

after Jesus announces the blessedness of Peter's testimony that he is "the Christ, the Son of the living God" (Matt 16:16), Jesus states that the blessedness only takes place within the corporate life of the successors of Peter and his interpretation. Jesus continues by saying: "And I also say to you that you are Peter and on this rock I will build my church, and the gates of Hades will not overpower it" (16:18). Christians are therefore only given a new perspective on life within "the house of the Rock."

As the first generations of witnesses to Jesus and his apostles passed away, the Scriptures were collected as the records about Jesus. The Trinitarian interpretation of Jesus continued, mediated by the Scriptures and the Trinitarian consensus of the early church. Importantly, it did so even in the context of horrors targeted at Christians. For example, Hippolytus of Rome (AD 170–235) was clearly dependent on the "livingness" of God for a blessed reading of Jesus. The livingness of God determined the context for understanding the goals and contours of the blessed reading. He calls on the Christian as follows: "Give me now your best attention, I pray you, for I wish to go back to the fountain of life, and to view the fountain that gushes with healing." The fountain is the life of God, and the Spirit is hence both life and life giver, "the Spirit that at the beginning 'moved upon the face of the waters'; by whom the world moves; by whom creation consists, and all things have life; who also wrought mightily in the prophets, and descended in flight upon Christ. ... By this Spirit Peter spake that blessed word, 'Thou art the Christ, the Son of the living God.' By this Spirit the rock of the Church was established."[31]

A second example can be seen in Irenaeus of Lyon (AD 130–200), who found himself leading the church only because the previous generation of leaders had been wiped out. He penned and commended one of the famous "rules of faith," which appeals to history's witness to the life of the Trinity for salvation and as the key to interpreting Scripture.[32]

31. Hippolytus, "The Discourse on the Holy Theophany," in *The Ante-Nicene Fathers*, 10 vols., ed. Alexander Roberts and James Donaldson (Buffalo, NY: Christian Literature, 1895–1896), 5:237.

32. See Irenaeus, *Against Heresies* 1.10.1–2, in *The Ante-Nicene* Fathers, 10 vols., ed. Alexander Roberts and James Donaldson (Buffalo, NY: Christian Literature, 1895–1896), 1:330–32; Irenaeus, *On the Apostolic Preaching* (Crestwood, NY: St. Vladimir's Seminary Press, 1997).

Importantly, the aims that directed the way that the early church interpreted Scripture were based on faith, hope, and love.[33] The blessed perspective therefore generates dispositions and perspectives that are consistent with developing the safety, story, and community required for recovery from trauma. Faith, hope, and love both will fuel recovery in the person who has been traumatized and will generate compassion and thoughtful care in those who accompany and support them. This involves the renewal of the moral and creative dimensions of those made in the image of God, which in turn heals and reestablishes relational aspects of personhood.

The Christian tradition, enshrined in the ecumenical creeds, therefore functions as an objective witness to the truth that stands outside the mind of the trauma survivor. The cluster of voices that comprises this witness remains with believers today, speaking across time and assuring them of the larger picture within which to interpret Jesus and ourselves.[34] This historical witness does not vacillate, and it emerged from the horrors of martyrdom. The creeds function as a guide to assuring people that they have been saved by the Trinitarian God and will one day participate in the new heavens and new earth, on the other side of God's final judgment of horrors.

MOVING FORWARD: A NEW PERSPECTIVE ON GOD, PERSONS, AND HISTORY

Perception is a way of seeing that draws into it our personal history and the perspective of others. Christians draw on the revelation that occurs through the incarnation and the work of the Spirit in order to be influenced by God's perspective on who Jesus is. This in turn renews and gives depth to their way of interpreting the world. As A. N. Williams expresses: "There is … a difference between Christian and secular *epistemology*, inasmuch as the Christian one acknowledges not only the frailty of the human

33. From the early church through to the Middle Ages, "The church does not, then, disdain the *sensus literalis* or *sensus historicus*, the literal or historical meaning, but learns of it and uses it as the point of departure for searching out the relation of the text to the Christian virtues [faith, hope and love]." Richard A. Muller, *Dictionary of Latin and Greek Theological Terms: Drawn Principally from Protestant Scholastic Theology* (Grand Rapids: Baker, 1985), 254.

34. Alois Grillmeier, *Christ in Christian Tradition* (New York: Sheed and Ward, 1965), 556. This ecclesial pressure on hermeneutics differentiates this approach from the one taken in Greg Forbes and Scott Harrower, *Raised from Obscurity: A Narratival and Theological Study of the Characterization of Women in Luke-Acts* (Eugene, OR: Pickwick, 2015).

mind, but its dependence on a mind greater than its own: the divinity that not only dwarfs the discourse that seeks to represent it, but lifts those who offer the discourse beyond themselves."[35]

Christians today may depend on God for interpreting the Bible, or Matthew more specifically, in a Trinitarian and blessed life-affirming manner. This is a counterhorror, posttrauma, and nonskeptical manner of interpretation that takes each of these seriously but is not overwhelmed by them. The term "reparative" is a helpful descriptor for this kind of perspective on what Scripture has to say.[36] It is a theological interpretation of Scripture that depends on the reality, activity, and presence of the God of Israel, who is God the Father, Son, and Spirit.[37] The living God accompanies, relates to, and aids readers and communities so that we may gain wisdom on God and on ourselves as we navigate skepticisms and recovery from trauma.[38] A blessed reading of Matthew reveals a Trinitarian view of God, revolving around the person and character of Jesus. It can determine the parameters for the kinds of questions about and responses given to the theological, anthropological, and existential issues that are raised by horrors and trauma. By means of this interpretation, the living God may restore some measure of human meaning, hope, and confidence in God's character in the context of horrors. These in turn may aid the journey toward the threefold goals of trauma recovery: the restoration of safety,

---

35. Italics original to Williams, *Architecture of Theology*, 221.

36. E. Sedgwick, "Paranoid Reading, Reparative Reading," in *Touching Feeling: Affect, Pedagogy, Performativity* (Durham, NC: Duke University Press, 2003), cited in Anne V. Murphy, "Founding Foreclosures: Violence and Rhetorical Ownership in Philosophical Discourse on the Body," *Sophia* 55, no. 1 (2016): 11–13.

37. See numerous works by Kevin Vanhoozer and Daniel Treier, including Kevin J. Vanhoozer, Craig G. Bartholomew, Daniel J. Treier, and N. T. Wright, eds., *Dictionary for Theological Interpretation of the Bible* (Grand Rapids: Baker Academic, 2005); Kevin J. Vanhoozer, Daniel J. Treier, and N. T. Wright, *Theological Interpretation of the New Testament: A Book-by-Book Survey* (Grand Rapids: Baker Academic, 2008); Kevin J. Vanhoozer and Daniel J. Treier, *Theology and the Mirror of Scripture* (Downers Grove, IL: InterVarsity, 2015). See also Charles E. Shepherd, *Theological Interpretation and Isaiah 53: A Critical Comparison of Bernhard Duhm, Brevard Childs and Alec Motyer* (London: Bloomsbury, 2014); Christopher B. Hays, "Bard Called the Tune: Whither Theological Exegesis in the Post-Childs Era?," *Journal of Theological Interpretation* 4, no. 1 (2010): 139–52; Hans Madueme, "Review Article: Theological Interpretation after Barth," *Journal of Theological Interpretation* 3, no. 1 (2009): 143–59.

38. David F. Ford, "In the Spirit: Learning Wisdom, Giving Signs," in *The Holy Spirit in the World Today*, ed. Jane Williams (London: Alpha International, 2011), 49–50.

healthy lament over the experience of trauma, and a return to community life embedded in healthy relationships.[39]

Interpreting life after trauma, cultivating safety, and making powerful decisions occur with the external perspectives provided by the Spirit and the interpretive matrices and creeds of the church.[40] By taking this pressure off the trauma survivor to interpret everything by themselves, God's own mind through the Spirit and the historical wisdom of the church supports the agency of the survivor. It allows room for empowerment in cooperation with God's grace.[41]

In part 3, I take three chapters to tease out the fruits of a blessed interpretation of Matthew's Gospel in relation to recovery from trauma. Each chapter carries out its interpretation in light of the living God with an eye to one of the key skepticisms that is a roadblock to recovery from horrors and trauma. First, I note God's historical actions to defeat horrors and show what possibilities this suggests for reestablishing safety and overcoming skepticisms about his character. Second, I examine the recovery of a coherent story and look at the anthropological question of whether there is hope for recovered personhood and flourishing. Third, I address the existential question of the meaninglessness/meaningfulness of human life and suggest prospects and means for recovery through a restoration to community.

---

39. Judith Lewis Herman, *Trauma and Recovery: From Domestic Abuse to Political Terror* (London: Basic Books, 2001), 155. My essay "God the Trinity and Christian Care for Those Who Lament," in *A Time for Sorrow: Recovering the Practice of Lament in the Life of the Church*, eds. Sean McDonough and Scott Harrower (Peabody, MA: Hendrickson, 2019) overlaps with, and complements, some of the central ideas of this book.

40. "Christ, in and of Himself, is the foundation; but the Apostles, not in and of themselves but through Christ's delegation, and through the authority given them by Christ, are foundations as well." Aquinas, *Commentary on the Gospel of St. Matthew*, 565. Aquinas draws on 1 Cor 3:11; 10:4 for this conclusion.

41. The clarity of this Christian account of perceiving is a stark contrast to the problems that contemporary philosophy faces today, as it has no grounds on which to argue for perception. All that contemporary philosophy can do is to talk about the current state of affairs *of the discussion itself*. See Lambert Wiesing, *Das Mich der Wahrnehmung: Eine Autopsie* (Frankfurt am Main: Suhrkamp, 2009), 14.

Part 3

—

HORRORS *and* **TRINITY**

9

RECOVERING SAFETY

Reestablishing Trust in God's Character

In order to recover from trauma, persons need to establish a sense of safety, lament their trauma in the context of a coherent story, and reconnect with their community.[1] This will aid the recovery of a person's relational, moral, and functional capacities as an image of God. It will also enable a sufferer to respond to skepticisms about God and his relationship to people and the world. In this chapter, we explore the ways that God brings about a renewed sense of safety through objective means.

A sense of safety is one of the most important dimensions for human flourishing. According to Judith Lewis Herman, "The sense of safety in the world, or basic trust, is acquired in earliest life in the relationship with the first caretaker. Originating with life itself, this sense of trust sustains a person throughout their lifecycle. It forms the basis of all systems of relationship and faith." If a person's basic experience of receiving human caregiving is a positive one, then a person may "envisage a world in which they belong, a world hospitable to human life."[2] From a theological point of view, Genesis 1–2 speaks of a heavenly caretaker of human beings who cares for creatures (including humans) through human caretakers. Humans were supposed to flourish and have a hopeful sense of themselves in the larger context of real-world safety in God's garden.

The loss of a sense of safety after the fall is one of the greatest problems facing humanity. The world is now unsafe, horrifying, and traumatic. In the absence of safe caretaking, Lewis Herman writes, "Trauma robs the

1. Judith Lewis Herman, *Trauma and Recovery: From Domestic Abuse to Political Terror* (London: Basic Books, 2001), 155.

2. Lewis Herman, *Trauma and Recovery*, 51.

victim of a sense of power and control: the guiding principle of recovery is to restore power and control to the survivor. The first task of recovery is to establish the survivor's safety. This takes precedence over all others, for no other therapeutic work can possibly succeed if safety has not been adequately secured."[3] Is the genealogy that opens Matthew's Gospel a story of safety or of a loss of divine control?

In the service of safety, a trauma survivor needs tangible historical facts and a healthy interpretation of them to justify not being overwhelmed by subjective experiences and fears. Objective historical events remain unchanged in themselves and may be trustworthy sources of knowledge despite the subjective and relational disruption the survivor experiences. Objective events also provide grounds for responding to problems generated by objective as well as subjective horrors and trauma.

How does the living, Trinitarian God act to establish a sense of safety for trauma survivors? First, through objective historical events. A Trinitarian and blessed interpretation of Matthew's Gospel presents historically tangible evidences of God's responses to horrors. God's providence, the incarnation of God the Son, Jesus' victories over horror makers, and his resurrection all historically demonstrate God's concern and powerful care toward his images. These are important objective events that secure a worldview posttrauma. They also resist skepticism about God's good nature and his care for human beings.

God can order historical events so that they mediate knowledge of himself. One way of doing this is by ordering patterns of events.[4] At the outset of his biography of Jesus, Matthew establishes God as a reliable character whose intentional acts in history provide confidence in the fuller message that is unpacked in the remainder of the story. Though God is not visibly discernible and at times elusive, the disclosure and consequences of God's character in the world are benevolent.[5]

---

3. Lewis Herman, *Trauma and Recovery*, 159.

4. "There is no reason to think that one cannot have an experience [of God] through many different sorts of mediums insofar as God's agency can order the patterns of many different kinds of mediums." Adam Green, "Reading the Mind of God (without Hebrew Lessons): Alston, Shared Attention, and Mystical Experience," *Religious Studies* 45, no. 4 (2009): 465.

5. Stephan Käufer and Anthony Chemero, *Phenomenology: An Introduction* (Cambridge, UK: Polity, 2016), 32–49, 66–78.

The theological dimensions of God's benevolence, or goodness, are expressed in a number of positive historical relationships in which God is related to beings.[6] These include general providence, incarnation, resurrection, indwelling, and the new creation. In addition, God stands in negative relationship with horrors: there will be a time and place further ahead in history in which horrors, unrelenting horror makers, and potential horror makers will be exposed, judged, and disallowed at the same time that all other persons will be remade into glorified human beings. I unpack these objective elements throughout the chapter.[7]

PROVIDENCE

A horror reading of Matthew's genealogy and much of Matthew's Gospel suggested that horrors and death overwhelm and determine the contours of human life. God appears to be a silent monster in this story, by either actively bringing calamities on his people's heads or passively failing to care for his people.

A blessed reading that interprets the Gospel with the living God in mind can recognize the real monsters for who they are. Parodies of perfect humans and angels are the enemies. Their actions and dispositions wrestle with the goodness of God and his invisible providence, and they result in destruction.[8]

---

6. Abraham Kuruvilla, "Pericopal Theology," ***Bibliotheca Sacra*** 173, no. 689 (2016): 3–17; Kuruvilla, "The Aqedah (Genesis 22): What Is the Author *Doing* with What He Is *Saying*?," *Journal of the Evangelical Theological Society* 55, no. 3 (2012): 489–508.

7. Here I will follow Green's methodology for relating biblical theology on one hand and theological interpretation on the other. "Biblical theology locates meaning in the past: theology is 'contained' within the biblical text; and the text's potential ongoing significance is discerned through a process that moves from left to right (historical description → theological synthesis → constructive theology) or from bottom to top (foundation to superstructure). Theological interpretation locates meaning in the dynamic interaction of the past and the present (and expectations of the future); theology (and thus ongoing significance) is the outcome of that interaction." Joel B. Green, "What You See Depends on What You Are Looking for: Jesus' Ascension as a Test Case for Thinking about Biblical Theology and Theological Interpretation of Scripture," *Interpretation* 70, no. 4 (2016): 457. Kevin J. Vanhoozer and Daniel J. Treier follow a similar approach in *Theology and the Mirror of Scripture* (Downers Grove, IL: InterVarsity, 2015).

8. Its plot sequence still has broad affinity with that of horror literature. Noël Carroll, *The Philosophy of Horror, or, Paradoxes of the Heart* (New York: Routledge, 1990), 99, 109.

Matthew's genealogy is riddled with people who did not worship Yahweh but who gave themselves and their nation over to those evil spirits who influenced and stood behind other religions.[9]

Though only the footprints of the devil are suggested in the Old Testament and Matthew's genealogy, his shadowy figure becomes clear immediately after Jesus' anointing. From then onward, the light of Jesus' life exposes the widespread presence, activity, and power of the devil or Satan himself (Matt 4:1–11; 12:26; 13:39; 16:23; 25:41) and his massive forces (12:24; 25:41).[10] He is an antilife figure who clearly wants to destroy people and separate them from God. Reading the story of the genealogy and what follows without an attunement to the devil as the one who brings devastation leads to a category confusion in which God is deemed responsible for the deathward, life-sapping works that delight the devil. When we look at horrors, we should see a reflection of the work of the enemy of life rather than God's nature or will. David Bentley Hart captured this in the wake of the 2005 South Asian tsunami:

> Our faith is in a God who has come to rescue His creation from the absurdity of sin and the emptiness of death, and so we are permitted to hate these things with a perfect hatred. ... When I see the death of a child, I do not see the face of God, but the face of his enemy. It is ... a faith that ... has set us free from optimism, and taught us hope instead.[11]

People are certainly influenced by demonic beings; however, their active will cannot be ignored, nor can its impact. "The will that chooses poorly," writes Hart, "through ignorance, maleficence, or corrupt desire, has not thereby become freer, but has further enslaved itself to those forces that prevent it from achieving its full expression."[12] History outside the

---

9. G. H. Twelftree, "Demon, Devil, Satan," in *Dictionary of Jesus and the Gospels*, ed. Joel B. Green and Scot McKnight (Downers Grove, IL: InterVarsity, 1992). See the mentions of "goat demons" (Lev 17:7)—also called Azazel (Lev 16:8, 10, 26) or Lilith (Isa 34:14)—the "horse leech or vampire" (Prov 30:15). See Twelftree, "Demon, Devil, Satan," 163–64.

10. Twelftree, "Demon, Devil, Satan," 169.

11. David Bentley Hart, *The Doors of the Sea: Where Was God in the Tsunami?* (Grand Rapids: Eerdmans, 2005).

12. Hart, *Doors of the Sea*, 71.

garden of Eden is a nexus of God's active and permissive power, demonic willing and limited power, and human action in the midst of this.

Providential Care and a Sense of Safety

Given Matthew's strongly Hebraic presuppositions, the author clearly works with an understanding of God as the divine caretaker of those made in his image. The genealogy of Matthew serves a powerful role for those reading the Gospel of Matthew with an eye to the character of God and human safety. Matthew's Gospel begins with a genealogy. It opens with the following line: "An account of the genealogy of Jesus Christ, the Son of David, the son of Abraham" (Matt 1:1). It ends with "so all the generations from Abraham to David were fourteen generations, and from David until the exile to Babylon, fourteen generations; and from the exile to Babylon until the Christ, fourteen generations" (1:17). This is important because it tells the reader that history has an order from a given perspective, and even a purpose, despite seemingly lacking these features sometimes.

There is a macro-order in place that preserves life. This helps the reader see that there may be deeper patterns to history because, historically speaking, the people of God survived despite Israel's failure as an independent national political-religious entity.[13] Surprisingly, human life and some culture survive historical processes, so perhaps there is hope for surprising forms of safety.

The value of the genealogy is limited for those who only read it as a description of horrors that take place during successive eras. But an outcome-driven perspective is also provided: there is life despite everything that has occurred. The suggestion of an invisible order that results in some life means that there is slightly more to the story so far than a series of horrors with occasional respite. The results are mild, yet worth attending to. That the people of God survive being harrowed by horrors points out other surprising signs of life in the genealogy. These high points occur in the context of significant threats and include occasional visible periods of individual personal, moral, and creative development. For example, Boaz;

13. "The repeated restarts of a movement back toward the new-creational kingdom were never irreversibly realized in the OT era. What seemed to be fulfilled faded and wilted like flowers without water." G. K. Beale, *A New Testament Biblical Theology* (Grand Rapids: Baker Academic 2011), 891.

his wife, Ruth (1:5); and their grandson Jesse (1:5–6) thrive despite the specter of death. On a national level, the references to David and Solomon point to cultural thriving and enjoyment of the land despite external affliction (1:7–8). These show that the benevolent divine disposition to bless and make the descendants of Abraham fruitful (Gen 12, 15) was not withdrawn by God, nor overcome by other cosmic forces.

These high points suggest a divine disposition toward preserving life within Israel despite the empires stacked against Abraham's descendants. The genealogy's long-term view on blessing and the guiding hand of God was most likely not seen this way by historical Israel or Jesus' contemporaries. This serves as a caution to those who expect immediate safety and resolution from horrors and trauma.

However, the presence of life amid God's covenant people at the time of Jesus' birth means that the sum of human destiny may be more than the phenomenon of persons maladapting to their hostile environment. At minimum, there is the possibility for life within and despite fluctuating degrees of chaos.[14]

Where to from here? The rest of Matthew's story could possibly confirm various degrees of divine safety. It could merely affirm a minimalist, survivalist kind of end-time safety in line with the mere survival offered by the genealogy. Yet it already suggests something stronger by bracketing the genealogy with the mention of Jesus Christ (Matt 1:1, 17), indicating that divine safety may be bound up with what Jesus does in the remainder of the story. Who Jesus is, what he did in his earthly life, and what he promises to do further in the plane of human time and space as we know it (and beyond) will be decisive.

The slim evidence and hope offered in the genealogy may indicate better things to come, but it requires a certain perspective to see. I call this a theological squint. It is like an artist squinting in order to determine areas of light and shade once the basic shapes and blocks of color have been laid out on the canvas. Under normal sight conditions, it is easy to miss the precise spaces that darkness and light occupy in a work. However, squinting makes these clear. Good artists always squint about one-third of the way into a work in order to make sure that they see areas of light that are

14. Beale, *New Testament Biblical Theology*, 16.

present yet subtle in the canvas. In the same way, reading the genealogy in Matthew with a theological squint from the living God allows us to see glimpses of life that may have been otherwise missed.

New Promises and Moderated Expectations

As Matthew's story progresses, there are cumulative indications of the benevolence of God's character, disposition, and promises to act in order to secure safety for people. These involve both visible and invisible acts of care, and their nature and mechanisms are surprising and sometimes unwelcome.

For example, Matthew affirms that God is a divine caretaker who is sufficiently powerful and intricately interested in the world in such a way that he benevolently establishes patterns of regularity and security. Matthew writes that even the hairs of a person's head are known and counted by God (Matt 10:29–31). This suggests that God sees, knows, and cares about everything that happens to a person. The value of a person is grander than that of the birds of the field and is never lost, and people are always God's concern (10:29–31).

The precise way this takes place is not known to us. There are secrets and mysteries to the kingdom of heaven, which people cannot understand without special divine insight (Matt 13:11). Indeed, the deep things and mysteries belong to God alone, even where many other things have been revealed (Deut 29:29). From a human perspective there will always be inaccessible knowledge that informs God's actions and his permission of events in the world. The point is that this restriction of information, or an incapacity to consciously perceive it, does not equate to an absence of God's care or interest in human beings. This draws on the disposition of God suggested in the genealogy and provides a fresh perspective on both the macro- and micro-picture of divine care for people. What's more, Jesus' teaching about the invisible providential care of God plays a very important role in slowly shaping the worldview of the reader, so that readers can consider that perhaps there is macro-safety.

Matthew the author was a former Roman tax collector, which means that he affirms God's sovereignty despite his own participation in traumatizing people and generating horrors as an active participant in the Roman oppression of his own people (Matt 9:9; 10:3). That he could pen the sovereignty-affirming genealogy despite being part of the regime that crushed Israel shows that his understanding of national and personal sovereignty was interpreted via a new perspective that originated with who Jesus is as the "Christ, the Son of David, the Son of Abraham" (1:1).

The author's personal experience and motivation enable an appropriation of the divine intent that echoes back to Genesis 1–2. It may be the case that, as Graham Cole writes, "the grand goal of the divine comedy is nothing less than to secure God's people in God's place under God's reign living God's way enjoying God's shalom in God's loving and holy presence as both family and worshippers, to God's glory."[15] God's purpose of establishing safety and shalom may become increasingly clear, enabling readers to resist skepticisms about God's character and care.

Taken together, these things prompt the reader to take a fresh step of confidence in God's care. It is not overconfidence, but it nonetheless exceeds the nihilism that experiencing horrors can yield. It does not do much, however, for the skepticism related to God's hiddenness. Visible confirmation of God's presence and care is required.

THE INCARNATION

God's providential omniscience and sovereignty push back against a totalizing horror perspective on reality. However, a general argument for these, based on the partial survival of Abraham's descendants, might not be sufficient to encourage people to seek safety in a personal relationship with God or others, as the answers provided so far do not overcome fears that the world is inherently hostile and dangerous at a personal and group level.[16]

From an existential and psychological perspective, it does not go far enough to reverse inappropriately intense desire for anxious attachments to other persons: as Judith Lewis Herman writes, "The terror of the traumatic event intensifies the need for protective attachments. The traumatized person therefore frequently alternates between isolation and anxious

15. Graham A. Cole, *God the Peacemaker: How Atonement Brings Shalom* (Downers Grove, IL: InterVarsity, 2009), 25.

16. "Trauma impels people to withdraw from close relationships and to seek them desperately. The profound disruption of basic trust, the common feelings of shame, guilt and inferiority, and the need to avoid reminders of the trauma that may be found in social life, all foster withdrawal from close relationships." Lewis Herman, *Trauma and Recovery*, 56.

clinging to others."[17] This means that healthy and flourishing relationships remain beyond perspective and grasp at this point.

Aside from strong visible and tangible historical evidence of God's presence and his "face," debates about the sovereignty of God and about safety take place under the shadow of the hidden God, *Deus absconditus*.[18]

Wolf Krötke captures this as follows:

> God is only truthfully called *God* insofar as we recognize that, in his power and supremacy, he affects everything that happens in the world. This means however, that he causes both good and evil, as his power is never idle. He drives the heels of the godly as well as the godless. He elects and rejects, as many biblical texts demonstrate, with a caprice that is impenetrable to us. He creates life, and he destroys life, just as he wills. One cannot have faith in him, that is, put one's trust in him. One cannot even preach him. Ultimately … he throws us into doubt, angst, and distress. Such a God cannot be a god who brings clarity to our lives. One can only flee before him.

The way back to the God known in power through history is christological. "In light of our inevitably fearful experiences of the hidden God," writes Krötke, "we ought to flee to the God who is revealed in Christ, the one who alone is able to be our God, in whom we place our trust, and who can be preached."[19]

This historical fact of the incarnation has intellectual, personal, relational, and moral consequences for refreshing and renewing a traumatized worldview. The visible presence of God himself in Jesus, appearing in human history, provides significant detail to the nature and extent of the safety provided by God's historical works. It gives grounding to objective intellectual truths for reorienting a worldview, such as God's ongoing commitment to those made in his image, his power to back up this commitment, and his condemnation of horrors.

17. Lewis Herman, *Trauma and Recovery*, 56.

18. Wolf Krötke, "God's Hiddenness and Belief in His Power: Essays in Honour of John Webster," in *Theological Theology*, ed. R. David Nelson, Darren Sarisky, and Justin Stratis (London: Bloomsbury, 2015), 141, italics original.

19. Krötke, "God's Hiddenness and Belief in His Power," 141–42.

Powerful interpersonal relationships go hand in hand with these. The most prominent is the offer of a secure and healing relationship with Jesus mediated by the Holy Spirit, which also provides at least one healthy person with whom we can all relate in the wake of suffering. These relationships provide decisive reorientation for traumatized persons who have lost "their trust in themselves, in other people, in God."[20]

God's Ongoing Commitment

The incarnation of God the Son demonstrates the Trinity's ongoing commitment to human beings. The unique value that God accords to his images is clear in Matthew's story of the virginal conception of Jesus (1:18–21). God revealed himself via angels in the past, and angels are prominent and positively portrayed in Matthew's Gospel. Angels are valuable to God and useful agents of God, and also have great insights into God and his workings. Despite his historic practice of revealing himself through angels or an angelic form, however, God took on a human nature and not an angelic one. He chose to be "God with us" in the person of Jesus (1:23).

Therefore, the incarnation affirms the basic dignity and value of his images over and above other creatures. Humans are particularly noble in God's eyes; they are precious images of God. This confirms Genesis's evaluation that humans are "very good" in comparison to other creatures, who are simply "good."[21] This sets up a train of thought that leads toward the divine judgment of horrors for what they are, yet offers to preserve the dignity and life of those who commit them—a thought we will pick up further below.

The reaffirmation of the dignity and value of images of God is crucial for people who currently experience or have experienced horrors and trauma. These people have, as Lewis Herman writes, "suffer[ed] damage to the basic structures of the self." Consequently, "the identity they have formed prior to the trauma is irrevocably destroyed."[22] The incarnation is a historical fact that points out God's care and valuation of all human beings

---

20. Lewis Herman, *Trauma and Recovery*, 56.

21. Ellen T. Charry, "Incarnation," in *Dictionary for Theological Interpretation of the Bible*, ed. Kevin J. Vanhoozer, Craig G. Bartholomew, Daniel J. Treier, and N. T. Wright (Grand Rapids: Baker Academic, 2005), 324–25.

22. Lewis Herman, *Trauma and Recovery*, 56.

regardless of the victimization and trauma that these persons suffer. This valuation exists in God's perspective and is independent of the subjective fears and misapprehensions of trauma survivors. This means that in reality a person's identity is always as an image of God and prized by God.[23]

This status also reflects something very attractive about God: the stability of his regard for people. The stability and consistency of God's perspective reflect his trustworthiness and the safety of his purposes. God's incarnation is an objective basis for orienting us to the fact that he cares about the safety and restoration of people's relational, moral, and creative aspects. His care is not undermined or overturned by horrors or traumas. God's actions, such as the incarnation, are historical and part of what make up reality; therefore, they cannot be ignored selectively but must be integrated with what we experience—even if it generates paradoxes. At a minimum, they invite us to consider that there is more to the world than horrors and trauma, and at the same time that we have not been wholly abandoned by God.

God's Power Demonstrated

God's benevolent posture toward people is existentially reassuring; however, a disposition in itself it not enough to actually secure a sense of safety. No matter what God's disposition may be, if he cannot bring about life where there is death, then there is little hope for the restoration and healing of the images of God. This is why the power that the incarnation demonstrates is very important. It is strong evidence of his power to carry out unexpected human works and personal realities that may be required in order to safely bring about their fullness of life. The confirmation of divine power in the incarnation is an instance of a true a story that offers "openings for new life," as Kathleen O'Connor puts it, even though it is accompanied by the themes of past disaster, fear, and the unknown.[24]

The connection between the power of the Holy Spirit and life is foremost in the incarnation. The Spirit brought about a new human life in the context of horrors and confusion. An important aspect of the incarnation is

23. Phillip Pettit, "Realism and Response-Dependence," *Mind* 100, no. 4 (1991): 587–626.

24. Kathleen M. O'Connor, "Stammering toward the Unsayable: Old Testament Theology, Trauma Theory, and Genesis," *Interpretation* 70, no. 3 (2016): 308.

that it highlights both the life of God and the lives of people to be signs and sources of light and life within the darkness of history. In Jesus, divinity and humanity are related to each other in order to point out God's power. In God's providence, Mary, Joseph, and the infant survive despite the malicious wills and actions of antilife forces.

By drawing our attention to the life-giving power of God's Spirit, the incarnation retrospectively strengthens a "blessed" interpretation of God's providence. The history of the Abrahamic people was ordered after all; it did have an invisible purpose that led to a visible incarnation. The process and order of history may not be as smooth as we would like it to be, but there are significant past public demonstrations of God's power and sovereignty that are sufficiently weighty to be objectively normative in a worldview, even in the case of serious subjective disruption from trauma.

The fact of an incarnation is a massive demonstration of power. God's power is not limited to this action. Rather, God promises to overcome objective and subjective horrors by rescuing people from the consequences of their horror-making and trauma-perpetuating attitudes and actions. He will provide the basis for rescuing people from their sins (Matt 1:21). This means that beyond the incarnation, God has the power to bring about a counterstory to the cross-generational horror-making genealogy that preceded Jesus.

This counterstory is cemented by the promise of a more intimate form of divine presence among his people: Jesus will also be called "Immanuel"—which means "God with us" (1:23). This means that for those who take the historical fact of the incarnation and what it means seriously, they may take a step closer to being in the life-giving and communicative presence of God, as humans were in the garden of Eden. The incarnation also demonstrates that God still treasures human beings, despite what they have done—an otherwise-dubious assumption, given the carnage humans have spread on earth.

THE LIFE OF JESUS: HISTORICAL ENGAGEMENT WITH HORROR MAKERS

In his earthly ministry, Jesus makes it objectively clear that God rejects horrors and trauma. He is morally and creatively opposed to them. In Christ,

God condemns both objective horrors and subjective trauma, at the same time as offering hope for human horror makers.

A significant aspect of Jesus' teaching ministry is to identify objective horrors and subjective trauma. He goes further and powerfully and meaningfully rejects them with God's own "No!" and he does something definitive about them. He is the teacher without comparison and the unique reference point for his Father's truth in a context where religious abuse appears to merely propagate relational, moral, and creative confusion and hurt (Matt 23:8–36).

This is not to say that Jesus was immune to horrors and trauma. One example of its impact on him is when Jesus hears about the horrific death of John the Baptizer, which generates subjective pain in Jesus. "When Jesus heard about it, he withdrew from there to a remote place to be alone" (14:13).

Jesus condemns both commonplace and gross horrors. They are equally putrid in his eyes. He rejects their source: all those things generated by the human heart that replace the expression of human nature. Another kind of nature is expressed: a defiled one. Jesus describes those things that "defile a person" and diminish the flourishing personhood of an image of God (Matt 12:34–35; 15:20): they are absences of the inclination, potential, and actuality of life. They are the transgressive replacements of good things. Though they are often expressed in sinful behavior, horror refer to absences as much as they do to actions. The things that defile us include "evil thoughts, murders, adulteries, sexual immoralities, thefts, false testimonies, slander" (15:19), dishonoring parents (15:3–9), religious abuse (15:1-9), and injustice (18:29–34).[25]

Jesus also redefines and intensifies what a horror is, thereby widening the category of thought and actions that he will actively judge, condemn, and accurse on behalf of the Father. "You have heard that it was said to our ancestors, 'Do not murder, and whoever murders will be subject to judgment.' But I tell you, everyone who is angry with his brother or sister, will be subject to judgment. ... Whoever says, 'You fool!' will be subject to hellfire" (Matt 5:21–22).

---

25. My thanks go to Kevin Anderson (Asbury University) for making me aware of this. Kevin L. Anderson, "Response to Dr. Scott Harrower, 'God, Horror, and Meaning'" (paper presented at Institute for Biblical Research research group "Suffering, Evil, and Divine Punishment in the Bible," San Antonio, TX, November 18, 2016).

Jesus rejects horrors so strongly that he ultimately and definitely will banish them and those who caused them. "The Son of Man will send out his angels, and they will gather from his kingdom all who cause sin and those guilty of lawlessness. They will throw them into the blazing furnace where there will be weeping and gnashing of teeth" (Matt 13:41–42).

Kevin Anderson writes that what I have categorized as commonplace horrors are just as heinous to Jesus as gross ones:

> I wonder if Jesus' use of horrific metaphors in the Gospel of Matthew in talking about the heinousness of sin taps into a similar perspective. Being in danger of hellfire for calling someone a fool; cutting off one's offending hand or gouging out one's eye rather than going to hell in one's whole body; it being better to be cast into the sea with a millstone around one's neck rather than causing a "little one" to stumble; God's warning to treat us like the unforgiving serving was treated in the parable of the unmerciful servant (tortured and imprisoned!) if we do not sincerely forgive those who have wronged us—these hyperbolic, horrific, traumatic images may well be designed to wield rhetorical power by properly and accurately identifying the weight of everyday sinful actions on the scale of horrors.[26]

In other words, Jesus is pro-life. He rejects gross and commonplace horrors as well as subjective traumas. But does this mean that all those human persons who are involved in horror making are ultimately condemned? Is the gospel about Jesus the horror defeater bad news for *everyone*?

Jesus' Substitutionary Death

Jesus' substitutionary experience of God's wrath on behalf of repentant horror makers offers a new possibility for life after horrors. Once Jesus has experienced divine abandonment on behalf of those who belong to the kingdom of the Father, there is no reason to fear the loss of God once again (Matt 27:46). Permanent relationship with him and membership in his kingdom allow people to be shaped by the Spirit's transformative work. When Jesus brings the influence of the Spirit to bear on people who

26. Anderson, "Response to Dr. Scott Harrower."

cannot enact their relational, moral, and creative capacities, "then the kingdom has come upon you" (12:28). The Spirit of God releases people from Satan's grip and the compulsion that the devil generates in a person's life. The Spirit indwells and inheres those who live under God the Father's influence.

The Trinitarian contours of this new hope and way of being human are consolidated and given clear direction as God the Son teaches people to live in a blessed manner. This is a virtuous way of life for images of God who are being enabled by the Spirit to recognize their poverty of Spirit: to mourn, to be humble, to desire and seek righteousness, to be merciful, pure in heart, peacemakers (Matt 5:3–10). Those who live this way are being restored to actualize their full potential as images of God and human persons in the fullest sense, which is Christlikeness. For this reason, they are "called sons of God," and "the kingdom of heaven is theirs" (5:9–10). Thus, the divine works that permit the reconstitution of each person have correlates in human action. These are focused on morally pure relationships with other persons and require giving oneself in the gift and service of one another and the fruitful use of our relational, moral, and creative capacities in order to bring about healthy personhood in each other (16:24–28; 18:15–20; 20:20–30).

Thus, the Trinity rescues God's precious images from Satan's control at the same time as beginning a work of inclusive restoration: it is a work of gathering people back to God, themselves, and one another. Whereas the work of Satan is described as scattering, God brings people back to themselves, himself, and each other in his kingdom through the Spirit working via the Son.

Unfortunately, these Trinitarian possibilities and works have received little acknowledgment in the work of those who deal theologically and pastorally with the problems of trauma and horrors. This is lamentable because God the Father, Son, and Spirit is the living God who intimately and powerfully brings human release from captivity and enables flourishing in its place. *Without an appreciation of the Trinitarian contours of this work, it is difficult to see how people will be brought into the kingdom of God and provided with safety and healing from traumas and horrors.* Indeed, Jesus himself warns that without the Spirit indwelling a person who was formerly influenced by the devil, people will only be more powerfully influenced by his destructive presence and power (Matt 12:43–45). For this reason, Jesus implores people not to resist the work of the Spirit, because God the Trinity is their only hope (12:31–32).

An important caveat needs to be clarified at this point. Many people already in the kingdom and who have the Spirit indwelling them will still experience horrors and trauma responses to these. They may struggle to move beyond a horror reading, but this does not mean that those who live with a horror hermeneutic are not Christians. In these cases, I would argue that the Spirit restrains the horror hermeneutic from being stronger than what it is. The Spirit is still operative, unperceived yet present and active in such a way that our theological, anthropological, and existential situations are "merely" experiences as a "void," and not the full extent of the foul abyss that often beckons us.

Jesus Overcomes Demonic Horror Makers

The extent of God's power to bring about new life is one of the key questions in trauma studies. The apparent lack of this power in everyday life raises the evidential problem of evil.

The Trinitarian theology in Matthew's Gospel makes a contribution to these issues as it describes God's disclosure of his series of defeats against the devil. The phenomena of horror and trauma are closely related to the devil's self-expression in history—he is one of the primary horror makers in the cosmos.

The Gospel of Matthew establishes Jesus, God the Son, as the one who can defeat horrors and bring about new life. The Father, Son, and Spirit are united in being and will. Trinitarian unity is affirmed by Jesus' baptism, anointing, and confirmation by God the Father—events that record that Jesus is the approved focal point for the historical revelation of the Trinity. This unity is consistent with and results from the unity of the divine name (Matt 28:19: "the name of the Father, Son, and Holy Spirit").

This unity of will, purpose, and power is immediately tested in a series of historical events. The particular unity of will between the Son and the Father is tested in the wilderness by extreme difficulties and temptation by the devil (Matt 4:1–11). However, the unity is unwavering. The victorious unity of will of purpose between Jesus, the Father, and the Spirit means that Jesus as the incarnate Son has at his disposal all the resources of the Trinitarian life. This is the foundation for his confrontation with agents of horror, both demonic and human.

Jesus is a horror defeater who expels demons from those people who are under their "evil" or "dirty" sway. This demonstrates God's intention to restore people to flourishing. For example, in the Gadarenes area Jesus liberates two demon-oppressed people who lived in tombs. He is able to help in a situation where others could not: these people "were so violent that no one could pass that way" (Matt 8:28). The demoniacs are not able to flourish as images of God; they are relationally cut off from others and are using their creative or functional human abilities in immoral ways by being violent toward other images of God. They are horror makers. However, this horror making is not their work alone, as shown by the fact that when the demons speak they do so through the voices of the demoniacs. The demons have taken over the faculties and abilities of the demonized persons. Thus, the demons are horror makers too; we could say they are the primary horror makers in this situation.

The way in which Jesus carries out distinct actions toward the demons versus the demonized people suggests once again that God accords great value to human beings. This is achieved by way of contrast with angels once again (as per Ps 8), though in this case they are fallen ones. The demons cry out: "What do you have to do with us, Son of God? Have you come to torment us before the time?" They acknowledge and anticipate Jesus' judgment of them in the future (Matt 8:29).[27] This is fleshed out in Matthew 13:36–43, where Jesus explains the parable of the sower (13:3–9) to his disciples. There will come a time when demons and their agents will no longer have humans within their reach because they will be condemned to fire (13:36–43).

In the Gadarenes story, the demons then make it clear that they must be judged and destroyed, because the demons destroy the animals and hurt the livelihoods of the herd keepers. They reveal their unchangeable nature and lack of repentance. They can only ever be destroyers. They are

27. Twelftree, "Demon, Devil, Satan," 169.

destroyers that do not change their course of action, even after a confrontation with God.

In contrast to this, there is no indication that the people involved will be judged and destroyed in the future. Indeed, Luke tells us that these images of God are restored to dignity (Luke 8:26–39). After their deliverance, one is described as "sitting at Jesus' feet, dressed and in his right mind" (8:35). Here we see God's intent for humanity revealed through Jesus the horror defeater: the man is an image of God who is restored to his relational, moral, and functional capacities, and therefore restored as a person. He is restored relationally because he is right with Jesus and no longer a threat to others (to the extent that he can return to his hometown). He is restored morally—a fact suggested by his getting clothed. Finally, he is functionally or creatively enlivened: not only does he learn at Jesus' feet, but he returns to his home and tells others "how much Jesus had done for him" (8:39). There is no anticipation of a future time in which this man will be judged, tormented, or destroyed. God aims to heal, renew, and restore these people.

RESURRECTION

The resurrection of Jesus is another historical instance through which God demonstrates his perspective on horrors. He rejects death as the great horror that it is. God bodily demonstrates his rejection and overcoming of death by means of the resurrection of Jesus. Jesus' victory over death—both his own death and death in general—overcomes death as the final horizon against which all life is lived, as Hans-Christian Kammler writes: "The gospel has its origin not in the world of death, but rather comes into this world marked by death as the word of the resurrected one from beyond, with transformative power. With Easter morning the dominion of death is broken; death no longer has the last word." As an historical event, it is a demonstration of God's power for a trauma survivor. It shows that despite the overwhelming fears and problems of trauma and horrors, God has had the ultimate victory over death and meaningless and hopelessness. How this is immediately related to the current difficulties and afflictions of Jesus' disciples may not always be clear. At least we can say that God may bring about life where there is death. However, it is more often than not an indirect comfort. Kammler continues, "The comfort of the gospel [that death is not the end of life] certainly remains a *contested* comfort, whose truth must always be authenticated by God himself against our own experience of self and world, and must be inscribed on our heart."[28]

At a minimum, the resurrection of Jesus amplifies the glimpses and glimmers of light to which God's providence points in the genealogy. It reveals the relevance of mentioning Jesus at the beginning and the end of this mostly sad account of history (Matt 1:1, 16). Jesus is the first light in the kingdom of the Father, who will ultimately draw to himself "the righteous," who "will shine like the sun in their Father's kingdom" (13:43). When the resurrection becomes part of the way we perceive the world, the world looks different indeed. There is hope for a better future, even if it may be years away from our present experience.

GOD'S ONGOING PRESENCE IN THE LIFE OF JESUS

Horrors do not prevent Jesus from being present with Christians today, not even those horrors that he himself endured before they killed him: "The brutal and sinful circumstances of the [crucified Christ's] human being do not prevent the fact that God is present with us in Christ," writes Ola Sigurdson.[29] The ascension and its outcome—Jesus is universally available to Christians—is often overlooked and misunderstood. The resurrection, ascension, session at the right hand of God, and sending of his Spirit to the church mean Jesus is available and present with billions of people at the same time across the world and in the intermediate state. After the resurrection and ascension of Jesus, the presence of God remains with his people.

The implications of this are decisive for life in the context of horrors and in the wake of trauma responses. The activity of Jesus continues today. Jesus' prayer is an example of this continuation, which has strong continuities with his life before the ascension. For example, Matthew 14:23 records that "after dismissing the crowds, he went up to the mountain by himself to pray. Well into the night, he was there alone." In the same way he prays for believers today: "Christ ... has been raised, he also is at the

28. Hans-Christian Kammler, "Der Trost des Evangeliums angesichts des Todes," *Kerygma und Dogma* 61 (2015): 69, italics original. See also Andreas Gössner, "Krankheit und Sterben in der reformationszeitlichen Seelsorge," *Kerygma und Dogma* 60 (2014): 75–91.

29. Ola Sigurdson, *Heavenly Bodies: Incarnation, the Gaze, and Embodiment in Christian Theology*, trans. Carl Olsen (Grand Rapids: Eerdmans, 2016), 493.

right hand of God and intercedes for us" (Rom 8:34). Given that prayer shapes historical situations and is a means by which God providentially orders events, we can say that Jesus is shaping our context and stories by means of his prayers for us.

Jesus is present with believers and may be glimpsed imperfectly in the kind of lives that his disciples live. Ever since he uttered them, the words of Jesus "I am with you always, to the end of the age" (Matt 28:20) have taken a near-visible form in the lives of those who are baptized in "the name of the Father and of the Son and of the Holy Spirit" (28:19). The living God dwells within every person who is baptized into his name and receives a new way of life from him. The indwelling presence of the Spirit in a believer is not the same as a direct embodiment of God, as was the case for Jesus as the incarnation of God. However, it is a reflection of God's active presence within them and other Christians. This enabling presence is appropriate and fitting because each disciple of God is being renewed in their orientation and potential to actualize the fullness of being an image of God. Therefore, as each image is aided to live up to its natural goal with the help of the Spirit of Jesus within, he or she gives to others an imperfect and indirect vision of God and of his desires for the world.[30] The resurrection of Jesus is also a corporate reality, in which the totality of the church embodies unique aspects and gifts of the life of the Christ.[31] Members of Christ's body need each other's presence and gifts in order to make disciples and teach them how to live Jesus' instruction.

However, the "grotesque" details of the passion of Christ remind us that Jesus' presence in the church (Matt 18:20) will take place amid suffering, death, and betrayal.[32] This dynamic of life-in-the-midst-of-death describes the historical expression of the life of the church in many of its various social and political expressions. As a theological category, Jesus' life-giving presence in the midst of social chaos and suffering explains the visible and unlikely historical survival of the Christian church. The success of the church through persecution and the trials of clarifying belief in unity via the seven ecumenical councils (AD 325–787) can be seen in

30. However, we need to note a key distinction: "That the church is the body of Christ does not mean that Christ is identical with the church." Sigurdson, *Heavenly Bodies*, 566.

31. Sigurdson, *Heavenly Bodies*, 566–68.

32. Sigurdson, *Heavenly Bodies*, 493–512.

the light of it being an extension of his life.[33] The church has a testimony to give about the Trinity, who brings about life despite persecution and trials. This is an interpretation of history that functions as a gift: it offers objectively grounded confidence in God despite immediate appearances to the contrary.[34]

Trauma survivors and many philosophers have strong skepticisms about God's care for human beings and his power to do anything about it. Yet there are historical reasons for interpreting that God provides safety to people, which is the first step to recovery from trauma. Historical self-disclosures of God through the phenomena of Israel's history, the incarnation, the life of Jesus, his resurrection, and his presence in the church point to past instances of God's care for people. These events are very important because all of them are historical facts that take place outside the mind of the trauma victim. This means that people are free to believe them and do not have to battle and wrestle with their own ideas as to whether or not they are true. These events take the pressure off the trauma survivor because they allow them to rest in the fact that in the past there have been instances of God's care for people, and therefore it is not true that God is entirely unconcerned for people generally or uncaring with respect to individuals specifically.

This is only the historical and visible part of God's response to horrors. These must be taken together with God's ongoing interaction with his disciples through his empathetic presence, indwelling by the Spirit, and his gift of hope for present, and ultimately healing. We turn to these invisible contemporary works in the next chapter.

33. Sigurdson, *Heavenly Bodies*, 566.

34. Jan Muis, "Die Rede von Gott und das Reden Gottes. Eine Würdigung der Lehre der dreifachen Gestalt des Wortes Gottes," *Zeitschrift für Dialektische Theologie* 16, no. 1 (2000): 68.

10

RECOVERING STORY

Reestablishing Hope

Having explored God's provision of safety by means of his objective disclosure in history and his rejection of horrors and trauma, we now turn to God's work that enables a trauma survivor to personally and subjectively engage with God in order to further develop the trauma narrative. This is one of the most important parts of our research because it helps overcome the fear that God is a neglectful and passive parent who does not intervene to actively care and protect his children from harm.[1] In particular, it helps to address the key anthropological question that arises from horrors: whether there is hope for a better personal future and restoration to full personhood.

A large element of recovering a coherent narrative is reestablishing hope—being a part of a story that accepts the realities of horrors and trauma but has reasonable expectation for change. The expectation of positive change is one foundational need of trauma survivors as they move from a numbed, death-like state to an authentic life posttrauma.[2] The detail and range of the positive consequences of hope are felt throughout the body and mind, ranging from improved resilience in ill health all the way to clearer thinking for navigating a new life.[3] Hope is therefore necessary to flourishing in a posttrauma life in which people can be in the world with others in ways that fulfill the relational, moral, and creative

1. Lauren E. Maltby and Todd W. Hall, "Trauma, Attachment, and Spirituality: A Case Study," *Journal of Psychology and Theology* 40, no. 4 (2012): 304.

2. Deborah van Deusen Hunsinger, "Bearing the Unbearable: Trauma, Gospel and Pastoral Care," *Theology Today* 68, no. 1 (2011): 18.

3. Kaethe Weingarten, "Reasonable Hope: Construct, Clinical Applications, and Supports," *Family Process* 49, no. 1 (2010): 5.

potentials within their human natures. In this way survivors can be influences and role models who reflect many of God's attributes for the sake of the common good.

The nature and actions of God the Trinity provide trustworthy reasons for hoping for and living into the reality of a better future for Christians affected by horrors and trauma. Providing hope that has real referents in the present and the future faces a number of challenges. Repairing these aspects of personhood will also respond to skepticisms about hope by arguing for safety with God and his community as well as for theological reorientations in the light of Jesus' historical resurrection and promises about the future. These provide the foundations for reasonable hope. Reasonable hope is the expectation of improvement based on a positive orientation to history, without requiring or demanding a certain set of feelings from trauma survivors.[4]

Alongside enabling reasonable hope, God reaches out into a world of trauma and relates to his children in a life-giving manner to transform the relational, moral, and creative aspects of his images. There are two invisible Trinitarian realities that come into play here, revolving around God the Son incarnate and his Spirit: the incarnate Son's empathetic understanding of human beings, and the Spirit's indwelling presence. The Son's understanding of the human experience of trauma as well as the permanence of his presence secured by the indwelling Spirit establish a safe yet vulnerable relationship between God and the trauma survivor.

Taken together with God's historic actions that establish safety, these subjective possibilities allow for the restoration of the relational aspect of what it is to be an image of God. By virtue of the Son's incarnation, when we are restored to God we are simultaneously restored to a human person: Jesus. This means that the trauma survivor may participate in a new personal story by healthily reconnecting to God in Jesus. A divine and a human relationship is established. The relational, moral, and creative outcomes of this will vary from person to person. The worldview and intellectual

4. Weingarten, "Reasonable Hope," 5.

consequences include acceptance of God's care and presence, and rejection of claims that God is uncaring and hidden from all people.[5]

In this chapter, then, we look at how God the Father, Son, and Spirit counters skepticisms toward hope and offers a positive orientation toward history. We also explore the subjective ways in which God as Trinity relates to trauma sufferers to enable relational restoration in the present. Finally, we look at how trauma survivors can establish a coherent trauma narrative that takes into account the tragedy of suffering within an overarching narrative of hope.

FUTURE HOPE

Hope as the Anticipation of a Perfect and Loving Future

Christian hope has classically hoped for intimacy and shalom with God in a renewed historical context. This communion with God is a state of intimacy described as seeing him face to face together with other heirs to his kingdom of light. The dynamic relationality this entails means there will be new ways in which the relational, moral, and creative aspects of human beings will be fulfilled and experienced as humans "shine like the sun in their Father's kingdom" (Matt 13:43).

The perfect Father-child relationship that is envisioned here is foundational for this is a face-to-face, loving relationship with God. Paul the apostle describes this in 1 Corinthians 13:12: "For now we see only a reflection as in a mirror, but then face to face. Now I know in part, but then I will know fully, as I am fully known." The context of this is Paul's expectation of God's love bringing about perfection for all things in love, which never ends (1 Cor 13:8, 10), but it generates faith and hope because the object of love is the loving and perfecting God. This approach is the result of a blessed perspective on the future. In the meantime, this will result in a way of life described as being light and salt in a decaying world (Matt 5:13–16), which involves dispositions and actions that express hope and result in positive change for other people.

---

5. Hilary of Poitiers, *Commentary on Matthew*, trans. D. H. Williams (Washington, DC: Catholic University of America Press, 2012), 179–80.

This ideal loving and perceptive relationship with God in God's perfect place has been described as the beatific vision by the greats of theology (Thomas Aquinas) and literature (Dante Alighieri). The beatific vision is the best possible kind of gazing on God by a human being. It involves looking on God in union with him. Such a vision is the perfected shared attention with God, being perfectly and securely in harmony with him. It is mediated to human bodies in union with God via the Son and Spirit. This is "a state of communion and not mere observation. ... The beatific vision is supposed to be a participation in the inner life of the Trinity which, in order to be consistent with the doctrine of perichoresis, the interpenetration of the divine persons, should involve the fullest possible expression of shared attention."[6] A successful relationship with, and perception of, God and all things as they relate to him requires human beings to have glorified bodies, souls, and minds in order to handle this vision and this place. Paul the apostle emphasized the discontinuity between our present bodies and those that are suited to handle the new knowledge and order of creation, thereby hinting at the heightened nature of the future (1 Cor 15:37–49; 2 Cor 12:3–4). Christian hope is therefore a future-oriented hope. This hope includes the prospect of one day understanding ourselves, our experiences, and our interactions with others within God's perspective. Only then will our lives "make sense"—divine sense.

Christians currently have limited knowledge of God and experience the frustrations of an imperfect understanding of God and what this perfect future for the world looks like. What is known is sufficient to contribute to recovering a larger story in which our own story makes sense. However, we need to acknowledge the obstacles to hope before we look at how God as Trinity overcomes them.

Skepticisms and Obstacles to Hope

One of the primary skepticisms about hope is that it is a fantasy with no basis in anything other than a person's mental state. This "hope is fiction" argument can be seen in Nietzsche's claim that "hope is the worst of evils

6. Adam Green, "Reading the Mind of God (without Hebrew Lessons): Alston, Shared Attention, and Mystical Experience," *Religious Studies* 45, no. 4 (2009): 459.

because it prolongs the torments of men."[7] It also is seen in J. L. Schellenberg's view that God does not seem to be bringing about the best for his followers.[8]

Perceiving our social environment through the eyes of faith and experiences of God mediated through the church will be one of the prominent ways forward.[9] However, it is a difficult process because of the role that a religious background may have in generating skepticism about hope.

Powerful skepticisms may be generated internally by the religious background of persons who have survived horrors inflicted on them and their communities. These are negative religious coping strategies and include questions such as "Has God abandoned me?" "What did I do to cause God to let this happen to us?" or statements such as "Whatever God is, he cannot have good plans for us."[10] Such people may blame themselves for God's abandonment, which, as Mary Patricia Van Hook writes, "increase[s] the sense of being abandoned, of being without support, of being a worthless person. Trauma can destroy a sense of trust in God and the higher power—a contract has been broken."[11]

The problem of Christian hopelessness after trauma is not uncommon because traumatic experiences often require revising beliefs, including those about the future, as Emma Hutchison and Roland Bleiker write:

> Traumatic experiences rupture the linear narratives through which one experiences the everyday. The comfort and stability of normal habits and expectations fall away. Commonly held assumptions and meanings that have, over the course of our lives, come to define us are stripped away. No longer can we envisage life as a smooth trajectory from here to there.[12]

---

7. Friedrich W. Nietzsche, *Human, All Too Human*, parts 1 and 2, trans. H. Zimmern and P. V. Cohn (Mineola, NY: Dover, 2006), 71.

8. J. L. Schellenberg, *The Hiddenness Argument: Philosophy's New Challenge to Belief in God* (Oxford: Oxford University Press, 2015); Schellenberg, *The Will to Imagine: A Justification of Skeptical Religion* (Ithaca, NY: Cornell University Press, 2009).

9. Ola Sigurdson, *Heavenly Bodies: Incarnation, the Gaze, and Embodiment in Christian Theology*, trans. Carl Olsen (Grand Rapids: Eerdmans, 2016), 275.

10. Adapted from Mary Patricia Van Hook, "Spirituality as a Potential Resource for Coping with Trauma," *Social Work & Christianity* 43, no. 1 (2016): 15.

11. Van Hook, "Spirituality as a Potential Resource for Coping with Trauma," 15.

12. Emma Hutchison and Roland Bleiker, "Emotional Reconciliation Reconstituting Identity and Community after Trauma," *European Journal of Social Theory* 11, no. 1 (2008): 388.

The context in which these questions are being asked skews the answers toward pessimism rather than optimism for a better immediate and ultimate future for people. For example, the claim has been made that the phenomenology of history resists prospects of hope. Damien Broderick suggests that existential hopelessness has been raised by an apparent malaise within human history itself:

> In the twenty-first century, we are ghosts haunting a futurist dream a century old. Reminded of the brash functionalist lines of "tomorrow's city," the clean Mondrian Formica kitchen surfaces, the sparkling electric railroads, we find that we accelerated by mistake into Gothic mode: Ground Zero at the heart of the world's capital of capital, jittery crack zombies in the skyscraper's shadows, the broken power plants of Iraq, the desolation of much of Africa, the last Space Shuttle hauled off to a museum, global economies a hairsbreadth from disaster.[13]

This hopelessness is compounded by the fact that trauma and horrors problematize how we interpret history due to the effect these have on memory. The horrors people experience have lasting effect in part because hope was threatened. That is, Judith Herman Lewis writes, "The 'very threat of annihilation' that defined the traumatic moment may pursue the survivor long after the danger has passed. ... The terror, rage, and hatred of the traumatic moment live on in the dialectic of trauma."[14]

Memories impede the ability to look forward into our individual and communal history. How we memorialize the past confers different degrees of meaning to it and frames how significant it is for generating as well as anticipating a certain kind of future.[15]

Trauma causes a number of compounding neurobiological and perceptive complications in a person's brain. This is particularly a problem with memory and how people remember events, other people, and themselves.

---

13. Damien Broderick, "Terrible Angels: The Singularity and Science Fiction," *Journal of Consciousness Studies* 19, nos. 1–2 (2012): 20.

14. Judith Lewis Herman, *Trauma and Recovery: From Domestic Abuse to Political Terror* (London: Basic Books, 2001), 50.

15. Duncan Bell, "Introduction: Violence and Memory," *Millennium: Journal of International Studies* 38, no. 2 (2009): 351, 360.

Post-traumatic stress disorder in particular "can be understood as a disorder of memory," write Lauren E. Maltby and Todd W. Hall. The knock-on effects of this for the present are that "memories take the form of habits and gut-level expectations and relational styles and they continue to influence one throughout life." This underscores why perspective is so important to this whole question of trauma and suffering. A large part of this for trauma survivors, and for those who work with them, is to explore and act in concert with how God the Trinity works to overcome the "dissolution of memory systems and ways of knowing," as Maltby and Hall put it, brought about by trauma.[16] Overcoming these memory dysfunctions is part of forming a coherent narrative in which to understand and integrate the experience of horrors and trauma responses. Overcoming these fragmented ways of remembering and being in the present open possibilities for life beyond continually reliving an ongoing horror narrative.

One of the primary steps to break these patterns of thinking and relating is to name horrors for what they are and to avoid confusing God with them. Writing soon after a devastating tsunami, David Bentley Hart stated that it is not God's face seen in such horrors but rather the face of the enemy of life.[17] This differentiation between the God of life and the enemy of life serves to establish trust in God, which hopefully goes some way to reestablishing safety and understanding horrors and trauma in the context of a larger story. These two outcomes of a clearer vision of God may generate hopeful expectations.

Trust: Security in the Character and Power Evident in Jesus' Death and Resurrection

A Christian perspective on hope needs to begin with the fact that God is the living God who pursues our life at the cost of trauma he need not have suffered. Deborah van Deusen Hunsinger writes: "If God in Jesus Christ descends into the worst hell imaginable in order to deliver us from the hells we inflict upon one another, then such a God is worthy of our trust. … in life and in death."[18]

16. Maltby and Hall, "Trauma, Attachment, and Spirituality," 304, 305.

17. David Bentley Hart, *The Doors of the Sea: Where Was God in the Tsunami?* (Grand Rapids: Eerdmans, 2005).

18. Van Deusen Hunsinger, "Bearing the Unbearable," 20.

God is also worthy of our trust because he is the living God who overcame death for human beings. Van Deusen Hunsinger continues: "Jesus Christ is not simply a human companion who comforts us by suffering trauma alongside us. As the creeds of the Church attest, he is known to us as the risen Lord, the very Wisdom and Power of God, through whom God will fulfill his purpose of redemption."[19] Trust in God's character and power are the starting points for reasonable hope because they answer "Yes!" to Joshua Seachris's pointed question: "Is there an intelligible, existentially satisfying narrative in which to locate the experience of pain and suffering and to give the sufferer some solace and hope? Evil in a meaningful universe may not cease from being evil, but it may be more bearable."[20]

One of the temptations faced on the journey to recovery is to take vengeful action. At the other end of the spectrum, giving up and entering a state of numb oblivion is attractive.[21] Both of these responses to the horrific conditions that attend much of individual and corporate human life fail to apprehend their futility and unconstructive nature. They also fail to do anything helpful about the profound mismatch between our great natures as images of God and our ravaged and meager realities.[22]

Safety requires trust, and we have established the safety available in relationship with a loving *and lovable* God. But will God ensure that traumas will not occur again? Will he protect his own people from horror makers and further trauma? When will afflictions in the forms of horrors, trauma, and death end?

Recognizing Those Who Resist the Kingdom

Fear of people shapes how we live in the world. We fear people and their action.

---

19. Van Deusen Hunsinger, "Bearing the Unbearable," 20.

20. Joshua W. Seachris, "Meaning of Life: Contemporary Analytic Perspectives," in *Internet Encyclopedia of Philosophy: A Peer Reviewed Academic Resource*.

21. Van Deusen Hunsinger, "Bearing the Unbearable," 16. Here the author cites Bessel van der Kolk from the dedication in his *Traumatic Stress: The Effects of Overwhelming Experience on Mind, Body, and Society*.

22. Paul Hinkley, *Beloved Community: Critical Dogmatics after Christendom* (Grand Rapids: Eerdmans, 2015), 602. See also Sarah Hinkley Wilson, "Jesus Christ, Horror Defeater," *Lutheran Forum* 47, no. 1 (2013): 2–10.

It is not unreasonable to fear people who resist the kingdom of God. Even those who knew Jesus best in his hometown rejected him and the kingdom of God he proclaimed (Matt 13:53–58). Sadly, at Nazareth, Jesus "did not do many miracles there because of their unbelief" (13:58). The unbelief of people means they missed out on an opportunity for restoration from the consequences of horrors in their lives and communities. Of course, they may have experienced healing by God at a later time, but this delays a qualitatively stronger involvement in pursuing the common good. They would have been more likely (though not guaranteed) to reflect much of God in their relational, creative, and moral capacities had the kingdom come near at that time.

Not all people are helpful in the reestablishment of safety and reconnection to a community in which trauma may be remembered and dealt with healthily (Matt 13:36–43). This point is brought home by Jesus' teaching that some people are evil trees that bring forth evil fruit (7:17–20) and that others are children of the evil one (13:38). Jesus' entirely realistic perspective on the range of people that inhabit this world avoids sentimentality and the false belief that all people are basically safe and intrinsically helpful for restoring others to health. For Jesus, not all people are safe. This is part of reasonable hope because it promotes safety first and prevents against unhealthy attachments in the context of trauma. This is especially important because predators often seek out vulnerable people to abuse, and these are often horror survivors.

However, beyond providing the wisdom to avoid vulnerability to all people, there is a stronger sense in which God will establish safety and life for his children.

Recognizing That There Will Be a Last Day of Horrors

Matthew's perspective on the future is that God has not abandoned human beings, and God will bring about their ultimate good beyond a world full of horrors. This includes overcoming all unrighteous horror makers by God's judgment and then bringing about a new creation. God promises to deal decisively with determined and unrepentant horror makers. Otherwise, in the light of their nonresponsiveness to God, the cosmos may become a macroreflection of the perpetuation of terror.[23]

23. Hutchison and Bleiker, "Emotional Reconciliation," 391.

For millennia, God's people have been holding onto this promise, the kind of everlasting shalom that would include the judgment of their enemies.[24] Two historical facts appreciated through the blessed reading give grounds for Christians to perceive this promise as true: the providential survival of Israel and the vicarious death of Christ.

First is the survival of Israel. Israel was on one hand an "ordinary nation"; however, as T. F. Torrance notes, it "became the means through which God worked out in the midst of the nations a way of reconciliation with himself in which the tensions embedded in man's alienated existence are resolved. ... Israel became the people impregnated with the promise of *shalom* for all humankind."[25]

Second is the representative abandonment of the Christ. Jesus' cry, "My God, my God, why have you abandoned me?" is representative of what awaits horror makers at the great judgment—those who do not know God and do not want to be "peacemakers" who "hunger and thirst for righteousness" as "sons of God" (Matt 5:3–10).

Jesus promised retributive justice and security from unremorseful horror makers upon his return to earth as the King.

> When the Son of man comes in his glory, and all the angels with him, then he will sit on his glorious throne. All the nations will be gathered before him, and he will separate them one from another, just as a shepherd separates the sheep and the goats. He will put the sheep on his right and the goats on his left. ... Then he will also say to those on his left, "Depart from me, you who are cursed, into the eternal fire prepared for the Devil and his angels." (Matt 25:31–33, 41–42)

These people did nothing to help those who were traumatized and needed restorative help; they did nothing to help others in the context of horrors. "You gave me nothing," Jesus will say to them. "I tell you, whatever you did not do for one of the least of these, you did not do for me" (Matt 25:45).

---

24. "Half a decade after 9/11 the spectre of terrorism remains as threatening and elusive as ever. ... Political elites have constituted a world where to be secure means to be cordoning off a safe inside—a sovereign state protected by military means—from a threatening outside." Emma Hutchison and Roland Bleiker, "Emotions in the War on Terror," in *Security and the War on Terror*, eds. Alex J. Bellamy, Roland Bleiker, Sara E. Davies and Richard Devetak (London: Routledge, 2008), 61–62.

25. T. F. Torrance, italics original, cited in Cole, *God the Peacemaker*, 102.

The consequence of this way of being in the world is that "they will go away into eternal punishment" (Matt 25:46). In these cases, these images of God have failed to flourish. These creatures will not reach their fitting, glorious zenith.[26]

Resurrection and Safety

People who are united to God the Father, Spirit, and Son and his life-giving love have nothing to fear with respect to their future in the new heaven and the new earth. A blessed reading of Matthew's Gospel generates the perspective that Jesus' cry "My God, my God, why have you abandoned me?" reflected an experience that he had on behalf of those who deserved exclusion from the kingdom of God. Jesus' perceived absence of God was a substitutionary one, rather than representative.[27] It is not representative of what awaits those who are baptized in the name of the Father, Son, and Spirit, but substitutionary, in order that they may receive the blessing of the kingdom. The return of Christ and his judgment of the nations is therefore a point in time toward which trauma survivors can look forward with great expectations of life, joy, and peace.

The resurrection of Jesus was a concrete event in history. It means that his life, ministry, words, and promises need to be interpreted in the light of that event. The resurrection provides the historical warrant for Christians to also interpret and perceive themselves as those who will be raised from the dead.

Consequently, this objective event provides a new, coherent narrative in which to reframe experiences of horror. It provides a metaphysical justification that disallows a person's subjectivity from being overwhelmed by deathly apprehensions and a deathly future. Christians cannot interpret their physical death as a horrific ending to life. Rather, their death is the beginning of a more intimate fellowship with Christ.[28] The doctrine of eternal life is also critical for reinforcing this point: Paul Griffiths argues

---

26. "Such last things are inglorious; they are indefectible endings-up of creatures that have, for one reason or another, failed to consummate, failed to reach their glory." Paul J. Griffiths, *Decreation: The Last Things of All Creatures* (Waco, TX: Baylor University Press, 2014), 11.

27. Susan Brower-Toland, "William Ockham on the Scope and Limits of Consciousness," *Vivarium* 52 (2014): 200–202.

28. Klaus Schawarzwaeller, "Johann Sebastian Bach: Actus Tragicus: evangelisches Requiem," *Kerygma und Dogma* 61 (2015): 26.

that the doctrine of eternal life means that it "is not open to Christians to say that death, understood as separation of soul from body, is necessarily the last thing of those who undergo it."[29]

Trinitarian renewal of all things and the concrete nature of eternal life in heaven (which I also refer to as the "new heavens and the new earth") reorients the disciple's perspective on the future. Heaven will be a physical place in which garden of Eden–like life will bloom, where God will be honored as he should be, and a place in which disciples will be rewarded by their heavenly Father (Matt 6:1). It will fulfill the promises, which came through God's prophets, of abundant life in a setting of peace, fellowship, and the knowledge of God. This is represented in Isaiah in a great banquet (Isa 25:6–8) in the kingdom of God, where death is no more and the land is enjoyed in shalom by all creatures (Isa 40–66).[30]

Just as the extent of our knowledge of horrors and their origin is limited, so is our understanding of heaven. However, in both cases what we have is sufficient to tell us about the problems that plague us as well as the kind of flourishing future that awaits us. Paul Fiddes captures the relationship between what we have known and what we do not know in the new earth: "We may trust God to remake our relationships with those whom we love, but it will not be just the same, a mere repetition. The adventure moves on into new regions, into deeper interweaving of persons."[31]

The belief in heaven proposes details for the nonhiddenness of God. Belief in a concrete reality called heaven resists both religious skepticism and Schellenberg's skeptical religion. Schellenberg's very vague and skeptical faith in "ultimism" merely offers what "all ... religious propositions can be seen as gesturing toward: that what is deepest in reality (metaphysically ultimate) is also unsurpassably great (axiologically ultimate) and the

29. Griffiths, *Decreation*, 46.

30. Andrew T. Abernethy, *Eating in Isaiah: Approaching the Role of Food and Drink in Isaiah's Structure and Message*, Biblical Interpretation Series 131 (Leiden: Brill, 2014); Abernethy, *The Book of Isaiah and God's Kingdom: A Thematic Theological Approach*, New Studies in Biblical Theology 40 (Downers Grove: IVP Academic, 2016).

31. Paul S. Fiddes, "Acceptance and Resistance in a Theology of Death," *Modern Believing* 56, no. 2 (2015): 235.

source of ultimate good."[32] Note how impersonal this is in contrast to the personalistic Trinitarianism we have been following.

A person who is united to the Trinity in the Son and in the Spirit will ultimately inherit fellowship with the glorified Christ. In the state of glorification, a person will be entirely healed physically, psychologically, relationally, morally, and creatively. A new physicality and psychology at glorification go in tandem with the perfect moral relationality in virtue of being part of Christ's bride, the church. These are the consequence of changes that mean we can be Christlike then in ways that are impeded by disabilities and deterioration in the present. Whereas we may be partly restored as images of God in the process of becoming Christlike, we are limited physically and by death. Paul describes this present tension: "Even though our outer person is being destroyed, our inner person is being renewed day by day" (2 Cor 4:16). On this side of glorification, we cannot expect all these perfections, but we may experience temporary approximations of them.

The whole-person recreation we can anticipate affirms the teleological goodness of God's will and actions. The final outcome of the entire process of each believing person's creation, disorientation through the course of their life, and death and resurrection will lead to full ontological reorientation as an image of God.[33]

The existential and pastoral consequences of the resurrection of Jesus as historical fact and as the expression of God's will are both far-reaching and immediate for believers. For Hildegard of Bingen, for example, the clearly visible actions of Christ in the past provide the basis for trusting that he is present and available to his disciples now: "Christ remains near, both through the sacraments of the Eucharist and confession and through the ardor of faith that brings about good works."[34]

32. J. L. Schellenberg, *The Will to Imagine: A Justification of Skeptical Religion* (Ithaca, NY: Cornell University Press, 2009), xii.

33. Schawarzwaeller, "Johann Sebastian Bach," 27.

34. Beverly Mayne Kienzle, *Hildegard of Bingen and Her Gospel Homilies* (Turnhout, Belgium: Brepols, 2009), 183.

PRESENT EXPERIENCE

The Trinitarian God does not leave his people to find a coherent story and renewed hope that is only based in past historical events and focused on future ideal relationships. He also establishes a present relationship through subjective means: the incarnate Son's empathetic understanding of human beings as well as the Spirit's indwelling presence. The Son's understanding of the human experience of trauma as well as the permanence of his presence, secured by the indwelling Spirit, establish a safe yet vulnerable relationship between God and the trauma survivor, allowing them to participate in a new personal story by healthily reconnecting to God in Jesus. We turn to these aspects now.

Shared Perspective with the Empathetic God

The phenomenon of shared attention and perspective between God and his images is not a one-way street. While God shares his attention with persons through his own perspective, he also attunes himself to human subjective experiences and perspectives. He disposes himself to share (in a limited way) in our consciences for the sake of understanding our perspective. God allows himself to share our experiences. Shared attention between God and people is thus more than intellectual; it is interpersonal and relational.

This is a relational epistemology, which Eleonore Stump describes as including both facts and a second-person perspective.[35] It is subjectively motivated by God's personal nature as the Trinity, and it is a fitting interpersonal goal that people know him and that he be known by people. For this reason, the worst thing a person can hear from God is "I never knew you. Depart form me" (Matt 7:23). God looks for a positive response to Jesus' invitation: "Come to me" (11:28).

Coming to God is helped by the fact that God has intimate personal knowledge of the horrors and the traumas of those made in his image. God's own experience of trauma through the incarnate Son's traumas allows him to empathize with us generally and know what it is like to struggle

35. Eleonore Stump, *Wandering in Darkness: Narrative and the Problem of Suffering* (Oxford: Oxford University Press, 2010); Stump, "Second-Person Accounts and the Problem of Evil," *Revista Portuguesa de Filosofia* 57, no. 4 (2001): 745–71.

as a human "from the inside." In Christ, God has knowledge of horrors and trauma from the perspective of the sufferer. As a wounded person, he perceives his and others' horrors and trauma through his own lived experience. God has experienced the fragmentation and partiality of human condition in the context of trauma and abandonment by other persons.

At the same time, God's Trinitarian nature also gives him person-specific, intimate knowledge of each individual who is personally indwelt by his Holy Spirit. God therefore knows about the particular as well as the general damage done to his own people by horrors.

The double effect of the incarnation of the Son and the indwelling of the Spirit means that God has access to two forms of empathy toward us. There is a form of empathy by which someone else imagines what it is like to be you and in your situation. However, the stronger form of it occurs when another person imagines *their own self* in your situation.[36] Via the incarnation, God can know what it is like to suffer as a human himself—he can have *general empathy* for all humans. In addition to having general empathy for us, the indwelling of the Spirit means that God really may have *specific empathy* for each particular Christian, and therefore knows from the inside what it is like for you to suffer as you do.[37] His knowledge of each indwelt person means that he is able to meet the criteria for empathetically knowing what it is like to suffer what you have suffered. Because of the incarnation of the Son and the indwelling of the Spirit, God has, as Frans de Waal puts it, "the capacity to (a) be affected by and share the emotional state of another, (b) assess the reasons for the other's state, and (c) identify with the other, adopting his or her perspective."[38] God can empathize with human persons with a full-orbed empathy because he is a Trinitarian God.[39] If he were not Trinitarian, he could not have the degree of empathy whereby he is "attuned and responsive to the affective states of those with whom they empathize."[40]

---

36. Ylwa Wirling, "Imagining Oneself Being Someone Else," *Journal of Consciousness Studies* 21, nos. 9–10 (2014): 205–25.

37. Wirling, "Imagining Oneself Being Someone Else," 221.

38. Frans de Waal, cited in Marion Hourdequin, "Empathy, Shared Intentionality, and Motivation by Moral Reasons," *Ethical Theory and Moral Practice* 15, no. 3 (2012): 408.

39. Pseudo-empathy is Coplan's concept. Wirling, "Imagining Oneself Being Someone Else," 223.

40. Hourdequin, "Empathy, Shared Intentionality, and Motivation by Moral Reasons," 409.

God's empathetic knowledge of each person he indwells is very important because it can overcome the difficulties that trauma survivors face when it comes to communicating what happened to them and what they are experiencing presently. "The problem of how to communicate the impact of trauma is considered common to survivors and witnesses," write Emma Hutchison and Roland Bleiker. Survivors and witnesses "tend to find that there are few words to adequately convey what has happened or even how it feels. Words suddenly seem incapable of representing the physical and emotional sensations experienced."[41]

In addition to understanding a person's present situation, God's empathy means he also knows what each person specifically requires in order to recover from horrors. Such therapeutic knowledge includes the negative, person-specific limitations and inhibitions to this process. Divine empathy of this kind means that God's therapeutic relationship to his images is person specific. In addition, as his providential power demonstrates, he may bring about restorative relationships between people that are perfectly appropriate to the posttraumatic needs of each individual or community. These may be surprising and not what people may initially expect, because part of healthily overcoming trauma involves breaking with some patterns of life that may have directly or indirectly fueled or perpetuated the underlying reasons for the traumatic events.[42] This helps to explain some of the frustration that people often feel with God when life does not return to its past state in the aftermath of traumatic events. God may be bringing about something new and better. This does not mean that God does not care; rather, it is evidence that he is the living God who works to bring full and concrete life even through traumatic situations.

Jesus the Safe Person and Relational Starting Point

Traumatized persons are often isolated, afraid, and relationally unable to make new friendships or to reengage with older relationships. This is because, as Lewis Herman writes, their "capacity for intimacy is compromised by intense and contradictory feelings of need and fear."[43] Jesus

41. Hutchison and Bleiker, "Emotional Reconciliation," 388.
42. Hutchison and Bleiker, "Emotional Reconciliation," 388–90.
43. Lewis Herman, *Trauma and Recovery*, 56.

provides corrective attachment experience for trauma survivors.[44] It is a relationship with him that over time shapes the survivor's perception on how to attach and relate to other people. This parallels what occurs within the therapeutic relationship with a therapist, in which a positive attachment renews a person's understanding of relationships, which in turn "will also extend into their relationship with God," as Maltby and Hall put it.[45] Jesus offers a relationship to himself as the starting point for trauma survivors to reengage with other people. Through him, the empathetic Trinitarian God is available by the Spirit to provide at least one real and healthy relationship for each traumatized person.

In Jesus, God offers himself to others as a person who is trustworthy. Jesus is a man who understands the depth of what happens in the hands of horrors and trauma: how overwhelming, disorientating, and limiting these experiences are, as well as what is required in order for recovery to occur. Jesus will not reject the traumatized person for the reasons others will, such as clinginess or evasive behaviors. Shame is particularly problematic for the trauma sufferer because it "reveals our inability to be solitary, isolated, atomic or disconnected," as Aislinn O'Donnell puts it, yet at the same drives home that we are often isolated in the wake of trauma.[46] Jesus' open empathy and intimate knowledge of the situation of those he indwells by his Spirit means that those who connect with him by faith and his Spirit may begin to overcome some of the isolation and the shame.[47]

Jesus is also a very safe person in whom to trust. As the human image of God par excellence, Jesus offers a relational starting point for reconnecting other images of God back to God, because Jesus is *the* righteous human person. He will always act in the right way for the right outcomes for God and human beings. He is always faithful to God and his mission to save people from horrors. This means he will act rightly with respect to a person's relational, moral, and creative capacities.

44. This relationship is often provided by attachment-theory clinicians. Maltby and Hall, "Trauma, Attachment, and Spirituality," 307.

45. Maltby and Hall, "Trauma, Attachment, and Spirituality," 307.

46. Aislinn O'Donnell, "Shame Is Already a Revolution: The Politics of Affect in the Thought of Deleuze," *Deleuze Studies* 11, no. 1 (2017): 7.

47. Lewis Herman, *Trauma and Recovery*, 133.

The righteousness of Christ becomes very clear in the series of temptations that the devil lays before him during his forty days in the wilderness. Jesus discloses that he really is worthy to be called the "Son of God," because he is faithful toward his mission, which requires being the perfect image of God. He is the image of God who can be trusted because of his nature and actions.

It is unsurprising that the persons who are most attracted to him are those who tend to suffer most from the anxieties that plague us: in the Gospel narratives, stories about vulnerable children, women, and men abound. In Jesus, God provides the first personal port in the rehabilitation of the relational aspect of being an image of God. As the ultimate image of God, Jesus is the one trustworthy image with whom other images should desire to connect relationally and intimately. Restoration via relationship with him is the best place to start the process of relating intimately with other human persons and trusting other human persons. A safe attachment to Jesus is the first step to healthy attachment to others and integration into communities, which is a vital part of the recovery process.

A common fear among trauma survivors is that attachments to other people are not safe, and therefore they do not have a stable web of relationships in which to healthily develop as persons. The invisible reality of union with God via the Spirit is critical at this point because the metaphysical reality of this union is the life of God himself. The life of God himself means that Christ unites survivors to himself via the Spirit, which is a union that cannot be broken or undone.

For this reason, Jesus promises his disciples, "I am with you always, to the end of the age" (Matt 28:20). Jesus remains with his disciples post-ascension. This works in tandem with Jesus' substitutionary suffering on the cross (27:46) and resurrection. His dying and rising means that a horror survivor who has faith in him need never fear that they will be rejected by God, even if their coping behaviors after trauma (such as addiction) may be less than ideal or even personally damaging.

REORIENTING NARRATIVE: DIFFERENTIATING TRAGEDY FROM PERPETUAL TRAUMA

In Paul's words, the atonement and union with Christ via the Spirit mean that a new life that is strongly discontinuous with the older one is possible for trauma survivors: "I no longer live, but Christ lives in me. The life I now live in the body, I live by faith in the Son of God, who loved me and gave himself for me" (Gal 2:20). In the light of this, a person may include their story in the larger story of what God is doing in the world. This is the first step in recovery from trauma: developing a personal trauma narrative.[48]

Confidence in God's character and his works of renewal is an important step toward living well in the aftermath of trauma. God's providential preservation of Abraham's descendants, his incarnation in Jesus, the resurrection, and promises for the future place our present personal and communal trauma within a larger story that enables meaning making to arise. This is called a trauma narrative.

A trauma narrative recounts the trauma within the frame of a larger (positive) worldview. Consequently, the interpretation of life in view of trauma does not *necessarily* have to conclude with toxic beliefs such as mistrusting and questioning the dignity and agency of the self or others.[49] Because the providential care of Israel, the incarnation, and the resurrection are historically verifiable events, reframing trauma within the Christian worldview and story arc has strong metaphysical grounding. This kind of reframing of trauma is not wishful thinking.

A Trinitarian reorientation does not abandon the memories of horrors and trauma. It remembers them, and remembers them well, yet within a framework of "tragedy" rather than "horrors." Horror and tragedy have been explored at length in Western literature. Such a sustained engagement has made it apparent that they are not equivalent but may be differentiated from each other. A Trinitarian reading of Matthew's Gospel provides the reader with some sense of reorientation in the context of the disorientations that are brought about by horrors and trauma.[50]

48. Lewis Herman, *Trauma and Recovery*, 133.

49. Christopher G. Frechette and Elizabeth Boase, "Defining 'Trauma' as a Useful Lens for Biblical Interpretation," in *Bible through the Lens of Trauma*, ed. Elizabeth Boase and Christopher G. Frechette (Atlanta: SBL Press, 2016), 6.

50. I am drawing on Bruggemann's use of orientation, disorientation, and new orientation as paradigms by which to understand a spirituality that attempts to hold onto God in the light of terror and trauma. Walter Brueggemann, *Spirituality of the Psalms* (Minneapolis: Fortress, 2002).

Tragedy as a Genre for Life

Horrific events and trauma, and their effects, do not have to have the last say. Distinguishing tragedies from horrors is helpful for focusing on what makes horrors so horrible. In genre terms, a tragedy is a story like a horror story, but it does not have the same ending as a horror story.[51]

Horrors and horror stories are events and experiences that are inconsistent with the created purpose of images of God for participation in God's shalom. Horror stories traumatize people, and their narrative arcs suggest that there is no future other than one that includes further horrors and additional trauma. Added to this, it is important to note that horror stories do not remain in the realm of reality.[52]

In contrast, a tragedy is a story set in reality of human rubble. Tragedies often provide a sense of hope and resolution because there may be a "way out of the cycle of revenge which seizes creator and creation," writes Curtis Smith. Tragedy may also provide a way for overcoming discord on the human level: the genre of tragedy offers the possibility of overcoming human-to-human alienation, isolation, and discrimination. There may be hope of recovering the "dignity," "majesty," or "transcendent order" that was once lost.[53]

It can be argued from the Christian worldview that human life can be seen in the genre of a tragic narrative arc, in which narrative has an "emphasis on violence during its first half, replaced with heroic drama, with its stylized conflict of love and honour, during the second half."[54] Historical disclosures of God establish this unquestionable direction for interpreting the story of God's life with human persons. These include the actions of God such as his providential power to bring about and maintain life in the context of death, the incarnation, the passion, resurrection, and ascension

51. Curtis C. Smith, "Horror Versus Tragedy: Mary Shelley's *Frankenstein* and Olaf Stapledon's *Sirius*," *Extrapolation* 26, no. 1 (1985): 72.

52. For example, this plays out in the contrast between Shelley's *Frankenstein* and Stapledon's *Sirius* as follows: "Shelley first conceived her story as in a 'waking dream' (Introduction), and all of *Frankenstein* has the unreality and exaggeration of dream. The mode of Sirius, by contrast, is realism. Sirius is no vampire." Smith, "Horror versus Tragedy," 72.

53. Smith, "Horror versus Tragedy," 72–73. For recent work on the interface between tragedy and theology see Kevin Taylor and Giles Waller, eds., *Christian Theology and Tragedy: Theologians, Tragic Literature, and Tragic Theory* (Burlington, VT: Ashgate, 2011).

54. William Holman and C. Hugh Harmon, "Tragedy," in *A Handbook to Literature*, ed. Harmon and Holman (Upper Saddle River, NJ: Prentice Hall, 1996), 521–23.

of the Son, together with the subjectively oriented works of God such as uniting people to himself and each other through the Spirit in anticipation of a future of "light." Therefore, the human story has a tragic form, though it needs to be interpreted in the light and ontology of Matthew's Trinitarian magical realism.[55] In this tragic context, there is room to act hopefully, meaningfully, and with integrity. Perhaps we can hazard to say that, from the perspective of our ultimate state, human beings experience horrible tragedies rather than permanent horrors per se.

The Emotions of Tragedy: Relocating Anger and Resentment

Recovering a narrative that embraces tragedy rather than horror as its narrative arc allows trauma sufferers to process their emotions and make sense of their stories in a coherent way.

What to do with anger and resentment before the final judgment and rejection of horrors and horror makers? How will God build a better future for human beings without dealing with the anger and fear that have been generated by horrors and trauma? The emotional life of early Christians was affected by their eschatological beliefs, including grief.[56] Trauma scholars have noted that fear and anger need to be recognized, for the reason that "when fear and anger remain unacknowledged and unaddressed, they can easily recreate a culture of anxiety and resentment."[57]

However, the recognition of fear and anger for what they are and what they may generate "brings them into the public sphere, and in so doing incorporates them into processes that aim to placate feelings of revenge and create a culture of healing and collaboration," as Hutchison and Bleiker write.[58] This is an important part of developing a personal narrative that makes sense of trauma; it also allows the expression of anger and fear to mature into different emotions when located in a longer-term view of a

55. Christopher Warnes, *Magical Realism and the Postcolonial Novel: Between Faith and Irreverence* (Basingstoke, Hampshire, UK: Palgrave Macmillan, 2009).

56. Stephen C. Barton, "Eschatology and the Emotions in Early Christianity," *Journal of Biblical Literature* 130, no. 3 (2011): 571–91.

57. Hutchison and Bleiker, "Emotional Reconciliation," 391.

58. Hutchison and Bleiker, "Emotional Reconciliation," 391.

person's life.[59] These emotions are more healthily incorporated into a life story and forward-looking life when they are reconstituted as grief.[60] This does not mean falling into sentimentality or antirealism, as there is a strong sense of grief, which is "grief for oneself."[61] This is more likely to prevent retaliation over past hurts and stop cycles of interpersonal aggression.[62]

Perspective is the key here: a Christian orientation may helpfully drive a primarily forward-looking perspective on the process of recovery and prospects for living with reasonable hope, rather than having a backward-looking perspective that stymies action.[63] This forward-looking perspective is in line with belonging in the present to the Father's kingdom, living in a time in which we may produce fruit in the lives of others (Matt 13:23), with the ultimate goal and expectation to "shine like the sun in their Father's kingdom" (13:43).

Integrity and Identity

The promise of shining like the sun in our Father's kingdom (Matt 13:43) suggests that people can have hope for a restored sense of personhood. Integrity entails coming to terms with who we are, as both trauma survivors and trauma inflictors. Self-perception occurs in tandem with God's incisive gaze or perspective that knows who we are as heirs of his kingdom of light.[64] In the context of trauma, God's gaze means that "neither what we do nor what we suffer defines us at the deepest level. Though the way we think of and treat ourselves and the way others think of and treat us does shape our identity, no human being can make or unmake us," writes Miroslav Volf. God's relationship to us is central to perceiving ourselves with integrity. Volf continues: "Instead of being defined by how human beings relate to us, we are defined by how *God* relates to us. We know that

59. Martha Craven Nussbaum, *Anger and Forgiveness: Resentment, Generosity, Justice* (Oxford: Oxford University Press, 2016), 93.

60. Nussbaum, *Anger and Forgiveness*, 105.

61. This comes especially to the fore as a person approaches death. Fiddes, "Acceptance and Resistance in a Theology of Death," 225.

62. Nussbaum, *Anger and Forgiveness*, 105.

63. Nussbaum, *Anger and Forgiveness*, 93.

64. Sigurdson, *Heavenly Bodies*.

fundamentally we are who we are ... because God loves us."[65] Thanks to the will and work of the Father, Son, and Spirit, people may employ new degrees of their creative and moral agency so that they may relate well to others.[66]

Memory and Eucharistic Remembrance

The healthy acceptance of tragedy within a blessed narrative is facilitated by a number of rituals. The Lord's Supper is an example of a ritual that is an avenue to a renewed point of view and grasp on the world. Elizabeth O'Donnell Gandolfo proposes that the Christian faith has far more than a future free from pain and sorrow to offer to those who have suffered. Her starting point echoes the Lord's Supper. "One of the defining characteristics of the Christian faith," she writes, "is the remembrance of suffering." However, Christian remembrance occurs in a particular perspective: suffering remembered in organic connection with hope, restoration, and a future promise of freedom from death and pain. Thus, Gandolfo writes that best-practice remembrance "reveals that hope in the memory of suffering does not arise simply and only from the pledge to make things right (though this pledge has hopeful effects, to be sure). Rather, there is something about the memory of suffering, *in and of itself*, which can produce hope."[67]

Gandolfo then proposes four results of suffering that are important for defining personal and corporate remembrance of suffering as an apologetic for hope. These are "interruption, identity, imagination and inspiration for action which this memory produces." With these four factors in place, these memories can "form and transform" Christians, even those who have been oblivious or shielded from the suffering of others. "Christians ... can be formed and transformed into a people of hope—moving from selfishness to freedom, from isolation to solidarity, and from fear to courageous confidence in the possibility of constructing a more just

65. Miroslav Volf, cited in Elizabeth O'Donnell Gandolfo, "Remembering the Massacre at El Mozote: A Case for the Dangerous Memory of Suffering as Christian Formation in Hope," *International Journal of Practical Theology* 17, no. 1 (2013): 76–77.

66. Gandolfo, "Remembering the Massacre at El Mozote," 77.

67. Gandolfo, "Remembering the Massacre at El Mozote," 63, italics original.

and peaceful world. It is from this memory of suffering that hope for this other world is born."[68]

As we will see in the following chapter, if God's presence, will, power to change, and perspective are offered by other helpful members of his kingdom, then the practical expression of this worldview and story has the possibility not only of qualifying horrors, but of giving the reframed trauma narrative substance. The trauma narrative will have substance because, by a number of means that include his images, God will actually restore and bring to new life the relational, moral, and creative aspects of human persons. This will hopefully place our lives in a context that supports "a sense of order, identity, agency, well-being, and solidarity, while also expressing the impossibility of fully comprehending the trauma. It is precisely the capacity to preserve such paradoxes that prevents a trauma narrative from slipping into banality."[69] Successful Christian trauma narratives affirm that "change is possible, and that light can enter places where there was only darkness."[70]

68. Gandolfo, "Remembering the Massacre at El Mozote," 87.
69. Frechette and Boase, "Defining 'Trauma' as a Useful Lens for Biblical Interpretation," 6.
70. Maltby and Hall, "Trauma, Attachment, and Spirituality," 310.

11

RECOVERING COMMUNITY

Reestablishing Meaning

This chapter describes how meaning and meaningful living are found in the context of the kingdom of God. This is the sphere of the living and loving care and actions of God, via the teaching of Jesus and the lives of other believers. In this context, believers may experience a profound transformation that leaves behind some of the enduring impact and consequences of trauma. New, meaningful attachments arise. These transformations include a new self-understanding, a new way of receiving morally pure relationships, and relating to others in ethically pure and creative ways. Meaning is implicitly and explicitly perceived in the process of participation in these news ways of being in the world. This offers a lived response to the question of living meaningfully in the aftermath of trauma.[1]

God offers people a meaningful life despite the presence of horrors and trauma in their lives. In the context of the kingdom of God, Jesus' disciples can represent him and his care to one another. God deputizes his images in order to make his character and engagement with a suffering world visible and available. The representation of God's kind face also serves as part of the restorative process for a person's relational, moral, and creative aspects. Representing it to others, as well as having it represented to us, play roles in this. In addition to God's visible mediation through the presence, prayer, and actions of his people, he also works invisibly though his Spirit.

1. It is a phenomenological disclosure of what is the case. It includes unconscious as well as conscious aspects.

A NEW CONTEXT

A religious transformation is defined as a drastic shift in religious attitudes and practices, which includes qualitative changes such as "a major shift toward sacred goals, values, and meanings, as well as the cognitive, behavioral, and social pathways that people follow to realize these goals."[2] Jesus called people to have a major religious transformation. Jesus' preaching was focused on religious attachment to God and God's life-giving transformation of people. The kingdom of heaven is the sphere in which people participate in a number of modes of knowing God's life-giving love, which leads to religious and personal transformation.

Christian trauma survivors are often haunted by the sense that they are not lovable by God: they do not merit it or are not worthy of it at all. This creates a "disconnection between [their] explicit and implicit knowledge of God," according to Lauren Maltby and Todd Hall.[3] Jesus' message of the kingdom of God is an announcement of love on God's behalf toward people. God is like the mother hen who seeks to gather the chicks into his arms (Matt 23:37); he is a Father in heaven who is good and wants to be generous toward his children (7:11). There are many modes of experiencing God's love: direct and indirect as well as visible and invisible ones. For example, actions and rituals that reflect God's love to others are ways in which believers come to experientially know what it is like to love and be loved. These all contribute to religious transformation (Matt 22:37–39; 26:17–30).

A Christian religious transformation in the context of trauma means that beliefs become, according to Neal Krause, Kenneth Pargament, and Gail Ironson, "more vibrant." This often includes positive coping mechanisms because Christian religious transformations "are associated with a number of psychosocial resources including a greater sense of meaning in life, a stronger sense of self-worth, greater optimism, and stronger social relationships with like-minded religious others; when coupled with the emotion and sense of commitment that are often part of the transformation

---

2. Neal Krause, Kenneth I. Pargament, and Gail Ironson, "Does a Religious Transformation Buffer the Effects of Lifetime Trauma on Happiness?," *International Journal for the Psychology of Religion* 27, no. 2 (2017): 105.

3. Lauren E. Maltby and Todd W. Hall, "Trauma, Attachment, and Spirituality: A Case Study," *Journal of Psychology and Theology* 40, no. 4 (2012): 307.

process, these changes suggest that religious transformations may be a potentially important coping resource."[4]

For this reason, religious transformation stops and reverses the correlation between trauma and a dampened degree of lifetime happiness. Researchers believe that the root reason for this may be that people who have had a religious transformation may have positive beliefs about God, such as him being a loving being.[5] These changes occur as a result of God's Spirit working to change a person's receptivity to him. This may often involve overcoming implicit, rather than explicit, resistance to accepting his love, which may arise from trauma.[6]

The kingdom of God's living and loving will is the invisible sphere where God is particularly and powerfully at work to bring life and light into people's lives. This is why it is also referred to as the kingdom of the Father of light, the living God (Matt 13:43; 16:16–17). He brings about a slow process of change to the end that believers will "shine like the sun in their Father's kingdom." This requires molding a person's perspectives to God. Despite resistance toward God, out of anger over trauma, for example, believers can come to attach themselves to him, and this will become a faithful allegiance marked by being humble and willing to learn like a child (Matt 13:43; 18:1–3). People can enter into the kingdom of the Father at the same time as they develop in faith, repent, and forgive others (18:21–35).

A NEW IDENTITY

God gives all his people a new identity that reflects their meaningfulness to him. God's perspective on a person is reflected in the kinds of words to describe those who are part of his people who strive for shalom. They are called the "heirs" to the kingdom and "sons" or children of God, those who will see God (Matt 5:3–10).

Disciples are called "sons of God" because they will reflect God's character to the world (Matt 5:9). The idea of sonship is not a gendered idea in this instance but rather speaks to the kind of character these people reflect. "Sons of" here is used to point out a certain kind of person rather

4. Krause et al., "Does a Religious Transformation," 112.

5. Krause et al., "Does a Religious Transformation," 112, 105.

6. Maltby and Hall, "Trauma, Attachment, and Spirituality."

than their gender. Sons of God belong to God, have their fate in his hands, and are mentored so as to reflect his character. In other words, "sons of" language is offspring language that refers to character matches between nonbiologically related "parents" and "children." Eli's sons are examples of the concept of "sonship" referring to what a person's character reflects and who their shaping influences were. Though biologically Eli's sons, the Hebrew texts describes them literally as "sons of Belial" (1 Sam 2:12). Sadly, Eli's sons are given this descriptor—meaning sons of foolishness or wickedness—due to their behavior and its effects on the worship of God and on God's people.[7] More positively, all those who seek God and act like him are "sons of God," regardless of being biologically male or female. Jesus' own sonship of God in part refers to his own reflection of God's character. A strong sense of identity that is grounded in God's own perspective drives his self-understanding and mission. At his baptism Jesus receives his identity as the Son and also God's own perspective on himself: "This is my Son, whom I love; with him I am well pleased" (Matt 3:17). The loving approval and specific identity conferred on him was affirmed by both a voice from heaven and the descent of the Spirit on him (3:16–17).

Every Christian also receives a new loving and affirming identity from God. The Father, Son, and Spirit view the believer as a "disciple" who has been baptized in the name of, or character of, the Father, Son, and Holy Spirit (Matt 28:19).

New life with God frees believers from being identified with the horrors they have committed. God offers all people a fresh start by way of a powerful break with their past identity. This is very important for all people because we have all—directly or indirectly, passively or actively—contributed to the trauma of others. One profound area of discontinuity with Jesus' baptism is that he was righteous before baptism, to the point that John tried to stop his baptism (Matt 3:14–15). Disciples of Jesus, however, are those who previously were sick and who need healing. They need a

7. "The designation 'wicked men' (lit., 'sons of Belial') in these opening chapters ... refers to cultic abuses, that is, a lack of regard for the proper worship of Yahweh." Bill T. Arnold, *1 & 2 Samuel* (Grand Rapids: Zondervan, 2003), 71. David W. Baker, "God, Names Of," in *Dictionary of the Old Testament: Pentateuch*, ed. T. Desmond Alexander and David W. Baker (Downers Grove, IL: InterVarsity, 2003), 359–68. See also Deut 13:13; Chrys C. Caragounis, "בֵּן (1201)," in *New International Dictionary of Old Testament Theology and Exegesis*, ed. Willem A. VanGemeren, 5 vols. (Grand Rapids: Zondervan, 1997), 1:671–77.

doctor in order to become merciful humans rather than horror makers and traumatizers of others (9:11–13). For this reason, their baptism includes the forgiveness of sins, the reception of the Spirit, and participation in Jesus' death, burial, and resurrection (Acts 2:38; Rom 6:3–11).

There have been a number of recent examples of owning this new identity at the same time as accepting the reality of suffering and its long-term consequences. Diverse and inspiring authors have written about living with a Christian identity in the context of both profound suffering and God's renewing perspective. One of these is Kathryn Greene-McCreight's biographical *Darkness Is My Only Companion: A Christian Response to Mental Illness*.[8] This book is a direct outcome of her struggles with bipolar disorder. Greene-McCreight's personal openness is a fruitful and arresting addition to pastoral theology. Whereas most writers in the field of trauma studies tend to describe and explore the profound struggles of others rather than their own, Greene-McCreight's narrative establishes the person-to-person interest and attention that is so important to recovery from trauma.[9] However, her work resonates with, and is consistent with, a number of key emphases in trauma studies.[10]

Todd Billings's book *Rejoicing in Lament* involves meditations on Scripture from the perspective of the sufferer. Billings writes in a similar manner to Greene-McCreight, yet differs in a number of ways that include his gender and the physical (rather than psychological) basis of his suffering. The achievement of this book is that he is able to articulate his subjective identity in a personalist manner that presumes both a direct mind-to-mind relationship with God and a mediated face-to-face relationship with God through people past and present as well as through sacred texts. How a person or a community remembers trauma is one of

8. Kathryn Greene-McCreight, *Darkness Is My Only Companion: A Christian Response to Mental Illness* (Grand Rapids: Brazos, 2006).

9. I know that this does not mean that most authors in the field of trauma studies have not suffered and been traumatized deeply. In private conversations it has become increasingly clear that this area of study tends to draws those who are "wounded healers." Henri Nouwen, *The Wounded Healer: Ministry in Contemporary Society* (Garden City, NY: Doubleday, 1972).

10. Kathryn Greene-McCreight, *Feminist Reconstructions of Christian Doctrine: Narrative Analysis and Appraisal* (New York: Oxford University Press, 2000). See also Susan Brison, *Aftermath: Violence and the Remaking of the Self* (Princeton, NJ: Princeton University Press, 2002).

the keys to self-understanding that is realistic about both trauma and the perspective of God.

Forgiveness

God is not shocked nor stumped by our own horror making. He does not have a trauma response but can act for the sake of life without rejecting the horror maker. This is shown in the scene in which one of the disciples "reached out his hand and drew his sword. He struck the high priest's servant and cut off his ear" (Matt 26:51). Jesus rebukes the disciple and then heals the man who has been injured (Matt 26:52–54; Luke 22:51). Jesus does not end his relationship with the disciple who does this; rather, he restores him despite even greater sins (John 21:15–25). An important part of this is forgiveness.

Forgiveness is declarative; it announces a state of affairs. It is not gradual but is declared to be the case or not to be the case. God declares that ungodly people who have faith in his work in Christ are justified, or in a right relationship with him, because their sins are forgiven. The fellowship that God creates between himself and the justified person is based upon God's gracious action of forgiveness that stems from his perspective on a person. This is not an arbitrary perspective but is based on the forgiveness and righteousness available to people in light of the crucifixion of Jesus. It is the reality on which a person's new identity is predicated. Past trauma and horrors committed are no longer the primary determiners of who a person is. These actions are considered actions of the past, not a person's present identity, nor a predictor of their future behavior. For the Christian, identity is based in God, his justifying action, and his inclusion of the justified person in the larger company of the "made-just-by-God," as Christiane Tietz terms it.[11]

Therefore, a human person does not need to manufacture or create a new identity or history for him- or herself in order to be right with God. People do not need to, nor can they, meaningfully reinvent themselves in God's eyes. Nor is identity equal to the trauma and negative coping strategies that result from the misdeeds of others. Rather, the entirety of who

11. Christiane Tietz, "Personale Identität und Selbstannahme," *Kerygma und Dogma* 61 (2015): 9, 7.

a person is, including all their history and their faults and strengths, is drawn into their new identity through righteousness in God's eyes and embrace by the Son and the Spirit.

Thus justification is a release from the individual and cumulative force of our misdeeds, while keeping our identity as unique persons with unique stories. God preserves our particularity as a person, yet he allows us to live beyond the condemnation that would arise from identifying us with our deeds.[12] This is not to say that the trauma survivor will not have to struggle through a very long process of recovery in which trauma may be manifested in a number of negative coping behaviors. Trauma is complex and entails ongoing brokenness, which is precisely why we need to be reminded that *every day and all day* our starting point is the profound assurance that we are accepted by and special to God.

The grace of God and its transforming power shine most brightly in the context of relationships that need to deal with one another's brokenness and sinfulness. Our ongoing sinfulness and the continual need for the grace of God and the grace of others drives home the depths of recovery from sin and trauma and the (frightening) need for one another and God's grace. Dietrich Bonhoeffer describes the unique possibilities of grace within Christian fellowship:

> Those who confess their sins in the presence of another Christian know that they are no longer alone with themselves; they experience the presence of God in the reality of the other. As long as I am by myself when I confess my sins, everything remains in the dark; but when I come face to face with another Christian, sin has to be brought to light. ... It is grace that we can confess our sins to one another.[13]

God's mercy will be reflected to various degrees in the lives of his images. It is a transformative love that cooperates with Christians who seek renewal. Cooperation between human love and divine love in the life of a person may possibly lead to the development of compassion and care toward other persons. Bonhoeffer writes: "It is God's own undertaking to

---

12. Tietz, "Personale Identität und Selbstannahme," 7.

13. Dietrich Bonhoeffer, *Works*, vol. 5, ed. Geffrey B. Kelly (Minneapolis: Fortress, 1996), 29.

teach such love. All that human beings can add is to remember this divine instruction and the exhortation to excel in it more and more. When God had mercy on us, when God revealed Jesus Christ to us and to our brother, when God won our hearts by God's own love, our instruction in Christian love began at the same time." Mercy for one another is shaped by forgiveness: "When God was merciful to us, we learned to be merciful with one another. When we received forgiveness instead of judgment, we too were made ready to forgive one another." Jesus' impact on the believer is the source of the close nature of Christian relationships and the Christlike manner in which they are carried out: "One is a brother or sister to another only through Jesus Christ. I am a brother or sister to another person through what Jesus Christ has done for me and to me."[14]

Therefore, God can change every horror maker in the world, including you and me and our communities. We can be freed from the tendency to traumatize and brutalize others, and from the guilt before God we incur for doing so. God's mercy can reach even the deepest and darkest aspects of who we are as people; there is no area of our lives that cannot be renovated by the power of Trinitarian grace. This means that Christians can grow, change, and become Christlike. Even very difficult Christian relationships can be handled appropriately in the context of costly grace. Bonhoeffer writes:

> As Christ bears our burdens, so ought we to bear the burdens of our fellow-men. The law of Christ, which it is our duty to fulfil, is the bearing of the cross. My brother's burden which I must bear is not only his outward lot, his natural characteristics and gifts, but quite literally his sin. And the only way to bear that sin is by forgiving it in the power of the cross of Christ in which I now share. Thus, the call to follow Christ always means a call to share the work of forgiving men their sins. Forgiveness is the Christlike suffering which it is the Christian's duty to bear.[15]

God's costly grace also has significant implications for the church's ministry priorities. The church only reflects God's will when it reminds its

14. Bonhoeffer, *Works*, 5:34.
15. Dietrich Bonhoeffer, *The Cost of Discipleship* (London: SCM, 2001), 45.

people of both the availability of grace and the need for continual repentance. Bonhoeffer writes that Jesus

> held that the only way to safeguard the gospel of forgiveness was by preaching repentance. If the Church refuses to face the stern reality of sin, it will gain no credence when it talks of forgiveness. Such a Church sins against its sacred trust and walks unworthily of the gospel. It is an unholy Church, squandering the precious treasure of the Lord's forgiveness.[16]

The treasure of forgiveness, which is essential for a sense of safety and for renewing the relational and moral aspects of ourselves as people made in God's image, is available from God. God cares about human repair and ending the deep-seated tendencies that perpetuate horrors and traumas in the world.

Spirit

The revelation of what true human persons look like via the incarnation, along with God's forgiveness of sins and welcoming into his kingdom, reveal that a new start is possible for human beings. By his Spirit, God affirms the potential for each person to live up to their nature as an image of God. The gift of the Spirit is the gift of God's power, which liberates and reorients people from trending toward death to trending toward fullness of life in the new heavens and new earth.[17]

The Spirit reestablishes the capacity within those made in God's image to relate to their Creator. The personal presence of God in his Spirit means that persons do not *necessarily* have to remain as victims and perpetrators of horrors. All persons may be vehicles of God's revelation and works in the world that he originally created to be coruled by his images. This means

16. Bonhoeffer, *Cost of Discipleship*, 219.

17. St. Augustine's *On the Trinity* focuses on the relationship between the Trinity and the images of God. Matthew Levering summarizes it as a work that "seeks to understand and to model what Christian life is all about. For Christians, the ascent to participation in God begins now: through the grace of the Holy Spirit, in faith and love, we are being conformed to the image of Jesus Christ, perfect wisdom and perfect love." Levering, *The Theology of Augustine: An Introductory Guide to His Most Important Works* (Grand Rapids: Baker Academic, 2013), 153.

that there is more to the basic human nature than the desire to impose our will on each other, which is what Nietzsche's *Wille zur Macht* claimed.

The Spirit also regenerates the creative capacities of each image. The ethical purity of the holy and living God directs this transformation so that the creative capacities of human beings may now lead to building life-giving cultures on earth.[18]

If the Spirit is at work in the lives of Christians, then particular communities of faith may move toward fullness. Trauma survivors do not have to treat all persons with extreme suspicion. This is because it may be the case that some people will not willfully (and pleasurably) victimize others because God is transforming them into people who do not inflict trauma on others. Those led by the Spirit will hopefully be less likely to overpower and impose their will and power on others.[19] At the same time, the Christian community may become more discerning with respect to perpetrators and survivors alike. We can suggest that new and powerful experiences of vulnerability, care, and trust may erode egotistic self-assertion, ultimately substituting it with loving care for others. The extension of this is the possibility of living a meaningful life that mediates God's presence, will, power to change, and perspective to other people, for the sake of their well-being. These enable the safety, sense-making story, and community reconnection required for recovery from trauma.[20]

Moral-perceptual transformation by the power of the Spirit also applies to Christian institutions. Though traumatic horrors such as sexual abuse have plagued many churches, there is room for hope. The disclosure of God's life-bringing culture in the world by the Spirit means that not all

18. John Paul II, *The Gospel of Life = Evangelium vitae* (New York: Random House Large Print in association with Times Books, 1995).

19. Friedrich W. Nietzsche, *The Gay Science* (Mineola, NY: Dover, 2006); Julian Young, *Friedrich Nietzsche: A Philosophical Biography* (Cambridge: Cambridge University Press, 2010); Nietzsche and Peter Fritzsche, *Nietzsche and the Death of God: Selected Writings* (Boston: Bedford/St. Martin, 2007).

20. Judith Lewis Herman writes, "Recovery unfolds in three stages. The central task of the first stage is the establishment of safety. The central task of the second stage is remembrance and mourning. The central task of the third stage is reconnection with ordinary life." She wisely adds: "Like any abstract concept, these stages of recovery are a convenient fiction, not to be taken too literally. They are an attempt to impose simplicity and order upon a process inherently turbulent and complex. But the same basic concept of recovery stages has emerged repeatedly." Judith Lewis Herman, *Trauma and Recovery: From Domestic Abuse to Political Terror* (London: Basic Books, 2001), 155.

human institutions must necessarily be treated with suspicion. For example, the historical community that generated Matthew's Gospel was probably not motivated by a drive to imprison others and treat them as objects.[21] I believe it was a safe and restorative community whose written record offers that possibility to its blessed readers.

Baptism

Baptism initiates people into a new identity: it breaks the old stories of who we are in the "devastation." Baptism allows for a new start and for the ongoing self-understanding that allows a lifelong narrative of grace in action. Baptismal practices have accented the dramatic nature of a new identity throughout Christian history by taking this action very seriously, as represented by periods of preparation and elaborate rituals.[22] Oils and water have symbolized the healing aspects of baptism, new identity, and incorporation into a new community of life.[23]

The frescoes and baptistery of the oldest surviving Christian house church at Dura-Europos reflect this new identity.[24] Built and decorated around AD 235, the baptistery was the site of the baptismal initiation ritual by means of water baptism. The room is decorated with frescoes centered on Jesus' uniqueness and thematically arranged to point to ideas of new life and God's care. The central feature of the baptistery was a pool of water in which people were baptized, which symbolized washing and cleansing by the Spirit (1 Cor 6:11). The central fresco above the pool of water where people were baptized is an image of the Good Shepherd holding a sheep on his shoulders. At the lower left of the image there is a picture of Adam and Eve in the idyllic garden of Eden. The combination of these two images in the context of baptism would have offered the initiate a new orientation,

---

21. Michel Foucault, *Madness and Civilization: A History of Insanity in the Age of Reason* (New York: Vintage Books, 1973); Alain Beaulieu and David Gabbard, *Michel Foucault and Power Today: International Multidisciplinary Studies in the History of the Present* (Lanham, MD: Lexington Books, 2006).

22. Everett Ferguson, *Baptism in the Early Church: History, Theology, and Liturgy in the First Five Centuries* (Grand Rapids: Eerdmans, 2009).

23. Michael Peppard, *The World's Oldest Church: Bible, Art, and Ritual at Dura-Europos, Syria* (New Haven, CT: Yale University Press, 2016).

24. Michael Peppard, "Illuminating the Dura-Europos Baptistery: Comparanda for the Female Figures," *Journal of Early Christian Studies* 20, no. 4 (2012): 573–74.

new life, and new identity. The other pictures that run along the walls leading to and from the baptistery serve to affirm the new worldview and set of relationships within which new Christians live. These include pictures of David defeating Goliath, the women at the tomb of Jesus, Jesus healing the paralytic, Jesus helping Peter walk on water, and the woman at the well. Baptism, and the Trinitarian powers of God at work through it, has the power to renew the subjective consciousness of trauma survivors with good, meaningful, and hopeful images that are relevant to people in the kingdom of God.

Lord's Supper

The Lord's Supper is the ritual that follows on from baptism and the new identity it establishes. Jesus initiated this ritual to demonstrate that his body was broken and his blood shed for the forgiveness of the horrors we commit against one another. The Lord's Supper reminds us that forgiveness is part of a greater motivation, which is to be in a new promise-keeping relationship with people in which horrors will not recur because the Lord's Supper anticipates a day in which there will be a fuller kind of feasting. Jesus says of the wine that he will "drink it new with you in my Father's kingdom" (Matt 26:26–29). It is a ritual that remembers horrors yet stops them from being taken as the final word about life. Because it affirms the future resurrection of all believers into a kingdom of banqueters, it affirms a deep connection between people that cannot be halted by horrors. Thus it stops horrors from necessarily preventing relationships between people who have suffered them. The Lord's Supper works both negatively and positively: negatively, it breaks down a number of false perceptions that may distort each person's story of their life with God; positively, it also allows for new insights into life with God in view of suffering.

First, it affirms the reality of suffering and does not let us pretend that life should be or is a life free from the obvious suffering in the world. This insight is helpful for all members of faith communities, not just those who have suffered obvious and crippling trauma. The Lord's Supper recalls Jesus' sufferings as well as our own and those around us. Memories of suffering, even if the suffering of others, serve to interrupt an oppressive and antirealist view of what human life looks like. These memories of trauma unmask what Jon Sobrino calls "the culture of concealment." By hiding horrors and trauma responses, opines Sobrino, we perpetuate a culture of "distortion," which if it is unchecked means we are "living a lie."[25] The Lord's Supper is a realist countermeasure to these "false realisms," as Elizabeth O'Donnell Gandolfo puts it. Its honest realism about suffering interrupts "received narratives about 'the way things are,' subvert[s] official versions of the past and uncover[s] reality for what it truly is." Second, "the memory of suffering in general [and of particular events] ... subverts the prevailing mores and values of a world order in which resignation, insensitivity, individualism, and an understanding of happiness as success are the norm." Finally, perpetrators cannot carelessly deny destruction they have wreaked on others. The practice of remembering suffering therefore makes the bold statement that those who have suffered are worth remembering.[26]

The positive aspect of the Lord's Supper for recovery from trauma by reintegration into a community relies on a number of aspects of that community's life. The first is that suffering is remembered in relation to the death and resurrection of Jesus, writes Gandolfo: "Remembering concrete suffering—past and present—is an essential corrective to this tendency [toward abstract hopes in the future]. It is even more so when situated within ... the dangerous memory of Jesus Christ and his Passion, Death, and Resurrection."[27]

By maintaining the ritual of the Lord's Supper, the Christian community affirms that the death and resurrection of Jesus made a difference in the world. It was not pointless but presses on us a particular ideology in which persons, horrors, time, and history are imbued with significance within a people set apart for God. They have new meaning in the context of a people group. They are the history, concern, memory, and past of a people group and not merely of an overwhelmed individual. This is

25. Jon Sobrino, *Where Is God? Earthquake, Terrorism, Barbarity, and Hope* (New York: Orbis, 2004), 33.

26. Elizabeth O'Donnell Gandolfo, "Remembering the Massacre at El Mozote: A Case for the Dangerous Memory of Suffering as Christian Formation in Hope," *International Journal of Practical Theology* 17, no. 1 (2013): 71–75. "The practice of remembering suffering can also be cause for hope insofar as it effects a rejection of received self-understandings which fragment, devalue, and destroy personal and communal identity." Gandolfo, "Remembering the Massacre at El Mozote," 74.

27. Gandolfo, "Remembering the Massacre at El Mozote," 80.

because the Lord's Supper points toward a corporate banqueting and final Trinitarian salvation.

Because Jesus blessed and sanctified this meal for all time and for all Christians, it perpetually serves as one of God's primary instruments for communicating his love for his people. God employs the broken and blessed bread and wine to confirm the blessed perspective within each community. The repetitive nature of this ritual reshapes the Christian imagination. This imagination is an essential part of the creative and functional dimensions of being an image of God. The Eucharist stretches our imaginations to the point that they may realistically accommodate "stretched" hopes for a different kind of life and future.[28] This imagination leads to discernment and wise actions in the world, a new set of purposes for God's children.[29]

A NEW PURPOSE

A new identity based on forgiveness, the gift of the Spirit, and initiation into a new community provide the believer a new general mission: to follow Jesus' teaching and to mediate God's presence in the world (Matt 28:20). In addition to a new, meaningful identity, believers are given a meaningful purpose. Mediating God's presence, character, and will to other persons adds a greater purpose to each human life. The particulars of this Trinitarian mission depend on each person and community's context and recovery from trauma. However, its core will include "teaching them to obey everything I have commanded you" (28:20). Teaching by means of word, deed, and community life will confirm to both believers and nonbelievers that Jesus really is with his people (28:19). Jesus' presence and instrumental use of these goods enable him to achieve his creational purpose of making a people for God who reflect who God is both in character and creativity. Rightly relating to God and others despite the mournful realities of life is the key to this (5:3–10).

This mission of mediation can be carried out in various degrees according to stages of recovery from trauma. God's empathy with his disciples means that he will not expect what is not possible, only what is relevant

28. Brison, *Aftermath*, cited in Gandolfo, "Remembering the Massacre at El Mozote," 77n30.
29. Gandolfo, "Remembering the Massacre at El Mozote," 79.

and helpful. This claim is substantiated by the gentle way in which Jesus gradually brings his disciples into the knowledge and lifestyle of the kingdom of heaven. He only gives them what they can handle at various stages of his time with them and their maturity. Jesus' interactions with children bring this to light. Jesus merely prays for them and blesses them; he does not even teach them (Matt 19:14–15). Jesus is aware of children's cognitive and social limitations, yet does not refuse them, whereas the disciples expect that their limitations mean that Jesus will not welcome, spend time with, or bless them. Indeed, the kingdom of God belongs to those who, like children, merely accept a relationship with Jesus and his power.

With respect to adults, Jesus also restrains his teaching and expectations compared to many of his contemporaries. For example, at times he encourages people to understand very basic matters in the Old Testament before he adds his own teaching: "Go and learn what his means: 'I desire mercy and not sacrifice.' For I didn't come to call the righteous but sinners" (Matt 9:13). On the other hand, he also recognizes great faith where he finds it, such as in the centurion whose servant Jesus heals (8:10). Jesus is also patient with those who, like most of us, are between the extremes of little understanding and great understanding. Notice Jesus' great patience with Peter's confused words at the transfiguration (17:1–13). Another important story of Jesus thoughtfully receiving whatever unique gift or service people may have to offer him occurs immediately before Jesus' Passover meal (26:6–7). An unnamed woman anoints Jesus' feet with expensive oil. Jesus accepts her gift in the best light possible, interpreting it as a service to God and to himself. He does not scold her for offering it in a dangerous context and setting off the course for Jesus' betrayal. Rather, he commends her to the memory of all Christians. "Truly I tell you," says Jesus, "wherever this gospel is proclaimed in the whole world, what she has done will also be told in memory of her" (26:13).

Jesus is also sensitive to the fact that his disciples, though keen to learn from him, are limited by their time and place with respect to how God the Trinity is at work in human history: "I still have many things to tell you, but you can't bear them now" (John 16:12). Jesus is sensitive to the fact that greater comprehension will be aided by the developing maturity of the Christian community under the guidance of the Spirit. The patience and sensitivity of God also applies today, as God works with the limitations of his people. God cooperates with the experiences, temperaments, and abilities of people at different life stages and life cycles.

The events and scars of horrors and trauma do not undermine the personal mission to mediate God's character and presence to people and societies. This truth resists powerful contemporary strands of folk wisdom that judge a meaningful life by the possibility of success in personal expression, career, fitness, or other areas. In this view, a life strongly scarred by trauma and possibly incapable of achieving "success" will have little meaning. Matthew's Gospel defines and gives meaning to people in relationship to God the Trinity. On this view, people who are traumatized neither are meaningless in themselves, nor are they incapable of positive influence on others. God the Trinity lets believers know that life in the kingdom of God is meaningful, providing some answer to this key existential question.[30]

The identity conferred on Christians in baptism is communal as much as individual; so too is the mission of Christians. This corporate mission is to make God's presence, perspective, disposition, will, and power to change visible and available for the sake of the well-being of others. By means of actively extending God's kingdom on earth, believers visibly mediate and reflect God's love, the gift of new life, and hope for the future to others. This offers a new horizon for human life in which there is the possibility for not only undoing horrors but restoring and even developing the relational, moral, and creative aspects of human persons.

Mediating God's Presence

Ola Sigurdson has noted that a theology of what is visible is very important for any theological account of reality:

> With what kind of gaze may humanity be said to behold the divine, and how does this gaze relate to the relationship between the visible and the invisible? If the gaze is a constitutive part of a person's being-in-the-world, through which she can express her relationality as such, how can a theology of the gaze, a theological "optics," be formulated such that it will manage to preserve humanity's

30. "Judging whether life is or is not worth living amounts to answering the fundamental question of philosophy. ... The meaning of life is the most urgent of questions." Albert Camus, *The Myth of Sisyphus and Other Essays* (New York: Vintage International, 1991), 1–2.

> relationship to the presence of God in a way that neither denies that it concerns *God's* presence nor denies *humanity's* relationship to this presence?[31]

For Sigurdson, this conundrum requires looking to the incarnation for what it determines about how the finite and contingent relate to the infinite and eternal.[32]

The incarnation reveals both humanity and divinity, as well as how they may relate to each other. Jesus is the twofold image of God par excellence: the human image of God, and God as image of God. He is both God and a human enfleshment that perfectly comports to what God requires of a human being. God the Son continues to be incarnated in Jesus Christ, and by his Spirit indwelling believers, he is also embodied indirectly in the church, which is his visible body in the world, through whom he acts. That is, through his Spirit he indwells those who belong to his kingdom, and through their actions he brings about change in the world.[33] However, we need to note that though the kingdom of God is closely identified with Jesus' church (Matt 16:18; 18:17), it is not identical to it (25:31–46).

Christians simultaneously participate in the kingdom and are ordinary people. Because they participate in the world of the kingdom and the world of the devastation, they are often the medium by which some realities of the kingdom of heaven are passed onto those who live only in the world. They also mediate these truths of the kingdom to each other. Because they are present in two kingdoms at once, both individuals and communities may do this with the result that meaning is communicated to others. Mediation does not happen for its own sake; rather, something is communicated in a manner that shapes the message received. Brent Plate writes, "Meaning never appears apart from its existence as a particular embodied

31. Ola Sigurdson, *Heavenly Bodies: Incarnation, the Gaze, and Embodiment in Christian Theology*, trans. Carl Olsen (Grand Rapids: Eerdmans, 2016), 3.

32. "The problem of the incarnation returns here as the question of the finite managing to behold the eternal within finite conditions, without in turn reducing the eternal to something finite, i.e., to behold the eternal as eternal." Sigurdson, *Heavenly Bodies*, 3.

33. Here I am applying the insights of Uro to God and his modes of acting and sharing knowledge. Risto Uro, *Ritual and Christian Beginnings: A Socio-Cognitive Analysis* (Oxford: Oxford University Press, 2016); István Czachesz, "The Promise of the Cognitive Science of Religion for Biblical Studies," *The Council of Societies for the Study of Religion Bulletin* 37, no. 4 (2008): 102–5.

form. Meaning does not exist apart from its mediation."[34] Mediators can be described metaphorically as bridges and bridge builders between persons. What is illuminating for Christian anthropology and pastoral care is that God's message of care is mediated through people. This in turn highlights the message that people matter to God.

Christian mediation demonstrates the presence of Christ through everyday actions, words, and attitudes. Jesus Christ may direct the empathy, attention, and acts of Christians in the world by his Spirit. Specific empathy and insights that the Spirit has about one believer whom he indwells (a believer who is suffering, for example) may be shared by the same Spirit with another Christian in whom he also dwells (a Christian who is open to help others). This sharing of attention between the Spirit and the second believer may lead to precise actions that are particularly relevant for the other Christian who suffers. In this way, divine empathy, attention, and intention are shared with people and become concrete actions in history for the benefit of others: this is a model for understanding how God's love is at work through his people.

I agree with Anthony Kelly, who draws on Trinitarian theology to write that the "Christian community lives the presence of Christ performatively, so to speak, through the mediations of liturgy and preaching, in its missionary outreach and dialogical encounters, in its serving Christ in the neighbor, and in loving him even in the enemy." Yet, this human performance of God's will and love on earth is imperfect: "The church ... is rather a 'live performance' of faith, however amateur and poorly produced it might be."[35]

It is appropriate that God is perceived (indirectly) through those made in his image and who respond to his kingdom with faith. Indirect perception is a feature of human relationships and perception of one another's mind and culture. These are mediated by the face, the voice, and the body.[36] Phenomenological approaches to psychology and personhood argue

34. "Meaning is mediated, which means it comes to individuals encapsulated and put into a format that we are taught to recognize, name, and engage." S. Brent Plate, "Introduction: The Mediation of Meaning, or Re-mediating McLuhan," *Cross Currents* 62, no. 2 (2012): 156.

35. Anthony J. Kelly, "The Body of Christ: Amen! The Expanding Incarnation," *Theological Studies* 71, no. 4 (2010): 799. For his Trinitarian theology, see 798.

36. Nivedita Gangopadhyay and Katsunori Miyahara, "Perception and the Problem of Access to Other Minds," *Philosophical Psychology* 28, no. 5 (2015): 695–714.

convincingly for this.[37] Indeed, a large part of how we perceive other persons, discerning their character traits and so forth, is communicated nonverbally. People's facial expressions and their body language relative to others have an enormous influence on how we perceive them.

This perceptive ability with respect to other persons is present from a person's earliest moments, before language acquisition.[38] In the same way, we can say that a large part of how God communicates to human beings is via the way his church, which is referred to as his body, acts on earth. We can use the metaphor of people as the "skin" of the Christian religion, the surface of the body indwelt by God the Trinity.[39] By extension of this metaphor, we may cautiously say that the church reflects God's "body language," though it falls short of Jesus' revelation of God's body language. However, there is a wonderful mystery here that cannot be cast aside or ignored: as Rupert of Deutz wrote, Jesus offers up to God the church as his body, of which he is the head: "'Here is bone of my bone, flesh of my flesh!' and making seen that he and her come together in a veritable unity of person, he says further, 'and the two will be one flesh.'"[40]

God enables mediated "face-to-face" impressions of himself, saying, "This is something of what I look like" via the embodied presence of believers to each other. Therefore, a prominent mode of God's presence in the world occurs through his embodiment via his disciples and their faces. This is a very important embodied reality and means of communication for trauma survivors. It contributes to cementing the belief that the risen

37. Stephan Käufer and Anthony Chemero, *Phenomenology: An Introduction* (Cambridge, UK: Polity, 2016), 94–121.

38. Green draws on mirror-neuron studies, which he takes to show that we do not perceive and understand people by mimicking them, but that mirror neurons enable us to perceive other persons by enabling us to interpret actions carried out with the same bodies as our own. Adam Green, "Perceiving Persons," *Journal of Consciousness Studies* 19, nos. 3–4 (2012): 49–64.

39. Here I draw on the phenomenological work of Brent Plate. He writes: "The skin ... [is the] liminal, semi-porous boundary between inner and outer worlds, between *self* and *world*. ... I articulate the beginnings of an approach to understanding religion in and through its skin, and through the sensually mediated experiences of religion. ... The study of religion has continued to focus heavily on the interpretation of sacred texts and intellectual exploration of philosophical doctrines. In contrast, experiencing religion through its sensual, material, and artistic practices challenges the student of religion to think through the seemingly mundane dimensions of religions: what religious people eat and taste and see in their sacred settings." Plate, "Skin of Religion: Aesthetic Mediations of the Sacred," *Cross Currents* 62, no. 2 (2012): 162, italics original.

40. Rupert of Deutz, *De divinis officiis* 1.2, cited in Kelly, "Body of Christ," 797.

Christ is unendingly present with his disciples (Matt 28:20). The power of this message also lies in what it undermines, namely: "You are utterly alone and abandoned by all."

Because persons need the embodied presence and activity of God in order to relate to him, they need other Christians in order to recover from trauma. Bonhoeffer writes, "It is impossible to become a new man as a solitary individual."[41] This process must overcome one of the most problematic aspects of trauma: its wounds leave gaping holes in persons and relationships, but they may not be overcome because trauma drives people away from one another.

God has not left his presence in the hands of people who are strangers to himself, but rather focuses his presence in the world in his restored images.[42] The indwelling of Jesus in the lives of his disciples follows on theologically from the incarnation, which demonstrated that a human being has the capacity to simultaneously be taken up by a divine person and be bound to a divine person. In best-case scenarios, images of God *who do image God* relationally, functionally, and morally will be vehicles of safety and stability for others. When members of the church of Christ are in person-to-person relationships, they may mediate God's presence to other people.[43]

Only those who have been transformed in the kingdom of heaven can uniquely and capably reflect God and mediate his presence to other images.[44] This is predicated on the Trinitarian reality that God the Son incarnate is present in and rules the church by his Spirit, according to the will of the Father. Sigurdson writes, "The presence of the risen Christ can ... be understood as a transformation of the material conditions we people live in, both socially and politically"; hence, the presence of God with people has the potential to reorder social relationships and relationships to power. The resurrection narratives all include an element that challenges the way

41. Bonhoeffer, *Cost of Discipleship*, 180.

42. Sigurdson, *Heavenly Bodies*, 568.

43. Thomas Aquinas, *Commentary on the Gospel of St. Matthew*, trans. P. M. Kimball (Bristol, UK: Dolorosa, 2012), 565.

44. "God often mediates His love for us through people." The authors apply this to the Christian therapist-client relationship. Maltby and Hall, "Trauma, Attachment, and Spirituality," 307.

people interpret being-in-the-world: "The meeting with the resurrected was a meeting with something that was able to challenge their understanding of themselves."[45] There will be an element of challenge when people mediate the presence of the living God to other people. However, because God is Trinitarian, he may work through his Spirit in such a way that this challenge is constructive rather than destructive.

These healing interactions with the world would not be possible if God were not God the Trinity and if people were not his images. Paul Griffiths brings both these points together: Matthew's God is the "triune Lord ... who redresses the devastation brought about by the angelic and human falls ... who guards and guides people as the means of healing the devastated world."[46]

This guidance is critical in order to make a difference to those who have suffered from horrors and trauma. Because people are the primary way by which God the Trinity works in the world, the church needs to own up to and live into its mediating mission to traumatized persons in particular. The body of Christ needs to able to articulate the following to traumatized people: "It's not just your problem. It's our problem—my problem, the church's problem, God's problem. You don't need to be alone, and I hope we can work on it together. That's what faith communities do."[47]

How people relate to one another in this mediating mission is important because beliefs about the possibility of attachment to God and attachment to people are related to each other.[48] By healing beliefs about attachment to God, God may heal beliefs related to attachment to people. And vice versa: as relationships to people are healed, or new ones are healthily promoted and carried out, then a more positive attachment to God may be developed. These require divine support.

Thoughtfully and willingly mediating God's presence to other people includes a work of re-creation: "In her renewed connections with other people, the survivor recreates the psychological faculties that were

45. Sigurdson, *Heavenly Bodies*, 567, 570.

46. Paul J. Griffiths, *Decreation: The Last Things of All Creatures* (Waco, TX: Baylor University Press, 2014), 3.

47. Serene Jones, *Trauma and Grace: Theology in a Ruptured World* (Louisville, KY: Westminster John Knox, 2009), 7.

48. Maltby and Hall, "Trauma, Attachment, and Spirituality," 305.

damaged or deformed by the traumatic experience. These include the basic capacities for trust, autonomy, initiative, competence, identity and intimacy," Lewis Herman writes.[49] At its best, the church may do this because it is sourced in the life and will of Christ. As the body of Christ, the powerful life of Jesus is the only special life the church has. It follows therefore that disciples of Jesus will become Christlike when they align their wills and lives with Jesus' will and life. This alignment takes place in the context of the presence of Jesus within the church. Bonhoeffer writes, "Just as the Holy Spirit is with the individual, so Christ makes himself present in the community of saints. ... From this conviction that Christ himself is the community, there arises the idea of an organic life in the community in accordance with the will of Christ."[50]

When the church deeply integrates Jesus' call to be Christlike, it is essentially allowing Jesus to shape it after himself. The church becomes the face (or faces) of Christ on earth, according to Bonhoeffer:

> Formation means ... Jesus's taking form in His Church. What takes form here is the form of Jesus Christ Himself. The New Testament states the case profoundly and clearly when it calls the Church the Body of Christ. The body is the form. So, the Church is not a religious community of worshippers of Christ but is Christ Himself who has taken form among men ... incarnate, sentenced and awakened to new life.[51]

These connections between Christians, Christ, and his body lead directly to a consideration of how disciples mediate the perspective of God the Trinity toward trauma survivors. Before turning to that, however, I want to touch on an often-overlooked consideration: the value of animals for mediating God's presence to horror and trauma survivors.

This short excursus on animals as "the paws of God" is motivated by my own experiences and observations of a number of other Christians

---

49. Lewis Herman, *Trauma and Recovery*, 133.

50. This is prefaced with "If we now look at the church ... as a unified reality, then the image of the body of Christ must dominate. What does this really mean? In the community Christ is at work as with an instrument. He is present in it." Dietrich Bonhoeffer, *The Communion of Saints (Sanctorum Communio)*, cited in Bonhoeffer, *A Testament of Freedom* (New York: HarperCollins, 1995), 56.

51. Dietrich Bonhoeffer, *Ethics* (New York: Touchstone, Simon and Shuster, 1995), 84–85.

living in quasi-anonymous Western cultures. We are accustomed to think of human persons as the "hands and feet of God in the world."[52] Alongside this, we need to pause and consider the important role of animals as reminders (not mediators) of God's presence to people in contexts where Christian care is not available or present. These contexts include prisons, institutions and clinics for the mentally ill, nursing homes, loveless communities, and uncaring marriages. In these situations, the absence of loving care only serves to underline the rampant breakdown in proper and healthy face-to-face relationships between images of God.[53]

The attention, affection, and actions of nonhuman animals toward people may be a means by which God communicates his love and embrace to people. The role of dogs in sustaining and developing a person's identity has been touched on in twentieth-century literature.[54] There is a theological precedent: in Mark's Gospel, the animals' presence with Jesus after his fasting and temptation by the devil recall and represent the ideal shalom to which we should return following trials (Mark 1:13). Exhausted and bereft of human company, animals communicate a number of realities to him. These echo the story of Genesis and suggest that animals may communicate the message that shalom between creatures is possible. There is a heightened need to appreciate this in the aftermath of horrors and trauma.

Given the horrors that human persons generate, animals may be a very valid, safe, and loving way by which God communicates to those who have been deeply and irreversibly traumatized by horrors at the hands of human animals.[55] On the basis of the personal experiences of many people and philosophical considerations around ethical protection afforded to dogs,

52. Often attributed to St. Teresa of Ávila.

53. "As modernity produces alienation from self and community … modernism's interrogation of human identity leads to a fresh recognition and reassessment of nonhuman beings." Joseph Anderton, "Dogdom: Nonhuman Others and the Othered Self in Kafka, Beckett, and Auster," *Twentieth-Century Literature* 62, no. 3 (2016): 272.

54. Anderton, "Dogdom," 272.

55. Root argues that dogs have a true capacity to love their owners. He then also proposes that because individual dogs are loving, they will enjoy the afterlife with God and those they love. The best of his arguments is a Trinitarian one that revolves around mediation: "We can claim that dogs will be swept up into the eternal, not because they're just so cute and good natured, but because in their face-to-face love, we experience a true manifestation of the relationship of God as Father, Son and Holy Spirit. They are walking, bouncing, wagging witnesses to the eternity we sense only fleetingly in our earthly day-to-day." Andrew Root, *The Grace of Dogs* (New York: Penguin, 2017), 155.

Joseph Anderton writes that "canines are sufficiently both close to and different from humans to also conjure reciprocity, inspire responsibility, and challenge a self-absorbed worldview."[56] Magnetic resonance imaging (MRI) studies show that dogs in particular have the neurological systems required for empathy and remembering especially significant people to them. These MRI studies show that dogs can translate our communication with them into their own language in the area of the brain that deals with mirror neurons, which is responsible for empathy. Consequently, they can comprehend humans and feel what humans feel as far as this is possible for a dog. This means that dogs can love their human family across the species barrier.[57]

We need to avoid two pitfalls in this area of theology and therapy: we must neither understate nor overestimate the potential benefits and roles of animals for people. Animals may indeed be loving and therapeutic for initiating a reordering and restoring of some of the relational, moral, and creative aspects of images of God that are damaged through horrors and trauma. However, we also need to recognize that animals may not be enough to comprehensively meet our needs and aid recovery. There is a species gap between people and dogs that cannot be overcome. We cannot access their conscious minds with the immediacy we crave and that we may have had the pleasure of experiencing with other persons.[58] However, because the immediate pressure they place on people is less than that imposed by other humans, they may be very helpful for establishing a relationship of trust and care that supports a number of positive coping strategies for people. Another positive coping strategy generated by dogs is that they enable pet owners (at a dog park, for example) to meet people with whom they would not otherwise socialize and get to know.

56. Anderton, "Dogdom," 274.

57. Root, *Grace of Dogs*, 114–15.

58. "Our intimacy with dogs appears obvious, and yet that very familiarity can make their difference all the more palpable, and ... painful. ... Its relative closeness strengthens the human desire to fully comprehend the dog ... but also underlies the fundamental separation." Anderton, "Dogdom," 274.

Mediating God's Perspective

The predatory nature of social and animal relationships has generated a number of perspectives on the value, meaning, and purpose of human lives. Secular sociologists, philosophers, and psychologists at times view people as little more than predators and victims in an animal world. This breeds deep skepticism to do with the special nature of human beings.[59] This view goes hand in hand with the absence of a substantial basis for an objective and epistemologically secure point of view on and valuation of human life.[60] Horrors and trauma responses to these appear to compound these fatalistic outlooks and conclusions. Christians have a lot to contribute to this perspective and may make a valuable contribution in preventing negative mental-health consequences in this context.

God shares his perspective on horrors and trauma with Christians so that they may helpfully share this with others, especially those who have suffered from horrors and trauma (these are the "poor in spirit" [Matt 5:3]). The Christian perspective on this is driven by the significance of the incarnation for affirming the universal value of human beings and the confidence in Trinitarian salvation that is expressed in the creeds. More immediately, God shares his interpretation of the world through the "gaze," or interpretive posture, of Jesus, as Sigurdson discusses. Jesus' gaze is a particular way of seeing the world that is at the same time a spiritual interpretation of it. His perspective looks for the saving presence of God and adopts a particular relational posture to other persons, events, and social constructs. This includes the emotional perception of people and trauma. Jesus experienced compassion as he perceived the truth about the crowds around him (Matt 9:36; 20:34). This shaped his positive actions toward them. On the other hand, he experienced anger at religious abuse, which also drove him to act, albeit in a different manner (Mark 3:5).[61]

Jesus' perspective, or gaze, is communicated most commonly through the Bible. Jesus' perspective is passed onto future generations by those

---

59. Recall the association between horrors and an evolutionary view of nature in Marilyn McCord Adams's work. See also Peter Singer, *Animal Liberation: The Definitive Classic of the Animal Movement* (New York: Ecco Book/Harper Perennial, 2009); Singer, *In Defense of Animals: The Second Wave* (Malden, MA: Blackwell, 2006).

60. Susan F. Krantz, *Refuting Peter Singer's Ethical Theory: The Importance of Human Dignity* (Westport, CT: Praeger, 2002), 56.

61. Sigurdson, *Heavenly Bodies*, 184–86, 243–92.

texts that God commissions or deputizes as his "speech."[62] They are God's authorized vehicles for communication between himself and people. The Spirit illumines these texts and enables us to understand Jesus' perspective on them. Hence, for the Christian, the interpretation of horrors and trauma can be shaped by Jesus' ongoing communication, which provides the basis for knowing the truth about the world despite the presence of horrors. Despite the fact that Jesus used historically and culturally conditioned language, and that language only has signifying value, he was able and is currently able to communicate truth to his followers.[63] Because the truths that Jesus speaks have real-world referents and refer to properties in the real world, they are more than mere intentions or hopes.[64] They can inform us how to manage the emotions and rituals that can either impede or support restoration after trauma.

Emotions play a significant role after trauma. As Emma Hutchison and Roland Bleiker write, they may have various outcomes: enabling healing, or creating further antagonisms or confusing perspectives. Yet emotions are often ignored by those who have the power to reestablish order after trauma. In the context of loss of trust and fear, "an active engagement with emotions can actually be a source of political imagination, inspiration and hope." Because this approach can reestablish trust, it is superior to trying to overcome trauma by inserting false or superficial dichotomies and barriers between "safe" and "unsafe" people via military enforcement or legal and economic arrangements.[65]

Members of God's kingdom play a significant role in mediating those emotions from God that will play an important role in restoring people and societies after trauma. They will not merely perpetuate the regnant and dominant emotions that lead to traumas in the first place. Rather, they may

62. Nicholas Wolterstorff, *Divine Discourse: Philosophical Reflections on the Claim That God Speaks* (Cambridge: Cambridge University Press, 1995).

63. Language only has signifying value because it only mediates information. It is not the reality about which it speaks.

64. Ana María Mora-Márquez, "Martinus Dacus and Boethius Dacus on the Signification of Terms and the Truth-Value of Assertions," *Vivarium* 52 (2014): 23–48.

65. Emma Hutchison and Roland Bleiker, "Emotional Reconciliation Reconstituting Identity and Community after Trauma," *European Journal of Social Theory* 11, no. 1 (2008): 385–87. "Trust becomes key, as individuals and groups divided by conflict search to build forms of community that allow them to heal their wounds in empathetic and humanizing ways." Hutchison and Bleiker, "Emotional Reconciliation," 387.

uniquely reflect God's emotional perspective on trauma. All the elements of Christian liturgy—the gathered body, the music, the creed, the Lord's Prayer, and all other ancient words and structures for gathering, preaching, confession, absolution, and blessing—play a unique role in recovering a sense of safety, self, and belonging after horrors.

A Trinitarian, spiritual, and interpersonal understanding of God is required in order to trust and understand that God does indeed share his perspective with believers in order that they can mediate his perspective and care to others.[66] However, an unaided, direct, and immediate access to God's unmediated mind or consciousness is not possible. God's consciousness is not commonly available to non-Christian people in a direct manner because of a natural distinction between God and people and because of spiritual blindness. The works of God in the Son and Spirit overcome the blindness and estrangement of sin, as well as the barrier between species. The incarnation and passion of Christ reconcile people to God (Matt 26:26–29), and the Spirit reveals the truth to believers (Matt 16).

Jesus is the one whom John promises will "baptize you with the holy Spirit and fire" (Matt 3:11)—referring to Pentecost (Acts 2:1–36). Jesus himself sends his Spirit so that believers may begin to understand the mind of God and adopt this mindset themselves (Phil 2:5–11). Because God the Spirit is the Holy Spirit, his holiness transforms and renews believing minds over time. Because he is God, the Spirit has the power to support our desires and will in order that we not only know God but are keen to act toward others in light of this.

Christians may be vessels though which God communicates his vision for life and light for the world (Matt 5:13–16). When people share attention and perspective with God, his perspective guides their thoughts in a relational and nudging manner. God enables direct mind-to-mind relationship and communication with us because persons who are in relationship with one another have at least some access to one another's minds.[67] Insight into

66. We can assume that God's consciousness is stable and continuous over time, and thus may be described as a single continuous stream of consciousness. I am developing this from William James, *Principles of Psychology*, cited with italics in Rebecca S. Ravue Davis, "Stream and Destination: Husserl, Subjectivity, and Dorothy Richardson's *Pilgrimage*," *Twentieth Century Literature* 59, no. 2 (2013): 312.

67. Davis, "Stream and Destination," 310. "Immanence is derived from the Latin verb 'manere,' to stay. In its broad sense, it means to stay within; it refers to the condition of existing

God's perspective shapes our ethical lives as God promotes virtues in place of the absences of character, which is what vices are.[68] Therefore Christians are likely to follow Jesus' lead to pursue justice for victims of horrors, as they imitate him about whom Isaiah wrote: "I will put my Spirit on him and he will proclaim justice to the nations" (Matt 12:18). The gentle manner by which this is done with respect to victims will also imitate Christ: "He will not break a bruised reed, and he will not put out a smoldering wick, until he has led justice to victory" (12:20).

A new purpose is given to believers in the context of trauma and horrors: to imitate Jesus' mission and manner under the guidance of God's Spirit.

Mediating God's Actions Today

When disciples of Jesus adopt his realist and Trinitarian perception and hope, they live lives of integrity.[69] In the field of trauma studies, integrity is a mature and nondefeatist approach to the world. It is a refusal to fall into oblivion. Herman writes that it "is the capacity to affirm the value of life in the face of death, to be reconciled with the finite limits of the human condition, and to accept those realities without despair. Integrity is the foundation upon which trust in relationships is originally formed, and upon which shattered trust may be restored."[70]

Integrity brings stability to the self. Just as significantly, it means that a person has the stability to be a trusted and steady person for those in recovery.[71] This stability, understood within the supportive desires and will of God, enables us to help others by adopting what trauma expert Kaethe Weingarten calls "reasonable hope." For her, reasonable hope is a guide to action posttrauma. Hope is best described as actions that express a perspective, rather than being understood as a feeling.[72]

---

inside a given sphere." Davis, "Stream and Destination," 310.

68. Andrew Pinsent, *The Second-Person Perspective in Aquinas's Ethics: Virtues and Gifts*, Routledge Studies in Ethics and Moral Theory 17 (New York: Routledge, 2012).

69. I also use Weingarten's notion of reasonable hope in tandem with this. Kaethe Weingarten, "Reasonable Hope: Construct, Clinical Applications, and Supports," *Family Process* 49, no. 1 (2010): 5–25.

70. Herman, *Trauma and Recovery*, 154.

71. Herman, *Trauma and Recovery*, 153–54.

72. Weingarten, "Reasonable Hope," 7.

This understanding sets people free from the expectation that one must feel or summon emotions and concentrates on actions instead. Reasonable hope is outward looking and relational, Weingarten continues: "Whereas hope is most often considered the attribute of an individual, reasonable hope can be the actions of one or many people." Reasonable hope tries to relate meaningfully to the present, with a secondary yet reasonable emphasis on the future. It is a perspective that recommends group and individual actions. These are carried out in the expectation that they may be at least partly successful and thus prepare people to consistently live hopefully in the future.[73]

A Christian version of reasonable hope has much to offer. To start with, it recognizes that working against injustice and cocreating a new world deploy the moral and functional dimension of being an image of God for the sake of justice. Without justice and social action, hope would be "incomplete."[74] Working toward concrete, here-and-now hope is sharpened christologically because hopeful actions recall Jesus' own actions, thereby demonstrating continuity with him in terms of outlook and behavior.[75] A stronger form of this continuity would claim that by means of putting into practice the promises Jesus made, disciples of Jesus as images of God partly complete the promises of Jesus to others. This aligns hope with the Trinity and with God's presence and power in the world through his people. It also aligns trust in the living God with the refusal to acquiesce to fatalistic belief.[76]

There is a call on the life of every Christian to embody the presence of the risen Christ in his church. This includes concrete, Spirit-enabled actions that renew, reorient, and remake the historical and cultural context: "One aspect of embodiment of this presence [of Christ] consists

73. It overlaps with the goal of creating a coherent narrative in which to locate our personal story of trauma because its "objective is the process of making sense of what exists now in the belief that this prepares us to meet what lies ahead. ... The present is filled with working not waiting; we scaffold ourselves to prepare for the future." Weingarten, "Reasonable Hope," 7.

74. Gandolfo, "Remembering the Massacre at El Mozote," 82.

75. Gandolfo, "Remembering the Massacre at El Mozote," 83.

76. Paul S. Fiddes, "Acceptance and Resistance in a Theology of Death," *Modern Believing* 56, no. 2 (2015): 225.

precisely in what this presence does with these concrete, material circumstances," Sigurdson writes.[77]

Mediating God's perspective and presence should also include mediating his will and care for people. There is a direct link between being "blessed by the Father," inheriting the kingdom prepared "before the foundation of the world" (Matt 25:34), and mediating God's actions in the world. Those who belong to the Father mirror his concern for the traumatized people who do not have safety and a community of care (25:35–46). God wants to provide food, shelter, and care for the sick and those in prison through those who reflect his will and character (25:45). This is theologically consistent with God being the loving and living God.

The ways God works through his people to provide some of this care is illustrated in the story of the feeding of the five thousand. This begins with God's orientation toward people: when Jesus "went ashore, he saw a large crowd and had compassion on them" (Matt 14:14). When the crowd's physical needs for food become clear, Jesus prevents the dismissal of the crowd and puts the onus of care onto the disciples: "They don't need to go away. You give them something to eat" (14:16). Taking the food brought forward by the boy (John 6:8), Jesus prays, blesses, breaks, and gives it to the disciples. It is the disciples who are responsible for the food distribution. God does not distribute the food directly, but rather carries out his work through the disciples. Jesus "broke the loaves and gave them to the disciples, and the disciples gave them to the crowds" (Matt 14:19). The result of God's miraculous work and the cooperation of his disciples is that "everyone ate and was satisfied" (Matt 14:20). The leftover food is in turn collected by those who were fed: the crowds thus complete a chain of action through which God's compassion is mediated by people.

The story of the good Samaritan also illustrates how God may indirectly bring about change in a person's situation (Luke 10:25–37). This is an important story because it deals with someone who was subject to horrors and may well have experienced a trauma response to being brutalized by thieves and abandoned by those who should have cared for him. In the story, God works to bring healing and recovery by means of the actions of the Samaritan. The Samaritan provides the safety needed for

77. Sigurdson, *Heavenly Bodies*, 567.

the process of recovery to begin. In addition, he embodies the virtues of love and justice, which are reflections of God's character. The concrete actions of the Samaritan are the only source of hope for the traveler. The important point is that Jesus uses the story of the good Samaritan in order to explain what the summary of the Old Testament looks like in practice. The good Samaritan is what "Love the Lord your God with all your heart, with all your soul, with all your strength, and with all your mind," and "Love your neighbor as yourself" look like. The practical consequence for those who take Jesus seriously is "Go, and do likewise" (Luke 10:37). They can do so because they are doing this in the power of the God into whom they are baptized and in whose name they act: the Father, Son, and Holy Spirit. That is, Christians "go and do likewise" only because they can do so by the enablement and cooperation of the Trinity.

The stories of the feeding of the five thousand and the good Samaritan demonstrate God's kind and merciful disposition toward those victimized and brutalized by horrors. They also illustrate the kind of kindness and care that Jesus' disciples should demonstrate. In the same way as Luke's Gospel, Jesus summarizes this with reference to the Old Testament in Matthew 7:12: "Whatever you want others to do for you, do the same for them, for this is the Law and the Prophets."

An important question for the followers of Jesus is whether his images will follow his teaching on this. Will they extend his care for others? One way that we may contribute to this kind of caring attitude is the cultivation of habits that contemplate God's care. This occurs at its best when it is sourced in contemplation on the nature of God and his grace, as Rik van Nieuwenhove emphasizes. Contemplation, particularly of God's nature and grace in spite of the presence of horrors in the world, is likely to lead to love and actions of charity. Such contemplation may renew Christ's disciples to the point that they may perform even small actions (such as giving, distributing, or collecting food) that serve as vehicles of the Trinity's loving service of humankind.[78] Matthew 7:24–27 is an important parable that suggests the importance of continual rumination on and reference to the

78. Rik van Nieuwenhove, "Recipientes per contemplationem, tradentes per actionem: the relationship between the active and contemplative lives in Aquinas," *The Thomist* 81, no. 1 (2017): 1–30, esp. p. 17.

words of Jesus as the foundation for a life that weathers horrors, a life that can provide shelter and security for others because it is a stable life: "Everyone who hears these words of mine and acts upon them will be like a wise man who built his house on the rock" (7:24).

God's grace is "concretely enacted or performed in people's lives," as Serene Jones puts it.[79] Often this takes the form of difficult and costly service of others. The weight of carrying the burdens of others as well as our own means that a "blessed" life is paradoxically a cross-bearing life. This is the enigma: a friendship with God somewhat lightens the burdens we carry because he helps us existentially and practically with these, yet carrying the burdens of others can lead to trauma responses of our own as well as bring us into righteous conflict with those who bring about horrors. Jesus promises his disciples that they will experience subjective horrors of persecution until he returns to earth (Matt 16:24–26). Moreover, the way power is enacted in the kingdom of God reflects God's other-person centeredness: "Whoever wants to become great among you must be your servant, and whoever wants to be first among you must be your slave" (20:27). This is modeled on the Son's own servant-shaped ministry: "Just as the Son of Man did not come to be served, but to serve, and to give his life as a ransom for many" (20:28).

Because the church is the earthly body of Christ, it will reflect his will for the world. This means it can never be only an inward-looking community. Gathering in the certainty of the presence of Christ and being Christlike generate a perspective that extends beyond our personal needs and desires. This is because by his Spirit Jesus shares his concerns and intentions with us. As a body of people whose life is patterned after Jesus, we will empathetically mirror his attention toward others, and so the church will reach out to the world in a manner that is best described as service. Bonhoeffer writes that the church "is a church only when it is there for others. ... The church must participate in the worldly tasks of life in the community—not dominating but helping and serving. It must

79. Jones, *Trauma and Grace*, x.

tell people in every calling what a life with Christ is, what it means to be 'there for others.'"[80]

Being there for others will take on various forms. At times it will involve challenging dominant cultural assumptions and behaviors, says Bonhoeffer: "In particular, *our* church will have to confront the vices of hubris, the worship of power, envy, and illusionism as the roots of all evil. It will have to speak moderation, authenticity, trust, faithfulness, steadfastness, patience, discipline, humility, modesty, contentment." In this way, the greatest witness to Jesus is the *kind* of life that Christians live. The church "will have to see that it does not underestimate the significance of the human 'example' (which has its origin in the humanity of Jesus and is so important in Paul's writings!); the church's word gains weight and power not through concepts but by example."[81]

Mediating God's Encouragement

Earlier I pointed out that God has the will and power to forgive and change even the deepest horror makers among us. This requires deep change, which is difficult and exhausting for the recovering horror maker and for those who are trying to care for them and mediate God's power to change them. Christians must continually rely on God the Trinity to uphold them in this work. The love of God the Trinity by the Spirit enables love for one another in a Christlike manner: "Christ opened up the way to God and to one another. Now Christians can live with each other in peace; they can love and serve one another; they can become one. But they can continue to do so only through Jesus Christ," Bonhoeffer writes.[82]

Therefore, the love and strengthening power of Christ is mediated through encouraging relationship with other people. Because Christians are united together in Christ by the Spirit, each aspect of their relationships with one another will only make sense when they are grounded in the person, presence, and intentional work of Christ through his Spirit.[83]

---

80. Dietrich Bonhoeffer, "Outline for a Book," in *Letters and Papers from Prison*, ed. Eberhard Bethge (London: SCM, 1967), 383.

81. Dietrich Bonhoeffer, *Letters and Papers from Prison*, in *Works*, vol. 8, ed. Christian Gremmels et al., trans. Isabel Best et al. (Minneapolis: Fortress, 2010), 503–4.

82. Bonhoeffer, *Works*, 5:33.

83. Bonhoeffer, *Works*, 5:29.

Living in a Christlike fashion therefore recognizes the need for Christian brothers and sisters in order to hold on to the promises God makes in his words to believers, as Bonhoeffer puts it:

> Help can only come from the outside; and it has come and comes daily and anew in the Word of Jesus Christ. ... God put His Word into the mouth of human beings in order that it may be communicated to others. Therefore, Christians need other Christians who speak God's Word to them. They need them again and again when they become uncertain and discouraged.[84]

Mediating God's Power to Change through Prayer

The Gospel of Matthew offers its readers a theology of prayer that generates intimacy with God and brings about change in time and space. It is a realist theology of prayer. By realist I mean a view that is determined by facts that are true phenomena in the world as it is.[85] This argues against skeptical, nonrealist approaches to God for Christian prayer.[86]

Jesus countered this view by encouraging his disciples to pray that God's will be done and to pray for things that will effect change in relation to human flourishing. Jesus' view of prayer was based on the expectations he had about the character and nature of God. The Lord's Prayer assumes a

84. Bonhoeffer continues: "Living by their own resources, they cannot help themselves without cheating themselves out of the truth. They need other Christians as bearers and proclaimers of the divine word of salvation. ... The Christ in their own hearts is weaker than the Christ in the word of other Christians." Bonhoeffer, *Works*, 5:32.

85. "[A] realist about X holds that discourse about X is apt for truth or falsity. ... The realist's opposite number is the non-cognitivist or non-factualist, who holds that seeming statements about X do not function in a generally descriptive way—do not, despite appearances, actually say what sort of things there are or actually ascribe properties—but rather have some other linguistic function." Peter Railton and Gideon Rosen, "Realism," in *A Companion to Metaphysics*, ed. Jaegwon Kim, Earnest Sosa, and Gary S. Rosenkrantz (Oxford: Wiley-Blackwell, 2009), 30. For the profound ethical implications of various forms of realism, see William Schweiker, "Love in Search of Realism," *Jahrbuch für Biblische Theologie* 29 (2014): 303–19; Timothy McGrew, "Convergence Model," in *Four Views on Christianity and Philosophy*, ed. Stanley N. Gundry, Paul M. Gould, and Brian Davis (Grand Rapids: Zondervan, 2016), 126–27.

86. Graham Robert Oppy and Nick Trakakis, "Religious Language Games," in *Realism and Religion*, ed. Andrew Moore and Michael Scott (Burlington, VT: Ashgate, 2007), 116. Based on these premises, the conclusion is that "we can see why Phillis develops this kind of non-realist account of religious language. ... For if theists—that is theists not blinded by philosophical prejudices—do not think of God as a metaphysically real subject, then they must thinking of God in some non-realist fashion." Oppy and Trakakis, "Religious Language Games," 116.

number of truths about God: he must be attentive to what occurs on earth; he must be a listener who is like a caring Father, who is holy, who has a will that entails the best possibilities for the world, who has mercy and is also just, who protects us from ourselves and our enemies, and who is more powerful than the evil one (Matt 6:9–13).

These beliefs about God explain the "who" and the "why" of prayer. Jesus himself clearly believes in prayer and encourages his disciples to pray because God is even better than a good parent: "If you then, who are evil, know how to give good things to your children, how much more will your Father in heaven give good things to those who ask him" (Matt 7:11).

The faith of the centurion demonstrates that prayer may be the instrument by which one person can work with God for the good of another. This is a historical case of one person asking Jesus to heal another (Matt 8:5–13). The centurion's servant is in a lamentable state: "at home paralyzed, in terrible agony" (8:6). "Lord," says the centurion, "just say the word and my servant will be healed" (8:8). Jesus commends this kind of faith: "Truly I tell you, I have not found anyone in Israel with so great a faith" (8:10). The petition is successful and serves as proof that God may work to heal people as a response to the requests of others.

The Psalms point out that in order for believers to speak to God and each other about Yahweh, they must be able to think back to stories of his relationships with others. We can speak about God meaningfully today by considering God's past patterns of behavior and modes of communication with others. This is what the psalmists did: in their own times they hoped in God based on their reflections on his previously observed relationships to the world and to people.[87]

Furthermore, the Psalms reflect an active dialogue between pray-ers and God. Those who pray are active persons and communities in a dynamic rather than passive relationship with God. This relationship is robust enough and dynamic enough to persevere throughout the whole gamut of historical pressures as well as the psalmists' joys and pains.[88]

So, what might a community living meaningfully, hopefully with a Christian identity in light of the "blessed reading," look like? Stian Eriksen

87. C. J. A. Vos, *Theopoetry of the Psalms* (Pretoria: Protea Book House, 2005), 28.

88. Vos, *Theopoetry of the Psalms*, 28–29.

describes the comprehensive extent of their faith across their lives, hopes, and fears:

> People relate to a living kind of religion, often marked by experiential dimensions of the faith that extend beyond mere confessional statements and habitation of religion. ... Interviewees have pointed to significant spiritual experiences or an everyday spiritual experiential dimension to life where faith represents a core life source intersecting with most other dimensions of everyday life, be it faith, family, finances, or general well-being. In my observations of churches, it is likewise common in many congregations to provide ample room for personal testimonies in the church services, where people willingly tell about "the goodness of God" or how they have experienced God's intervention, blessing or felt help during daily life or through personal crisis.[89]

THE WAY FORWARD: MEANINGFUL LIVING THROUGH PARTICIPATION IN GOD'S KINGDOM

Throughout Matthew's Gospel, Jesus offers his disciples the possibility of belonging to the kingdom of heaven. At the end of the Gospel, Jesus clarifies the identity of those who belong. They are those whose life is based on the reality of the one God who is Father, Son, and Spirit. Consequently, they accept Jesus' teaching.

The dialectic of living under and in the kingdom of God with a new identity establishes that there is a meaningful life to be lived, even if it does not look like what we had hoped for. The kingdom is an active realm that is advanced through human agency in the presence, power, and will of the Trinity. When people live obediently, the kingdom advances. The identity that Jesus gave his disciples at the Great Commission is fulfilled by word and deed as his people embody and pass on "everything" that Jesus taught. In other words, when life is lived according to the identity the disciples have as those who belong to the Father, Son, and Spirit, then they are living in a manner consistent with God's active reign.

---

89. Stian Eriksen, "The Epistemology of Imagination and Religious Experience: A Global and Pentecostal Approach to the Study of Religion?," *Studia Theologica* 69, no. 1 (2015): 47.

Life is therefore meaningful because it can fit within the best possible scenario for this kind of world. There is a best way to live, and there are many lesser ways to live.

If reconnection with everyday life is a key factor of recovery, and if this is possible as a disciple who participates in the gradual healing and preservation of the world, then this reconnection may be done in a meaningful manner. This means that people who have been traumatized by horrors may reconnect with ordinary life without becoming prey to distorted forms of mundane life, such as the unrighteous pursuit of goods, fame, and power. Life may be ordinary, but it is by no means meaningless. Meaning is not invented but received, supported, and put into practice by disciples.

CONCLUSION

I'd like to end this book with a couple of suggestions, some unresolved questions that I have, and an appropriate blessing taken from the Bible.

Allow me first to encourage you to consider what this book suggests for engaging with God via a blessed perspective on both biblical texts and people. In this book, we have discussed the difference that God being Trinitarian makes for how he is involved in the recovery of human personhood after horrors and trauma. We have fleshed out the various ways by which God may provide the sense of safety, a coherent retelling of personal trauma, and integration into a community, which are the foundation for recovery from trauma. And we have found that, although the nature of horrors does not change, the blessed perspective given by God the Trinity changes our understanding of them.

If you are a horror and trauma survivor yourself, I hope this book has helped you by providing some useful integration between theology and your experiences. I am sorry if I have missed the mark and hope that I can continue to learn how to empathize with those who have experienced trauma.

My hope is that many of us can take our learnings about trauma and Trinity a step further and begin to think about how we currently relate to people who have experienced horrors and had trauma responses. This is not an abstract question for me. Writing this book has urged me to be more available to other people in an open and caring manner. The particulars of what this looks like in practice will probably continue to revolve around support groups and mentoring, and possibly extend to caring for unsupported children. Hopefully the interpersonal and Trinitarian emphasis of the book will assure you that we can connect with God meaningfully, so that you may at once both understand horrors and trauma for what they are, and not give up on hope and meaningful living.

This work in no way resolves all issues around horrors and trauma neatly, and many questions linger in my mind. I need to explore these further, and I would encourage you to pursue them also.

Some of these questions are existential: for example, How do we live in the knowledge that we have committed gross and commonplace horrors that appear to have damaged and stunted another person or community's future? This is especially the case when we know we have not been forgiven and the other person or community still bears resentment toward us.

Some are related practical, "how-to" questions: for example, What should one do when one person who wants to express remorse at past horrors they have committed may not do so because they fear the anger and revenge of those they have hurt? How do we ask for forgiveness from those we have wronged when they may in turn use this apology and request against us in law court?

Other questions are more philosophical or to do with the nature of persons (though they have pragmatic outcomes): Are there sufficient reasons for continuing to live in the company of others when we appear to contribute more to commonplace horrors and trauma responses than we do to the greater good? Is a secluded life away from people (isolated, hermit-like monasticism) a strong option for Christians because it reduces the likelihood of our own horror-making actions, especially unintentional ones? Is it true that pets and artificially intelligent machines are not, in the overall scheme, more conducive to recovery from horrors than people are?

I also have theological questions that are equally soul wrenching, but they are for another time, when the dark night of the soul hopefully passes somewhat. Despite these questions, the sum of this book's engagement with Matthew suggests that survivors of horrors and trauma may be renewed along a trajectory in which their personhood increasingly reflects aspects of God's nature and character. This does not negate the fundamentally life-altering ramifications of experienced horrors and trauma. However, it does weaken the suggestion that horrors and traumas must result in *impenetrable* skepticism concerning God's character, the potential for flourishing of persons, and a meaningful existence. And in doing so, it echoes the interpersonal (face-to-face), historical, and existential perspectives expressed in the blessing that God gives to his people to pronounce on one another in Numbers 6:24–26:

May the Lord bless you
and protect you;
may the Lord make his face to shine on you
and be gracious to you;
may the Lord look with favor on you
and give you peace.

Oh, that this would be so for you, and me, and our communities!

BIBLIOGRAPHY

Abernethy, Andrew T. *Eating in Isaiah: Approaching the Role of Food and Drink in Isaiah's Structure and Message*. Biblical Interpretation Series 131. Leiden: Brill, 2014.

———. *The Book of Isaiah and God's Kingdom: A Thematic Theological Approach*. New Studies in Biblical Theology 40. Downers Grove, IL: IVP Academic, 2016.

Albiston, Jordie, and Kevin Brophy. *Prayers of a Secular World: Australian Poems for Our Times*. Carlton South, Victoria: Inkerman & Blunt, 2015.

Adams, Marilyn McCord. *Christ and Horrors: The Coherence of Christology*. Cambridge: Cambridge University Press, 2006.

———. "Horrors in Theological Context." *Scottish Journal of Theology* 55, no. 4 (2002): 468–79.

American Psychiatric Association. *Diagnostic and Statistical Manual of Mental Disorders: DSM-5*. Washington, DC: American Psychiatric Association, 2013.

Anderson, A. K. "Review: Marilyn McCord Adams, Christ and Horrors: The Coherence of Christology." *International Journal for Philosophy of Religion* 64, no. 3 (2008): 161–65.

Anderson, Kevin L. "Response to Dr. Scott Harrower, 'God, Horror, and Meaning.'" Paper presented at Institute of Biblical Research research group "Suffering, Evil, and Divine Punishment in the Bible." San Antonio, TX, November 18, 2016.

Anderton, Joseph. "Dogdom: Nonhuman Others and the Othered Self in Kafka, Beckett, and Auster." *Twentieth Century Literature* 62, no. 3 (2016): 271–88.

Appelros, Erica. *God in the Act of Reference*. Aldershot, UK: Ashgate, 2002.

Aquinas, Thomas. *Commentary on the Gospel of St. Matthew*. Translated by P. M. Kimball. Bristol, UK: Dolorosa, 2012.

———. *Summa Theologiae*. Vol. 8. London: Eyre & Spottiswoode, 1967.

———. *Summa Theologiae*. Vol. 18. London: Eyre & Spottiswoode, 1966.

Arnold, Bill T. *1 & 2 Samuel*. Grand Rapids: Zondervan, 2003.

Baker, David W. "God, Names Of." Pages 359–68 in *Dictionary of the Old Testament: Pentateuch*. Edited by T. Desmond Alexander and David W. Baker. Downers Grove, IL: InterVarsity, 2003.

Ball, Brian. "Knowledge Is Normal Belief." *Analysis* 73, no. 1 (2013): 69–76.

Ballaban, Steven. "The Use of Traumatic Biblical Narratives in Spiritual Recovery from Trauma: Theory and Case Study." *The Journal of Pastoral Care & Counseling* 68, no. 4 (2014): 1–11.

Banner, Michael. "Scripts for Modern Dying: The Death before Death We Have Invented, the Death before Death We Fear and Some Take Too Literally, and the Death before Death Christians Believe In." *Studies in Christian Ethics* 29, no. 3 (2016): 249–55.

Barton, Stephen C. "Eschatology and the Emotions in Early Christianity." *Journal of Biblical Literature* 130, no. 3 (2011): 571–91.

Beale, G. K. *A New Testament Biblical Theology*. Grand Rapids: Baker Academic, 2011.

Beaulieu, Alain, and David Gabbard. *Michel Foucault and Power Today: International Multidisciplinary Studies in the History of the Present*. Lanham, MD: Lexington Books, 2006.

Bell, Duncan. "Introduction: Violence and Memory." *Millennium: Journal of International Studies* 38, no. 2 (2009): 345–60.

Belliotti, Raymond. *Power: Oppression, Subservience, and Resistance*. Albany: State University of New York Press, 2016.

Benedict XVI. *Licht der Welt*. Freiburg im Breisgau: Herder GmbH, 2010.

Benton, Matthew A. "Epistemology Personalized." *Philosophical Quarterly* 67, no. 269 (2017): 813–34.

———. "Expert Opinion and Second-Hand Knowledge." *Philosophy & Phenomenological Research* 92 (2016): 492–98.

Beveridge, Andrew. "Social Theory Two Ways: John Levi Martin's Structures and Actions." *Historical Methods* 45, no. 4 (2012): 179–82.

Bonhoeffer, Dietrich. *The Cost of Discipleship*. London: SCM, 2001.

———. *Ethics*. New York: Touchstone, Simon and Shuster, 1995.

———. *Letters and Papers from Prison*. In vol. 8 of *Works*. Edited by Christian Gremmels et al. Translated by Isabel Best et al. Minneapolis: Fortress, 2010.

———. "Outline for a Book." In *Letters and Papers from Prison*. Edited by Eberhard Bethge. London: SCM, 1967.

———. *A Testament of Freedom*. New York: HarperCollins, 1995.

———. *Works*. Vol. 5. Edited by Geffrey B. Kelly. Minneapolis: Fortress, 1996.

Boxall, Ian. *Discovering Matthew: Content, Interpretation, Reception*. London: SPCK, 2014.

Brison, Susan. *Aftermath: Violence and the Remaking of the Self*. Princeton, NJ: Princeton University Press, 2002.

Broderick, Damien. "Terrible Angels: The Singularity and Science Fiction." *Journal of Consciousness Studies* 19, nos. 1–2 (2012): 20–41.

Brower-Toland, Susan. "William Ockham on the Scope and Limits of Consciousness." *Vivarium* 52 (2014): 197–219.

Brueggemann, Walter. *Spirituality of the Psalms*. Facets. Minneapolis: Fortress, 2002.

Bruner, Frederick Dale. *Matthew: A Commentary*. Rev. and expanded ed. Grand Rapids: Eerdmans, 2004.

Buijs, Govert, and Simon Polinder. "Concluding Reflections: Christian-Philosophical Reflection and Shalom Searching Wisdom." *Philosophia Reformata* 81, no. 1 (2016): 89–109.

Burgos, Juan Manuel. *Introducción al personalismo*. Madrid: Ediciones Palabra, 2012.

Burns, Charlene P. E. *Christian Understandings of Evil: The Historical Trajectory*. Minneapolis: Fortress, 2016.

Camus, Albert. *The Myth of Sisyphus and Other Essays*. New York: Vintage International, 1991.

Caracciolo, Marco. "Fictional Consciousness: A Reader's Manual." *Style* 46, no. 1 (2012): 42–65.

Caragounis, Chrys C. "בֵּין (1201)." Pages 1:671–77 in *New International Dictionary of Old Testament Theology and Exegesis*. Edited by Willem A. VanGemeren, 5 vols. Grand Rapids: Zondervan, 1997.

Carlson, Nathaniel A. "Lament: The Biblical Language of Trauma." *Cultural Encounters* 11, no. 1 (2015): 50–68.

Carman, Taylor. "Phenomenology." Pages 179–92 in *The Oxford Handbook of Philosophical Methodology*. Edited by Herman Cappelen, Tamar Gendler, and John Hawthorne. Oxford: Oxford University Press, 2016.

Carroll, Noël. *The Philosophy of Horror, or, Paradoxes of the Heart*. New York: Routledge, 1990.

Carson, D. A. *Matthew*. The Expositor's Bible Commentary. Grand Rapids: Zondervan, 2010.

Cason, Thomas Scott. "Victims and Not Violators: Scapegoat Theory and 3 Maccabees 7:10–17." *Journal for the Study of the Old Testament* 41, no. 1 (2016): 117–33.

Cave, Nick. *And the Ass Saw the Angel*. London: Penguin, 1998.

———. *The Death of Bunny Munro*. 1st American ed. New York: Faber and Faber, 2009.

Charry, Ellen T. "Incarnation." Pages 323–25 in *Dictionary for Theological Interpretation of the Bible*. Edited by Kevin J. Vanhoozer, Craig G. Bartholomew, Daniel J. Treier, and N. T. Wright. Grand Rapids: Baker Academic, 2005.

Christie, Douglas E. "The Night Office: Loss, Darkness, and the Practice of Solidarity." *Anglican Theological Review* 99, no. 2 (2017): 211–32.

Clark, James Kelly, and Michael C. Rea. "Introduction." In *Reason, Mind, Metaphysics, and Mind: New Essays on the Philosophy of Alvin Plantinga*. Edited by James Kelly Clark and Michael C. Rea. Oxford: Oxford University Press, 2012.

Clute, John. "Horror." Page 478 in *The Encyclopedia of Fantasy*. Edited by John Clute and John Grant. Exeter, UK: Orbit, 1997.

Colavito, Jason. "Oh, the Horror!" *Skeptic* 15, no. 3 (2010): 21–23.

Cole, Graham A. *God the Peacemaker: How Atonement Brings Shalom*. Downers Grove, IL: InterVarsity, 2009.

———. "Personalism." Page 667 in *New Dictionary of Theology*. Edited by Martin Davie, Tim Grass, Stephen R. Holmes, John McDowell, and T. A. Noble. Downers Grove, IL: IVP Academic, 2016.

Colyer, Elmer M. *How to Read T. F. Torrance: Understanding His Trinitarian and Scientific Theology*. Downers Grove, IL: InterVarsity, 2001.

Cotnoir, A. J. "Mutual Indwelling." *Faith and Philosophy* 34, no. 2 (2017): 123–51.

Crisp, Oliver. "Analytic Theology as Systematic Theology." *Open Theology* 3, no. 1 (2017): 156–66.

———. *Divinity and Humanity: The Incarnation Reconsidered*. Current Issues in Theology. New York: Cambridge University Press, 2007.

———. *God Incarnate: Explorations in Christology*. New York: T&T Clark, 2009.

Czachesz, István. "The Promise of the Cognitive Science of Religion for Biblical Studies." *The Council of Societies for the Study of Religion Bulletin* 37, no. 4 (2008): 102–5.

Damschen, Gregor. "Dispositional Knowledge-How versus Propositional Knowledge-That." Pages 278–95 in *Debating Dispositions: Issues in Metaphysics, Epistemology and Philosophy of Mind*. Edited by Robert Schnepf and Karsten Stueber Gregor Damschen. Berlin: de Gruyter, 2009.

Dauphinais, Michael. "The Difference Divine Mercy Makes in Aquinas' Exegesis." *The Thomist* 80, no. 3 (2016): 341–53.

Davidson, E. T. A. "The Comedy of Horrors." *Proceedings* 23 (2003): 39–54.

Davies, Brian. *Thomas Aquinas on God and Evil*. Oxford: Oxford University Press, 2011.

Davis, Rebecca S. Ravue. "Stream and Destination: Husserl, Subjectivity, and Dorothy Richardson's Pilgrimage." *Twentieth Century Literature* 59, no. 2 (2013): 309–42.

De Jaegher, Hanne. "How We Affect Each Other." *Journal of Consciousness Studies* 22, nos. 1–2 (2015): 112–32.

Dennis, John A. "Glory." Pages 313–15 in *Dictionary of Jesus and the Gospels*. Edited by J. B. Green, Jeannine K. Brown, and Nicholas Perrin. Downers Grove, IL: IVP Academic, 2013.

Deusen Hunsinger, Deborah van. "Bearing the Unbearable: Trauma, Gospel and Pastoral Care." *Theology Today* 68, no. 1 (2011): 8–25.

Eckert, Rebekah. "Preaching to Horror-Struck People." *Consensus* 31, no. 1 (2006): 91–105.

Eller, Vernard, Johann Christoph Blumhardt, and Christoph Blumhardt. *Thy Kingdom Come: A Blumhardt Reader*. Grand Rapids: Eerdmans, 1980.

Embry, Brian. "An Early Modern Scholastic Theory of Negative Entities: Thomas Compton Charleton on Lacks, Negations and Privations." *British Journal for the History of Philosophy* 23, no. 1 (2015): 22–45.

"EN DIRECT – Attentats de Paris: des proches d'un terroriste arrêtés." *Le Figaro*. November 26, 2015. http://www.lefigaro.fr/actualites/2015/11/13/01001-20151113LIVWWW00406-fusillade-paris-explosions-stade-de-france.php.

Erickson, Millard J. *Christian Theology*. 3rd ed. Grand Rapids: Baker Academic, 2013.

Eriksen, Stian. "The Epistemology of Imagination and Religious Experience: A Global and Pentecostal Approach to the Study of Religion?" *Studia Theologica* 69, no. 1 (2015): 45–73.

Eslinger, Lyle M. "The Enigmatic Plurals Like 'One of Us' (Genesis i 26, iii 22, xi 7) in Hyperchronic Perspective." *Vetus Testamentum* 56, no. 2 (2006): 171–84.

Fahy, Thomas Richard. *The Philosophy of Horror: The Philosophy of Popular Culture*. Lexington: University Press of Kentucky, 2010.

Farris, Joshua Ryan. *The Soul of Theological Anthropology: A Cartesian Exploration*. London: Routledge, 2016.

Farris, Joshua Ryan, and R. Keith Loftin, eds. *Christian Physicalism? Philosophical Theological Criticisms*. Langham, MD: Lexington Books, 2017.

Felch, Susan. "Dialogism." Pages 173–75 in *Dictionary for Theological Interpretation of the Bible*. Edited by Kevin Vanhoozer. Grand Rapids: Baker Academic, 2005.

Ferguson, Everett. *Baptism in the Early Church: History, Theology, and Liturgy in the First Five Centuries*. Grand Rapids: Eerdmans, 2009.
Fiddes, Paul S. "Acceptance and Resistance in a Theology of Death." *Modern Believing* 56, no. 2 (2015): 223–36.
Finnern, Sönke. *Narratologie und biblische Exegese*. Tübingen: Mohr Siebeck, 2010.
Forbes, Greg, and Scott Harrower. *Raised from Obscurity: A Narratival and Theological Study of the Characterization of Women in Luke-Acts*. Eugene, OR: Pickwick, 2015.
Ford, David F. "In the Spirit: Learning Wisdom, Giving Signs." Pages 42–63 in *The Holy Spirit in the World Today*. Edited by Jane Williams. London: Alpha International, 2011.
Foucault, Michel. *Madness and Civilization: A History of Insanity in the Age of Reason*. New York: Vintage Books, 1973.
Frame, John M. *The Doctrine of God: A Theology of Lordship*. Phillipsburg, NJ: P&R, 2002.
Frechette, Christopher G., and Elizabeth Boase. "Defining 'Trauma' as a Useful Lens for Biblical Interpretation." Pages 1–27 in *Bible through the Lens of Trauma*. Edited by Elizabeth Boase and Christopher G. Frechette. Atlanta: SBL Press, 2016.
Frey, Jörg, and Uta Poplutz. *Narrativität und Theologie im Johannesevangelium*. Biblisch-theologische Studien. Neukirchen-Vluyn: Neukirchener Verlagsgesellschaft, 2012.
Galbusera, Laura. "The (Temporal) Constitution of the 'We' between Connectedness and Differentiation." *Journal of Consciousness Studies* 22, nos. 1–2 (2015): 107–11.
Gandolfo, Elizabeth O'Donnell. "Remembering the Massacre at El Mozote: A Case for the Dangerous Memory of Suffering as Christian Formation in Hope." *International Journal of Practical Theology* 17, no. 1 (2013): 62–78.
Gangopadhyay, Nivedita, and Katsunori Miyahara. "Perception and the Problem of Access to Other Minds." *Philosophical Psychology* 28, no. 5 (2015): 695–714.
Gerleman, G. "שָׁלֵם *šlm* to Have Enough," Pages 1337–48 in *Theological Lexicon of the Old Testament*. Edited by Ernst Jenni and Claus Westerman. 3 vols. Peabody, MA: Hendrickson, 1997.
Goldman, David P. "Be Afraid—Be Very Afraid." *First Things* (October 2009): 41–43.
Gordon, James R. *The Holy One in Our Midst*. Minneapolis: Fortress, 2016.
Gössner, Andreas. "Krankheit und Sterben in der reformationszeitlichen Seelsorge." *Kerygma und Dogma* 60 (2014): 75–91.
Graff, Beatrice de. "An End to Evil: An Eschatological Approach to Security." *Philosophia Reformata* 81, no. 1 (2016): 70–88.
Green, Adam. "Perceiving Persons." *Journal of Consciousness Studies* 19, nos. 3–4 (2012): 49–64.
———. "Reading the Mind of God (without Hebrew Lessons): Alston, Shared Attention, and Mystical Experience." *Religious Studies* 45, no. 4 (2009): 455–70.
Green, Adam, and Keith A. Quan. "More than Inspired Propositions: Shared Attention and the Religious Text." *Faith and Philosophy* 29, no. 4 (2012): 416–30.
Green, Joel B. "What You See Depends on What You Are Looking for: Jesus' Ascension as a Test Case for Thinking about Biblical Theology and Theological Interpretation of Scripture." *Interpretation* 70, no. 4 (2016): 445–57.

Greene-McCreight, Kathryn. *Darkness Is My Only Companion: A Christian Response to Mental Illness*. Grand Rapids: Brazos, 2006.

———. *Feminist Reconstructions of Christian Doctrine: Narrative Analysis and Appraisal*. New York: Oxford University Press, 2000.

Griffiths, Paul J. *Decreation: The Last Things of All Creatures*. Waco, TX: Baylor University Press, 2014.

Grillmeier, Alois. *Christ in Christian Tradition*. New York: Sheed and Ward, 1965.

———. *Christ in Christian Tradition*. Atlanta: John Knox, 1975.

———. "The Reception of Chalcedon in the Roman Catholic Church." *The Ecumenical Review* 22, no. 4 (1970): 383–411.

Gruijters, Rochus-Antoin. "Solidarity, the Common Good and Social Justice in the Catholic Social Teaching within the Framework of Globalization." *Philosophia Reformata* 81, no. 1 (2016): 14–31.

Güney, Zeynep Okur. "Collective Affinity as a Flux of You, Me and We." *Journal of Consciousness Studies* 22, nos. 1–2 (2015): 102–6.

Hannett, Lisa L. "Wide Open Fear: Australian Horror and Gothic Fiction." This Is Horror. http://www.thisishorror.co.uk/columns/southern-dark/wide-open-fear-australian-horror-and-gothic-fiction/. Accessed December 12, 2015.

Harmon, William, and C. Hugh Holman. "Tragedy." Pages 521–23 in *A Handbook to Literature*. Edited by William Harmon and C. Hugh Holman. Upper Saddle River, NJ: Prentice Hall, 1996.

Harris, Robert. "Elements of the Gothic Novel." Virtual Salt. June 15, 2015. https://www.virtualsalt.com/gothic.htm.

Harrower, Scott. "God the Trinity and Christian Care for Those Who Lament." In *A Time for Sorrow: Recovering the Practice of Lament in the Life of the Church*. Edited by Sean McDonough and Scott Harrower. Peabody, MA: Hendrickson, 2019.

Harry, Michael. "Bourke Street Tragedy: Witness Recalls Walking into a Scene of Confusion and Horror." *Sydney Morning Herald*. January 21, 2017. http://www.smh.com.au/comment/bourke-street-tragedy-witness-recalls-walking-into-a-scene-of-confusion-and-horror-20170120-gtvyom.html.

Hart, David Bentley. *The Doors of the Sea: Where Was God in the Tsunami?* Grand Rapids: Eerdmans, 2005.

Hart, Kevin, ed. *Marion, Jean-Luc: The Essential Writings*. New York: Fordham University Press, 2013.

Hasker, William. "Analytic Philosophy of Religion." In *The Oxford Handbook of Philosophy of Religion*. Edited by William Wainwright, 421–26. Oxford: Oxford University Press, 2005.

Hays, Christopher B. "Bard Called the Tune: Whither Theological Exegesis in the Post-Childs Era?" *Journal of Theological Interpretation* 4, no. 1 (2010): 139–52.

Herman, Judith Lewis. *Trauma and Recovery: From Domestic Abuse to Political Terror*. London: HarperCollins, 1992.

Hilary of Poitiers. *Commentary on Matthew*. Translated by D. H. Williams. Washington, DC: Catholic University of America Press, 2012.

Hinkley Wilson, Sarah. "Jesus Christ, Horror Defeater." *Lutheran Forum* 47, no. 1 (2013): 2–10.

Hinkley, Paul. *Beloved Community: Critical Dogmatics after Christendom*. Grand Rapids: Eerdmans, 2015.

Hippolytus. "The Discourse on the Holy Theophany." In *The Ante-Nicene Fathers*. 10 vols. Edited by Alexander Roberts and James Donaldson, 5:234–37. Buffalo, NY: Christian Literature, 1895–1896.

Hogle, Jerrold E. "Introduction: The Gothic in Western Culture." Pages 1–20 in *The Cambridge Companion to Gothic Fiction*. Edited by Jerrold E. Hogle. Cambridge: Cambridge University Press, 2002.

Horton, Michael Scott. *The Christian Faith*. Grand Rapids: Zondervan, 2011.

Hourdequin, Marion. "Empathy, Shared Intentionality, and Motivation by Moral Reasons." *Ethical Theory and Moral Practice* 15, no. 3 (2012): 403–19.

Howard-Snyder, Daniel, and Adam Green. "Hiddenness of God." *Stanford Encyclopedia of Philosophy*. April 23, 2016. https://plato.stanford.edu/entries/divine-hiddenness/.

Hutchison, Emma, and Roland Bleiker. "Emotional Reconciliation Reconstituting Identity and Community after Trauma." *European Journal of Social Theory* 11, no. 1 (2008): 385–403.

Irenaeus. *Against Heresies*. In *The Ante-Nicene Fathers*. 10 vols. Edited by Alexander Roberts and James Donaldson, 1:315–567. Buffalo, NY: Christian Literature, 1895–1896.

———. *On the Apostolic Preaching*. Crestwood, NY: St. Vladimir's Seminary Press, 1997.

Jensen, Rasmus Thybo. "Merleau-Ponty and McDowell on the Transparency of the Mind." *International Journal of Philosophical Studies* 21, no. 3 (2013): 470–92.

John Paul II. *The Gospel of Life = Evangelium Vitae*. 1st large print ed. New York: Random House Large Print in association with Times Books, 1995.

Johnson, Dru. *Knowledge by Ritual*. Winona Lake, IN: Eisenbrauns, 2016.

Jones, Serene. *Trauma and Grace: Theology in a Ruptured World*. Louisville, KY: Westminster John Knox, 2009.

Kain, Phillip J. "Nietzsche, Virtue and the Horror of Existence." *British Journal for the History of Philosophy* 17, no. 1 (2009): 153–67.

Kalmanofsky, Amy. *Terror All Around: Horror, Monsters, and Theology in the Book of Jeremiah*. The Library of Hebrew Bible/Old Testament Studies 390. New York: T&T Clark International, 2008.

Kammler, Hans-Christian. "Der Trost des Evangeliums angesichts des Todes." *Kerygma und Dogma* 61 (2015): 48-69.

Kang, Aimee. "Review of Serene Jones, *Trauma and Grace: Theology in a Ruptured World*." *Practical Matters*. March 1, 2011. http://practicalmattersjournal.org/2011/03/01/trauma-and-grace/.

Käufer, Stephan, and Anthony Chemero. *Phenomenology: An Introduction*. Cambridge, UK: Polity, 2016.

Keller, Albert. "Der Mensch ohne Alternative." Pages 65–76 in *Structuren der Wirklichkeit: Leben im Geist*. Edited by Paul Imhof and Gabriel-Alexander Reschke. Taufkirchen: Via Verbis Verlag, 2005.

Kelly, Anthony J. "The Body of Christ: Amen! The Expanding Incarnation." *Theological Studies* 71, no. 4 (2010): 792–816.

Kienzle, Beverly Mayne. *Hildegard of Bingen and Her Gospel Homilies*. Turnhout, Belgium: Brepols, 2009.

Krantz, Susan F. *Refuting Peter Singer's Ethical Theory: The Importance of Human Dignity*. Westport, CT: Praeger, 2002.

Krause, Neal, Kenneth I. Pargament, and Gail Ironson. "Does a Religious Transformation Buffer the Effects of Lifetime Trauma on Happiness?" *International Journal for the Psychology of Religion* 27, no. 2 (2017): 104–15.

Krötke, Wolf. "God's Hiddenness and Belief in His Power: Essays in Honour of John Webster." Pages 137–48 in *Theological Theology*. Edited by R. David Nelson, Darren Sarisky, and Justin Stratis. London: Bloomsbury, 2015.

Kuruvilla, Abraham. "The Aquedah (Genesis 22): What Is the Author Doing with What He Is Saying?" *Journal of the Evangelical Theological Society* 55, no. 3 (2012): 489–508.

———. "Pericopal Theology." *Bibliotheca Sacra* 173, no. 689 (2016): 3–17.

Lehmann Imfeld, Zöe, Peter Hampson, and Alison Milbank. "Hospitable Conversations in Theology and Literature: Re-opening a Space to Be Human." Pages 1–11 in *Theology and Literature after Postmodernity*. Edited by Zöe Lehmann Imfeld, Peter Hampson, and Alison Milbank. London: T&T Clark, 2015.

Levering, Matthew. *The Theology of Augustine: An Introductory Guide to His Most Important Works*. Grand Rapids: Baker Academic, 2013.

Levinas, Emmanuel. *Totality and Infinity: An Essay on Exteriority*. Duquesne Studies Philosophical Series 24. Pittsburgh: Duquesne University Press, 1969.

———. *Trauma and Recovery: From Domestic Abuse to Political Terror*. London: Basic Books, 2001.

Lohrey, Amanda. "Introduction." In *Best Australian Stories (2015)*. Edited by Amanda Lohrey, vii–ix. Collingwood, Victoria: Black, 2015.

Lommel, Pim van. "Non-local Consciousness." *Journal of Consciousness Studies* 20, nos. 1–2 (2013): 7–48.

Long, Thomas G. "Essential Books on God and Suffering (Theodicy)." *Christian Century* 130, no. 21 (2013): 33.

Lowe, Matthew Forrest. "Book Review: Marilyn McCord Adams, Christ and Horrors: The Coherence of Christology." *Religious Studies and Theology* 26, no. 2 (2007): 267–69.

Madueme, Hans. "Review Article: Theological Interpretation after Barth." *Journal of Theological Interpretation* 3, no. 1 (2009): 143–55.

Maguen, Shira, and Brett Litz. "Moral Injury in Veterans of War." *PTSD Research Quarterly* 23, no. 1 (2012): 1–3.

Maltby, Lauren E., and Todd W. Hall. "Trauma, Attachment, and Spirituality: A Case Study." *Journal of Psychology and Theology* 40, no. 4 (2012): 302–12.

Marion, Jean-Luc. *Prolegomena to Charity*. Perspectives in Continental Philosophy 24. New York: Fordham University Press, 2002.

Matthiae, Gisela, Renate Jost, Claudia Jeanssen, Annette Mehlhorn, and Antje Röckemann, eds. *Feministische Theologie: Initiativen, Kirchen, Universitäten – eine Erfolgsgeschichte*. Gütersloh: Gütersloher Verlagshaus, 2008.

McCall, Thomas. *An Invitation to Analytic Christian Theology*. Downers Grove, IL: IVP Academic, 2015.

McDonough, Sean, and Scott Harrower, eds. *A Time for Sorrow: Recovering the Practice of Lament in the Life of the Church*. Peabody, MA: Hendrickson, 2019.

McGowan, Michael W. "Trauma and Grace: Psychology and Theology in Conversation." *Pastoral Psychology* 58, no. 2 (2009): 167–80.

McGrath, Alister E. *A Scientific Theology*. 3 vols. Grand Rapids: Eerdmans, 2003.

McGrew, Timothy. "Convergence Model." Pages 123–50 in *Four Views on Christianity and Philosophy*. Edited by Stanley N. Gundry, Paul M. Gould, and Brian Davis. Grand Rapids: Zondervan, 2016.

McKeown, James. "Blessings and Curses." Pages 83–87 in *Dictionary of the Old Testament: Pentateuch*. Edited by T. Desmond Alexander and David W. Baker. Downers Grove, IL: InterVarsity, 2003.

Merleau-Ponty, Maurice. *Phenomenology of Perception*. Translated by Donald A. Landes. New York: Routledge, 2012.

Mora-Márquez, Ana María. "Martinus Dacus and Boethius Dacus on the Signification of Terms and the Truth-Value of Assertions." *Vivarium* 52 (2014): 23–48.

Moreland, J. P. "Oppy on the Argument from Consciousness." *Faith and Philosophy* 29, no. 1 (2012): 70–83.

Morris, Thomas V. *The Logic of God Incarnate*. Ithaca, NY: Cornell University Press, 1986.

Mounier, Emmanuel. *Personalism*. Notre Dame, IN: University of Notre Dame Press, 1970.

Muis, Jan. "Die Rede von Gott und das Reden Gottes. Eine Würdigung der Lehre der dreifachen Gestalt des Wortes Gottes." *Zeitschrift für Dialektische Theologie* 16, no. 1 (2000): 59–70.

Muller, Richard A. *Dictionary of Latin and Greek Theological Terms: Drawn Principally from Protestant Scholastic Theology*. Grand Rapids: Baker, 1985.

Murphy, Anne V. "Founding Foreclosures: Violence and Rhetorical Ownership in Philosophical Discourse on the Body." *Sophia* 55, no. 1 (2016): 5–14.

Nagel, Thomas. *The View from Nowhere*. New York: Oxford University Press, 1986.

Nauta, Lodi. "The Order of Knowing: Juan Luis Vives on Language, Thought and the Topics." *Journal of the History of Ideas* 76, no. 3 (2015): 325–45.

Nel, Phillip J. "שָׁלֵם (8966)," Pages 130–35 in *Dictionary of Old Testament Theology and Exegesis*. Edited by Willem A. VanGemeren. 5 vols. Grand Rapids: Zondervan, 1997.

Ng, Andrew. "Revisiting Judges 19: A Gothic Perspective." *Journal for the Study of the Old Testament* 32, no. 2 (2007): 199–215.

Nickel, Phillip J. "Horror and the Idea of Everyday Life." Pages 14–32 in *The Philosophy of Horror*. Edited by Thomas Richard Fahy. Lexington: University Press of Kentucky, 2010.

Nietzsche, Friedrich W. *Human, All Too Human*. Parts 1 and 2. Translated by H. Zimmern and P. V. Cohn. Mineola, NY: Dover, 2006.

———. *The Gay Science*. Dover Philosophical Classics. Mineola, NY: Dover, 2006.

Nietzsche, Friedrich Wilhelm, and Peter Fritzsche. *Nietzsche and the Death of God: Selected Writings*. Bedford Series in History and Culture. Boston: Bedford/St. Martin, 2007.

Nieuwenhove, Rik van. "Recipientes per contemplationem, tradentes per actionem: The Relationship between the Active and Contemplative Lies in Aquinas." *The Thomist* 81, no. 1 (2017): 1–30.

Nolan, Daniel. "Method in Analytic Metaphysics." Pages 159–78 in *The Oxford Handbook of Philosophical Methodology*. Edited by Herman Cappelen, Tamar Gendler, and John Hawthorne. Oxford: Oxford University Press, 2016.

Nouwen, Henri J. M. *The Wounded Healer: Ministry in Contemporary Society*. 1st ed. Garden City, NY: Doubleday, 1972.

Nussbaum, Martha Craven. *Anger and Forgiveness: Resentment, Generosity, Justice*. Oxford: Oxford University Press, 2016.

O'Connor, Kathleen M. *Jeremiah: Pain and Promise*. Minneapolis: Fortress, 2011.

———. "Stammering toward the Unsayable: Old Testament Theology, Trauma Theory, and Genesis." *Interpretation* 70, no. 3 (2016): 301–13.

O'Donnell, Aislinn. "Shame Is Already a Revolution: The Politics of Affect in the Thought of Deleuze." *Deleuze Studies* 11, no. 1 (2017): 1–24.

O'Donovan, Oliver. *Self, World and Time*. Grand Rapids: Eerdmans, 2013.

Olds, Tim. "The History of the Future in Five Words." *New Philosopher* 15, no. 2 (2017): 88–89.

Ollenburger, Ben C. "Creation and Peace: Creator and Creature in Genesis 1–11." Pages 143–58 in *The Old Testament in the Life of God's People: Essays in Honour of Elmer A. Martens*. Edited by Jon Isaak. Winona Lake, IN: Eisenbrauns, 2009.

Oppy, Graham Robert, and Nick Trakakis. "Religious Language Games." Pages 103–30 in *Realism and Religion*. Edited by Andrew Moore and Michael Scott. Burlington, VT: Ashgate, 2007.

Owens, Joseph. "Aristotle and Aquinas." Pages 38–59 in *The Cambridge Companion to Aquinas*. Edited by Norman Kreutzmann and Eleonore Stump. Cambridge: Cambridge University Press, 2005.

Parrott, Jill M. "How Shall We Greet the Sun?: Form and Truth in Gwendolyn Brook's Annie Allen." *Style* 46, no. 1 (2012): 27–41.

Peppard, Michael. "Illuminating the Dura-Europos Baptistery: Comparanda for the Female Figures." *Journal of Early Christian Studies* 20, no. 4 (2012): 543–74.

———. *The World's Oldest Church: Bible, Art, and Ritual at Dura-Europos, Syria*. New Haven, CT: Yale University Press, 2016.

Pettit, Phillip. "Realism and Response-Dependence." *Mind* 100, no. 4 (1991): 587–626.

Pfenniger, Jennifer. "Bakhtin Reads the Song of Songs." *Journal for the Study of the Old Testament* 34, no. 3 (2010): 331–49.

Pinsent, Andrew. *The Second-Person Perspective in Aquinas's Ethics: Virtues and Gifts*. Routledge Studies in Ethics and Moral Theory 17. New York: Routledge, 2012.

Plantinga, Cornelius. *Not the Way It's Supposed to Be: A Breviary of Sin*. Grand Rapids: Eerdmans, 1995.

Plate, S. Brent. "Introduction: The Mediation of Meaning, or Re-mediating McLuhan." *Cross Currents* 62, no. 2 (2012): 156–61.

———. "The Skin of Religion: Aesthetic Mediations of the Sacred." *Cross Currents* 62, no. 2 (2012): 162–80.

Polanyi, Michael, and Amartya Sen. *The Tacit Dimension*. Chicago: University of Chicago Press, 2009.

Polanyi, Michael. *Personal Knowledge: Towards a Post-critical Philosophy*. London: Routledge, 1997.

Poplutz, Uta. *Erzählte Welt: Narratologische Studien zum Matthäusevangelium*. Biblisch-theologische Studien. Neukirchen-Vluyn: Neukirchener Verlag, 2008.

Proházková, Viktória. "The Genre of Horror." *American International Journal of Contemporary Research* 2, no. 4 (2012): 132–42.

Railton, Peter, and Gideon Rosen. "Realism." Pages 533–37 in *A Companion to Metaphysics*. Edited by Jaegwon Kim, Earnest Sosa, and Gary S. Rosenkrantz. Oxford: Wiley-Blackwell, 2009.

Rambo, Shelly. "Spirit and Trauma." *Interpretation* 69, no. 1 (2015): 7–19.

———. *Spirit and Trauma: A Theology of Remaining*. Louisville, KY: Westminster John Knox, 2010.

———. "'Theologians Engaging Trauma' Transcript." *Theology Today* 68, no. 3 (2011): 224–37.

Rea, Michael C. "Authority and Truth." Pages 872–98 in *The Enduring Authority of the Christian Scriptures*. Edited by D. A. Carson. Grand Rapids: Eerdmans, 2016.

Reichberg, Gregory M. "Beyond Privation: Moral Evil in Aquinas's 'De Malo.'" *Review of Metaphysics* 55, no. 4 (2002): 751–84.

Reinhartz, Adele. "Incarnation and Covenant: The Fourth Gospel through the Lens of Trauma Theory." *Interpretation* 69, no. 1 (2015): 35–48.

Riches, John. "Reception History as a Challenge to Biblical Theology." *Journal of Theological Interpretation* 7, no. 2 (2013): 171–85.

Rodríguez Lizano, Jesús. "El personalismo. Sus luces y sus sombras." Pages 301–7 in *El Primado de la persona en la moral contemporánea*. Edited by Augusto Sarmiento et al. Navarra, Spain: Servicio de Publicaciones de la Universidad de Navarra, 1997.

Root, Andrew. *The Grace of Dogs*. New York: Penguin, 2017.

Roth, Sesshu. "Intention, Expectation, and Promissory Obligation." *Ethics* 127, no. 1 (2016): 88–115.

Rowe, C. Kavin. "Biblical Pressure and Trinitarian Hermeneutics." *Pro Ecclesia* 11, no. 3 (2002): 295–312.

Rowe, Christopher Kavin. *Early Narrative Christology: The Lord in the Gospel of Luke*. Beihefte zur Zeitschrift für die neutestamentliche Wissenschaft und die Kunde der älteren Kirche 139. Berlin: de Gruyter, 2006.

———. *World Upside Down: Reading Acts in the Graeco-Roman Age*. Oxford: Oxford University Press, 2009.

Schaefer, Frauke C., and Charles A. Schaefer, eds. *Trauma and Resilience*. Condeo, 2012.

Schawarzwaeller, Klaus. "Johann Sebastian Bach: Actus Tragicus: Ein evnagelisches requiem." *Kerygma und Dogma* 61 (2015): 22–47.

Schellenberg, J. L. *The Hiddenness Argument: Philosophy's New Challenge to Belief in God*. Oxford: Oxford University Press, 2015.

———. *The Will to Imagine: A Justification of Skeptical Religion*. Ithaca, NY: Cornell University Press, 2009.

———. *The Wisdom to Doubt: A Justification of Religious Skepticism*. Ithaca, NY: Cornell University Press, 2007.

Schrauzer, Michael. "Sin Is the True Horror." *The Catholic Answer* (September-October 2012): 30–33.

Schweiker, William. "Love in Search of Realism." *Jahrbuch für Biblische Theologie* 29 (2014): 303–19.

Seachris, Joshua W. "Life, Meaning of." Pages 1–7 in *New Catholic Encyclopedia: Supplement 2012–2013: Ethics and Philosophy*. Edited by Robert L. Fastiggi. Detroit: Gale/Catholic University of America Press, 2012.

———. "Meaning of Life: Contemporary Analytic Perspectives." In *Internet Encyclopedia of Philosophy: A Peer Reviewed Academic Resource*. https://www.iep.utm.edu/mean-ana/. Accessed January 10, 2018.

Sedgwick, E. "Paranoid Reading and Reparative Reading, or, You're So Paranoid, You Probably Think This Essay is About You." In *Touching Feeling: Affect, Pedagogy, Performativity*, 123–52. Durham, NC: Duke University Press, 2003.

Shepherd, Charles E. *Theological Interpretation and Isaiah 53: A Critical Comparison of Bernhard Duhm, Brevard Childs and Alec Motyer*. London: Bloomsbury, 2014.

Shessu Roth, Abraham. "Intention, Expectation, and Promissory Obligation." *Ethics: An International Journal of Social, Political and Legal Philosophy* 127, no. 1 (2016): 88–115.

Sigurdson, Ola. *Heavenly Bodies: Incarnation, the Gaze, and Embodiment in Christian Theology*. Translated by Carl Olsen. Grand Rapids: Eerdmans, 2016.

Singer, Peter. *Animal Liberation: The Definitive Classic of the Animal Movement*. Updated ed. New York: Ecco Book/Harper Perennial, 2009.

———. *In Defense of Animals: The Second Wave*. Malden, MA: Blackwell, 2006.

Smith, Curtis C. "Horror versus Tragedy: Mary Shelley's *Frankenstein* and Olaf Stapledon's *Sirius*." *Extrapolation* 26, no. 1 (1985): 66–73.

Sobrino, Jon. *Where Is God? Earthquake, Terrorism, Barbarity, and Hope*. New York: Orbis, 2004.

Stålsett, Sturla J. "Non/Human: Overcoming the Fatal Separation, without Diffusing the Crucial Distinction." *Studia Theologica* 69, no. 1 (2015): 25–31.

Stump, Eleonore. *The God of the Bible and the God of the Philosophers*. The Aquinas Lectures. Milwaukee: Marquette University Press, 2016.

———. "The Problem of Evil: Analytic Philosophy and Narrative." Pages 251–64 in *Analytic Theology: New Essays in the Philosophy of Theology*. Edited by Oliver D. Crisp and Michael C. Rea. Oxford: Oxford University Press, 2009.

———. "Second-Person Accounts and the Problem of Evil." *Revista Portuguesa de Filosofia* 57, no. 4 (2001): 745–71.

———. *Wandering in Darkness: Narrative and the Problem of Suffering*. Oxford: Oxford University Press, 2010.

Swenson, Adam. "Privation Theories of Pain." *International Journal for Philosophy of Religion* 66, no. 3 (2009): 139–54.

Taliaferro, Charles, and Paul J. Griffiths. *Philosophy of Religion: An Anthology*. Blackwell Philosophy Anthologies 20. Malden, MA: Blackwell, 2003.

Taylor, John G. "The Problem of 'I.'" *Journal of Consciousness Studies* 19, nos. 11–12 (2012): 233–64.

Taylor, Kevin, and Giles Waller, eds. *Christian Theology and Tragedy: Theologians, Tragic Literature and Tragic Theory*. Burlington, VT: Ashgate, 2011.

Thomas, Oral A. W. *Biblical Resistance Hermeneutics within a Caribbean Context*. BibleWorld. Oakville, CT: Equinox, 2010.

Tietz, Christiane. "Personale Identität und Selbstannahme." *Kerygma und Dogma* 61 (2015): 3–21.

Torrance, Thomas F. "The Reconciliation of the Mind: A Theological Meditation on the Teaching of St. Paul." Pages 196–204 in *Theology in the Service of the Church*. Edited by M. Alston Wallace Jr. Grand Rapids: Eerdmans, 2000.

Trible, Phyllis. *Texts of Terror: Literary-Feminist Readings of Biblical Narratives*. Philadelphia: Fortress, 1984.

Twelftree, G. H. "Demon, Devil, Satan." Pages 163–72 in *Dictionary of Jesus and the Gospels*. Edited by Joel B. Green and Scot McKnight. Downers Grove, IL: InterVarsity, 1992.

Uro, Risto. *Ritual and Christian Beginnings: A Socio-Cognitive Analysis*. Oxford: Oxford University Press, 2016.

Valent, Paul. "Bearing Witness to Trauma." Pages 37–41 in *Encyclopedia of Trauma: An Interdisciplinary Guide*. Edited by Charles R. Figley. London: Sage, 2012.

Van Dijk, Teun A. "Narrative Macro-Structures: Logical and Cognitive Foundations." *Poetics and Theory of Literature* 1 (1976): 547–68.

Van Hook, Mary Patricia. "Spirituality as a Potential Resource for Coping with Trauma." *Social Work & Christianity* 43, no. 1 (2016): 7–25.

Vanhoozer, Kevin J. "Love's Wisdom: The Authority of Scripture's Form and Content for Faith's Understanding and Theological Judgement." *Journal of Reformed Theology* 5 (2011): 247–75.

———. "May We Go Beyond What Is Written after All? The Pattern of Theological Authority and the Problem of Doctrinal Development." Pages 747–92 in *The Enduring Authority of the Christian Scriptures*. Edited by D. A. Carson. Grand Rapids: Eerdmans, 2016.

———. *Remythologizing Theology: Divine Action, Passion, and Authorship*. Cambridge Studies in Christian Doctrine 18. Cambridge: Cambridge University Press, 2010.

———. "Theological Commentary and 'The Voice from Heaven': Exegesis, Ontology, and the Travail of Biblical Interpretation." Pages 269–98 in *On the Writing of New Testament Commentaries: Festschrift for Grant R. Osborne on the Occasion of His 70th Birthday*. Edited by Eckhard Schnabel. Leiden: Brill, 2013.

Vanhoozer, Kevin J., Craig G. Bartholomew, Daniel J. Treier, and N. T. Wright, eds. *Dictionary for Theological Interpretation of the Bible*. Grand Rapids: Baker Academic, 2005.

Vanhoozer, Kevin J., and Daniel J. Treier. *Theology and the Mirror of Scripture*. Downers Grove, IL: InterVarsity, 2015.

Vanhoozer, Kevin J., Daniel J. Treier, and N. T. Wright. *Theological Interpretation of the New Testament: A Book-by-Book Survey*. Grand Rapids: Baker Academic, 2008.

Vos, C. J. A. *Theopoetry of the Psalms*. 1st South African ed. Pretoria: Protea Book House, 2005.

Waldenfels, Bernhard. "Levinas and the Face of the Other." Pages 63–81 in *The Cambridge Companion to Levinas*. Edited by Simon Critchley and Robert Bernasconi. Cambridge: Cambridge University Press, 2002.

Ward, Peter, and Heidi Campbell. "Ordinary Theology as Narratives." *International Journal of Practical Theology* 15, no. 2 (2011): 226–42.

Warnes, Christopher. *Magical Realism and the Postcolonial Novel: Between Faith and Irreverence*. Basingstoke, Hampshire, UK: Palgrave Macmillan, 2009.

Webster, John. *Theological Theology*. Oxford: Clarendon, 1998.

Weingarten, Kaethe. "Reasonable Hope: Construct, Clinical Applications, and Supports." *Family Process* 49, no. 1 (2010): 5–25.

Welz, Claudia. *Love's Transcendence and the Problem of Theodicy*. Tübingen: Mohr Siebeck, 2008.

Werner, Roland. *Die Christus-Treff Story – Die Geschichte einer Gemeinschaft im Aufbruch*. Neukirchen-Vluyn: Neukirchener Aussaat, 2002.

Wiesing, Lambert. *Das Mich der Wahrnehmung: Eine Autopsie*. Frankfurt am Main: Suhrkamp, 2009.

Williams, A. N. *The Architecture of Theology: Structure, System, and Ratio*. Oxford: Oxford University Press, 2011.

Wirling, Ylwa. "Imagining Oneself Being Someone Else." *Journal of Consciousness Studies* 21, nos. 9–10 (2014): 205–25.

Wolterstorff, Nicholas. *Divine Discourse: Philosophical Reflections on the Claim That God Speaks*. Cambridge: Cambridge University Press, 1995.

———. *Until Justice and Peace Embrace: The Kuyper Lectures for 1981 Delivered at the Free University of Amsterdam*. Grand Rapids: Eerdmans, 1983.

Wortham, Amanda. "Reading Sideways: How Fiction Helps Us Navigate the Maze of Tragedy." Christ and Pop Culture. July 28, 2016. http://christandpopculture.com/reading-sideways-how-fiction-helps-us-navigate-the-maze-of-tragedy/.

Yeago, D. S. "The New Testament and the Nicene Dogma: A Contribution to the Recovery of Theological Exegesis." Pages 87–102 in *The Theological Interpretation of Scripture: Classic and Contemporary Readings*. Edited by Stephen E. Fowl. Oxford: Blackwell, 1997.

Young, Julian. *Friedrich Nietzsche: A Philosophical Biography*. Cambridge: Cambridge University Press, 2010.

"Your Definitive Guide to 2017: A Year of Hope and Horror." *USA Today*. December 28, 2017. https://www.usatoday.com/story/news/2017/12/28/definitive-guide-reflecting-horrific-and-hopeful-2017/987241001/.

Zahavi, D. "You, Me, and We: The Sharing of Emotional Experience." *Journal of Consciousness Studies* 22, nos. 1–2 (2015): 84–101.

Zündel, Friedrich, Christian T. Collins Winn, and Dieter Ising. *Pastor Johann Christoph Blumhardt: An Account of His Life*. Blumhardt Series. Eugene, OR: Cascade Books, 2010.

SUBJECT INDEX

M

SCRIPTURE INDEX

The Old Testament

The New Testament

Mark

Luke

John